LC 1039.5 .R44 2011

Recognizing and Serving Low-Income Students in Higher Education

Recognizing and low

Written for administrators, faculty, and staff in Higher Education who are working with low-income and first-generation college students, *Recognizing and Serving Low-Income Students in Higher Education* uncovers organizational biases that prevent postsecondary institutions from adequately serving these students. This volume offers practical guidance for adopting new or revised policies and practices that have the potential to help these students thrive.

This contributed volume is based on empirical studies that specifically examine the policies and practices of postsecondary institutions in the United States, England, and Canada. The contributing authors argue that discussions of diversity will be enriched by a better understanding of how institutional policies and practices affect low-income students. Unlike most studies on this topic, this volume focuses on institutional rather than federal, state, and public policy. Institutional policies and practices have been largely ignored and this volume lifts the veil on processes that have remained hidden.

Recognizing and Serving Low-Income Students in Higher Education:

- showcases an often-overlooked issue in diversity discussions;
- outlines how post-structuralism can elucidate the concepts and issues examined;
- highlights organizational policies and practices that can hold back low-income students;
- provides a comprehensive approach to low-income student success;
- offers practical solutions and advice to professionals in Higher Education.

This volume presents tremendous insight and valuable guidance for working within new institutional policy and practice frameworks and will undoubtedly reshape the future of educational opportunities for low-income students in Higher Education.

Adrianna Kezar is Associate Professor for Higher Education at the University of Southern California.

WITHDRAWN

Recognizing and Serving Low-Income Students in Higher Education

An Examination of Institutional Policies, Practices, and Culture

Edited by

Adrianna Kezar

Routledge
Taylor & Francis Group

NEW YORK AND LONDON

First published 2011
by Routledge
270 Madison Avenue, New York, NY 10016

Simultaneously published in the UK
by Routledge
2 Park Square, Milton Park, Abingdon, Oxon OX14 4RN

Routledge is an imprint of the Taylor & Francis Group, an informa business

© 2011 Taylor & Francis

Typeset in Minion by EvS Communication Networx, Inc.
Printed and bound in the United States of America on acid-free paper by Edwards Brothers, Inc.

All rights reserved. No part of this book may be reprinted or reproduced or utilised in any
form or by any electronic, mechanical, or other means, now known or hereafter invented,
including photocopying and recording, or in any information storage or retrieval system, without
permission in writing from the publishers.

Trademark Notice: Product or corporate names may be trademarks or registered trademarks,
and are used only for identification and explanation without intent to infringe.

Library of Congress Cataloging-in-Publication Data
Recognizing and serving low-income students in higher education : an examination of institutional
policies, practices, and culture / edited by Adrianna Kezar.
p. cm.
Includes bibliographical references and index.
1. Postsecondary education—United States. 2. Educational equalization—United States.
3. People with social disabilities—Education (Higher)—United States. I. Kezar, Adrianna J.
LC1039.5.R44 2010
378.1'9826942—dc22
2009047575

ISBN 13: 978-0-415-80321-2 (hbk)
ISBN 13: 978-0-415-80322-9 (pbk)
ISBN 13: 978-0-203-85125-8 (ebk)

CONTENTS

Preface   vii
ADRIANNA KEZAR WITH ASSISTANCE
FROM MARYBETH WALPOLE

Part I: Background and Context   1

1 Rethinking Postsecondary Institutions for Low-Income
   Student Success: The Power of Post-Structural Theory   3
   ADRIANNA KEZAR

Part II: Access to Postsecondary Institutions   27

2 Lessons Learned from Indiana's Twenty-First Century
   Scholars Program: Toward a Comprehensive Approach
   to Improving College Preparation and Access for
   Low Income Students   29
   EDWARD P. ST. JOHN

3 Chances and Choices of Low-Income Students in Canada
   and England: A Post Structuralist Discussion
   of Early Intervention   49
   TONY CHAMBERS AND FIONA DELLER

4 Showing Them the Money: The Role of Institutional
   Financial Aid Policies and Communication Strategies
   in Attracting Low-Income Students   72
   LAURA PERNA, VALERIE LUNDY-WAGNER, APRIL YEE,
   LEYKIA BRILL, AND TERAN TADAL

Part III: Entering and Transitioning to College 97

5 **Academics, Campus Administration, and Social Interaction: Examining Campus Structures Using Post-Structural Theory** 99
MARYBETH WALPOLE

6 **Strangers in a Strange Land: Low-Income Students and the Transition to College** 121
JULIA COLYAR

7 **Welfare Students in Community Colleges: Policy and Policy Implementation as Barriers to Educational Attainment** 139
JOHN S. LEVIN, VIRGINIA MONTERO-HERNANDEZ, CHRISTINE CERVEN, AND GENEVIEVE SHAKER

Part IV: Persistence, Success, and Graduation 159

8 **Demography is Not Destiny: What Colleges and Universities Can Do to Improve Persistence Among Low-Income Students** 161
JENNIFER ENGLE AND MARY G. LYNCH

9 **Minority Serving Institutions—What Can We Learn?** 176
ALISA CUNNINGHAM AND LACEY LEEGWATER

10 **The Hidden Curriculum: The Difficulty of Infusing Financial Education** 192
ADRIANNA KEZAR AND HANNAH YANG

Part V: Transfer and Moving on to Graduate School 215

11 **Improving Transfer Access for Low-Income Community College Students** 217
ALICIA DOWD

12 **Post-Baccalaureate Preparation and Access for Low-Income Students and the Myth of a Level Playing Field** 232
ALEX JUN AND KRISTIN PAREDES-COLLINS

13 **Re-Orienting Our Understanding of Colleges in Relation to Low-Income Students** 247
ADRIANNA KEZAR

List of Contributors 254

Index 262

PREFACE

ADRIANNA KEZAR
WITH ASSISTANCE FROM MARYBETH WALPOLE

PURPOSE AND FOCUS

In the last 30 years, colleges and universities have worked to diversify the student populations that attend and succeed in college. Campus dialogues about diversity and multiculturalism tend to focus most on race and ethnicity, to a lesser extent on gender and sexual orientation, and often provide little if any attention to socioeconomic status. Programs, centers, and policies help students of color to succeed, reach out and recruit students from disadvantaged high schools, ensure affirmative action, and provide a bridge between high school and college. Though these efforts are extremely important, campus leaders are beginning to realize that socioeconomic status is largely missing from the policies and practices in place in most college campuses. During a recent interview study regarding advancing diversity agendas on campuses, college presidents expressed comments similar to this sentiment:

> while we need to continue to advance the racial and ethnic demographics of the students and faculty on campus and ensure their success, we largely ignore social class or income and its impact on students. This impacts our success with students of color as well and makes us blind to important issues that may be shaping how students perform, and how we shape (or do not) that success.

A recent study by Bowen, Chingos, and McPherson (2009) underscores how important it is to focus on social class. They document that over the last 30 years low-income access rates have dropped and middle- and high-income rates have gone up, making the gap larger than in previous time periods.

vii

Even though postsecondary institutions today generally ignore social class, there is a tradition within higher education of recognizing the impact of social class or income on access and success in college. Efforts to improve low-income[1] student success began many years ago with a few pioneering institutions such as Oberlin and Antioch that allowed students to work to pay tuition, and special mission institutions such as tribal colleges and Historically Black Colleges and universities that tried to create environments where individuals, who are from low-income populations, could be successful. Tribal colleges have emergency funds for students—knowing the precarious condition of their finances— offering financial education, and providing high touch programs for their first-generation college students, not expecting that they understand scholarship applications or financial aid policy. In the early 1970s, federal policy turned to social class with the passage of the TRIO programs that aim to help first-generation and low-income students to gain access to and be successful in college. TRIO programs offer mentoring, academic support, and assistance with college-going knowledge important to gain access and transition successfully to college. Federal financial aid, and in particular the Pell grant program, provided funding for low-income students to attend college based on financial need and not necessarily merit. State programs, such as Indiana's Twenty-First Century Scholars Program, offer particular support to low-income students by providing an early commitment of funding, raising expectations for college, and providing mentoring. These various federal and state programs acknowledge that low-income students have particular needs to be successful in the college environment.

Much of policy related to low-income students continues at the federal and state levels. These important dialogues help to ensure funding for low-income students and support programs that identify academically strong low-income students and help them successfully gain access to college. However, there has been little examination or recognition of the impact of campus-specific institutional policies and practices on low-income students. Prior to the federal and state infrastructures, there was an understanding that for low-income students to be successful, institutions needed to examine their policies and practices and try to create an environment where such students could thrive. In more recent years, individual colleges and universities have come to depend on federal and state programs to provide support for low-income students. As a result, institutional policies and practices generally go unexamined, and if there are any unintended negative effects on low-income students, these practices typically do not come to light. For example, the cost of college textbooks has gone up 600 percent in the last 30 years (Government

Accountability Office, 2005). College textbooks have gone up more than any other type of book on the market. Institutions generally do not examine the cost of books, do not encourage faculty to explore and look at the impact of the cost of textbooks assigned, and do not encourage faculty to list scholarship funds available to support low-income students who may not be able to afford books. In addition, campus dialogues around diversity have often focused on race and ethnicity and not looked at the intersection of race and social class. Programs and centers established for students of color generally do not make a distinction between the varying needs of African American students from upper-middle-class, middle-class, or low-income backgrounds. The absence of these conversations and programs means that the particular needs of low-income students are often overlooked.

In this book, we examine institutional policies and practices, and critique and make visible practices that negatively affect the success of low-income students. We also showcase practices that work well for low-income students and that can serve as models for campuses trying to make changes. Post-structuralism is the theoretical foundation for the book and it is reviewed thoroughly in Chapter 1. Post-structuralism examines how existing practices, policies, and structures embed certain normative and dominant values, and only by deconstructing these values can we change the policies and practices to make them more inclusive. For example, feminist post-structuralists have been very successful using this lens to uncover bias in organizations around hiring and promotion of women. This same lens can be used to demonstrate how postsecondary institutions have underlying norms and values that support middle and high-income students, but not low-income students. The purpose of the book is to expose these underlying practices and assumptions that disadvantage low-income students, and the chapters are aimed at developing awareness of practices that work against low-income students.

We believe that discussions of diversity can be enriched by adding an understanding of how institutional policies and practices affect low-income students. Because the majority of emphasis on serving low-income students has been through federal and state policy, most of the research in the last 30 years related to low-income students has focused on public policy—Pell grant trends, impact of specific state programs targeted for low-income students, or changes in or evaluations of TRIO programs. There have been only a handful of studies that have focused on the policies and practices of postsecondary institutions. This book is based on these empirical studies that have been done in recent years, focusing on the organizational practices of colleges and universities related to low-income students. We recommend ways that institutions can change their policies and practices to better serve low-income students. We also highlight future research that is needed because this topic has been underexplored by researchers and scholars, and we need more research to better inform organizational policies and practices.

RESEARCH ON LOW-INCOME STUDENTS: PLACING THE BOOK IN CONTEXT[2]

Before describing the organization of the book, it is important to briefly note previous research on low-income students that helps contextualize what we know for the reader. Researchers have explored the experiences of low-income students in three broad areas: college access, college experiences, and college outcomes. In all three areas, the research has most often utilized a deficit approach—focusing on what these students lack rather than on how colleges and universities can successfully educate them.

COLLEGE ACCESS

Low-income students are less likely to attend college, in part because our current admissions system works to disadvantage low-income students in several ways (Bowen, Kurzweil, & Tobin, 2005; Karabel, 2005). The way in which merit is constructed privileges high-income students because it places weight on access to rigorous coursework, grades, and test scores (Karabel, 2005). Early admission systems, legacy admits, admission based on athletic prowess (Karabel, 2005), and merit awards also work in concert to disadvantage low-income students in the admissions process (Heller & Rasmussen, 2002). For example, low-income students often do not have access to rigorous coursework like advanced placement as it is not offered in the schools they attend. However, rather than focus on how the system works to disadvantage low-income students, much of the research has focused, instead, on what these students lack.

For example, research has found that low-income students are less likely to attend college because they have lower aspirations and are more likely to lack access to rigorous coursework (honors and Advanced Placement courses) than high-income students (Adelman, 2006; Akerhielm, Berger, Hooker, & Wise, 1998; Paulsen & St John, 2002; Wei & Horn, 2002, 2009). In fact, low-income students are less likely to enter college than are high-income students, even with high test scores, rigorous academic programs, advanced coursework, and Algebra I in eighth grade (Akerhielm et al., 1998; Bowen et al., 2009). Even when controlling for test scores, low-income students are still less likely to attend college than high-income students.

Although academic preparation is key to increasing the prospects of low-income youth attending college, these students' expectations about the necessity of college preparation for their desired career is also critical (Bedsworth, Colby, & Doctor, 2006; Stitt-Gohdes, 1997). Bedsworth and colleagues additionally found that low-income students need more information about academic requirements, and that while parental involvement was important, having a peer group that was planning on attending college was more important than parental encouragement.

Financial aid availability is, of course, critical for low-income students to attend college (Akerhielm et al., 1998; DesJardins, Ahlburg, & McCall, 2006; Paulsen & St. John, 2002). Low-income students need more information and may believe that a college education is not financially possible (Bedsworth et al., 2006; Tierney & Venegas, 2007, 2009). In a sample of almost 100,000 students, DesJardins and colleagues (2006) found that low-income students, across all racial and ethnic groups, were less likely to enroll and that the expectation of aid, as well as the actual award received, affected students' enrollment behaviors. Moreover, even when receiving aid, low-income students are more likely than their peers to have a financial need that is unmet by aid (Choy & Carroll, 2003). Paulsen and St. John (2002) also found that financial factors affected the types and locations of the institutions low-income students attended. Low-income students attend less expensive community colleges and regional institutions where tuitions are lower to reduce debt or perceived debt. These students sometimes do not realize that their tuition might be covered by financial aid at a more expensive institution because they are shocked by the college's quoted sticker price (Tierney & Venegas, 2009).

Some research has also focused on college access for low-income students from different racial or ethnic backgrounds. Hurtado, Inkelas, Briggs, and Rhee (1997) found that low-income White and Latino students submitted the fewest college applications, and the number of applications increased as income did. Income did not affect the number of applications Asian American students submitted, and only the lowest income African American students applied to fewer institutions than other African American income groups. Perna (2000) also found that a higher family income increased the probability of Latino students attending four-year institutions. Teranishi, Ceja, Antonio, Allen, & McDonough (2004) investigated college choice among Asian American and Pacific Islander ethnic groups and found that low-income Chinese and Korean Americans were the most likely to attend highly selective institutions, while low-income Southeast Asian and Filipino Americans were most likely to attend public colleges. Additionally, low-income Chinese, Korean, and Filipino Americans reported choosing a college based on low tuition.

COLLEGE EXPERIENCES

Clearly, according to National Center for Education Statistics (NCES) data, low-income students have much less of a chance to attend college. NCES data indicated that in 2007, 55 percent of low-income high school graduates attended college (Wei & Horn, 2009). However, although some research has been conducted regarding the types of institutions they attend, little research has examined their experiences in college compared to their high-income peers, and the research that exists has again taken a deficit approach.

According to the research, when they do attend college, low-income students are more likely to attend less selective, less costly institutions than their peers (Bailey, Jenkins, & Leinbach, 2005; Berkner, He, & Cataldi, 2002; Steinburg, Piraino, & Haveman, 2009). Additionally, low-income students were less likely to enroll full time, to live on campus, or to enroll continuously than high-income peers (Berkner et al., 2002; Paulsen & St. John, 2002). Moreover, low-income students work more and are less involved in extracurricular or political activities than their peers from higher-income families (Arzy, Davies, & Harbour, 2006; Paulsen & St. John, 2002; Seider, 2008). Low-income students attributed their cautious social and co-curricular involvement to their lack of comfort with their peers and with the campus environment (Arzy et al., 2006). Similarly, they interacted little with faculty inside or outside the classroom, although they did not see this as interfering with their academic focus. We know much less though about their experiences and several authors in this volume conduct research on the experiences of low-income students, so that we can learn from them and change campuses' policies and practices.

COLLEGE OUTCOMES

Once again the research on college outcomes has found that low-income students are less likely to persist and graduate from college, take longer to complete their degrees, and earn less money than their higher-income peers (Choy & Carroll, 2003; Paulsen & St. John, 2002; Perna, 2000; Wei & Horn, 2009). Moreover, low-income students are more likely to receive Associate's degrees and less likely to receive Bachelor's degrees (Department of Education, 2003), and have lower career aspirations than their higher-income peers (Aries & Seider, 2007). This research has again primarily utilized a deficit model, explaining that low-income students lack something necessary for persisting and graduating.

In reports focusing on low-income students, more selective institutions and institutions with smaller cohorts of low-income students had higher graduation rates (Bowen et al., 2009; Horn, 2006). As selectivity declined, the proportion of low-income students grew, and the six-year graduation rates fell (Horn, 2006). Moreover, at low-income serving institutions—institutions that have 25 percent or more of their students Pell grant eligible—those with relatively high graduation rates tended to be private, secular, with large undergraduate populations, and lower enrollments of students of color. A recent study suggests that low-income students are more likely to graduate and in four years if they go to the most selective institution that they can get admitted (Bowen et al., 2009). Engle and O'Brien (2007) found that institutions that have high graduation rates for low-income students maintain close personal contact with students, create supportive campus communities, maintain a focus on undergraduate education, and create a campus culture focused on retention and graduation.

Several authors (Cabrera, Nora, & Castaneda, 1992; Paulsen & St. John, 2002; St. John, Cabrera, Nora, & Asker, 2000) focused on connecting low-income students' persistence to financial aid using the financial nexus model. Cabrera et al. (1992) found that financial aid had an indirect effect on persistence. Paulsen and St. John (2002) found that, overall, low-income students were less likely to persist if they were cost conscious when choosing a college. They also found that low-income students' attrition increased when tuition increased.

Paulsen and St. John (2002) found that among their two lowest-income groups, African American students persisted at higher rates than White students, although higher-income African American students have higher persistence rates than their lower-income peers (St. John, Paulsen, & Carter, 2005). They found Latino students chose colleges that had lower costs and were less likely to take out loans than other racial and ethnic groups. Further, compared with other groups in the study, low-income Asian American students were the least likely to persist. They also found low-income women were less likely to persist than low-income men.

Thus, while it is clear that low-income students are not as successful as their high-income peers in enrolling in, persisting in, or graduating from colleges and universities, most of the research has focused on factors highlighting the differences between low-income and high-income students, and the opportunities, characteristics, or achievements that low-income students have not had. More recently, research has begun to highlight the campuses that are successful with low-income students and the factors that they have in common (Engle & O'Brien, 2007; Horn, 2006). This research is most promising because in order to enroll and graduate more of these students, knowledge about what we can do as educators on our campuses is critical, and thus the focus of this book.

ORGANIZATION OF THE BOOK

The book is organized into five major parts: I. Background and Context (reviewing the analytic framework); II. Access to Postsecondary Institutions (early intervention programs, financial aid, and admissions practices); III. Entering and Transitioning to College (covering bridge programs, residence halls, and first-year practices); IV. Persistence, Success, and Graduation (covering learning and classroom experiences, commitment to undergraduate teaching, campus community, engagement practices, and successful models for engaging low-income students); and, V. Transfer and Moving on to Graduate School (moving between institutional contexts, socialization processes). This organization helps administrators within different departments and divisions to examine their policies and practices. Part II on access to postsecondary institutions provides specific advice for individuals in financial aid and admissions while Part III on entering and transitioning to college provides advice for staff who work with first-year experience programming and courses, student support services, and academic affairs administrators. Not only do the different parts speak to different audiences, but the book is organized to provide a comprehensive approach to low-income student success. Policies need to be examined that impact access, transition, persistence, graduation, transfer, and graduate school, helping to change the entire pipeline.

We recommend that readers first review Part I which provides necessary context information for understanding low-income students and the analytic focus of the book. In Chapter 1, Kezar provides an introduction to the analytic framework: post-structuralism. The chapter introduces the three prongs of the framework (revelation, deconstruction, reconstruction), provides examples, and applies the framework so that readers can fully understand the value. This chapter draws on historical analysis to describe the ways that postsecondary institutions emerged as middle-class/upper-middle-class institutions, and how policies and practices in place support middle- and upper-class students and ignore the needs of low-income students. Both the historical analysis and the deconstruction of current practices serve to provide a context for the following chapters that critique certain campus practices in-depth such as financial aid, orientation programs, curricular requirements, and the like.

Part II focuses on access issues ranging from early intervention programs to admissions and financial aid policies. Access has become the major focus of federal, state, and institutional policymakers. In this book, we provide examples of federal and state initiatives aimed at access examining the role that individual colleges play or (more appropriately) do not play in helping make these programs and policies successful. The major policies to address access among low-income youth have been early intervention for college programs, financial aid packaging, and admissions practices.

In Chapter 2, St. John reviews the Twenty-First Century Scholars Program—summarizing research from over a decade. This informative chapter looks at one of the most well-conceived state-level efforts to create greater access, and the project has been heavily researched, providing much empirical data to draw upon. This statewide early intervention for college program targeting low-income youth has been extremely successful in improving access. Yet, by critically examining the program, St. John demonstrates how postsecondary institutions fall short of helping students transition and persist in college. Colleges need to provide support services critical for making students more successful, not just funding and financial aid guarantees. Colleges also need to be more strongly linked to school reform efforts and communicate more with high schools. The chapter provides a comprehensive guide for how colleges could be meaningfully involved to support low-income, first-generation college students in the future.

In Chapter 3, Chambers and Deller review early intervention programs in Canada and England, providing lessons and insights that can come from comparative educational studies. Their chapter provides a helpful framing of concepts used in post-structural analysis such as "social capital" and "habitus." The authors take a critical lens to notions like whether access for low-income students can be so easily provided and the constraints that are often not examined (such as inter-generational poverty or lack of parental guidance because they did not attend college) in access discourses. They also argue for the need to look systemically at the problem—not too much focus on any one dimension such as finances, social supports, peer group or family influence, student's self-confidence, etc. While research points to systemic barriers, programs typically address few areas or address a variety of areas, but in superficial ways. Chambers and Deller then use the analytic concepts to deconstruct early intervention programs in two countries showing the need for more work to develop truly effective programs that address systemic barriers to low-income student success.

In Chapter 4, Perna, Lundy-Wagner, Yee, Brill, and Tadal provide an overview of the role of financial aid to low-income students' attendance in college, demonstrating low-income students' sensitivity to cost, loans, and tuition increases. They then examine the ways that institutions have "no loan policies" for low-income students and how institutions communicate this policy. While this is a policy among mostly highly selective colleges, these are also colleges that have historically not served low-income students and are a gateway to success in society. Through an analysis of campus websites, the authors demonstrate how the no loan policies are poorly communicated to students and that it would be unlikely that they would find, understand, or use this information/policy. The chapter draws a larger critique about the importance of not just having policies, but being careful to implement them in a way that will be successful.

In Part III, the book moves on to issues of entering and transitioning to college as this is often a critical time period where students drop out, particularly low-income, first-generation college students. For many years, access was such a strong focus that college leaders did not think about whether low-income students were persisting. In recent years, there has been more attention to transition, as researchers demonstrated the high attrition rates of low-income students. As a result, institutions are developing more support for students as they enter college. Bridge programs are perhaps the most common strategy in place that are aimed at low-income students. Colyar reminds us in her chapter that, for many students from low-income backgrounds, the transition to college is analogous to foreign travel: the location is unfamiliar, the language is difficult to understand, and the traveler is clearly identified as a tourist, a temporary visitor in the spaces that belong to locals. Transitions to college are not simply geographic, or even academic; they are also complicated by institutional values and practices that challenge students' self-concepts and sense of belonging. As low-income students locate their classrooms on campus maps, they also work to redefine themselves within the middle-class norms of the academic setting.

Chapter 5 provides a comprehensive examination of the way institutional policies, particularly in the first year, can impact low-income student success. Walpole's study of private liberal arts colleges shows that admissions, housing, social support, academic support, academic requirements, and even specific policies such as study abroad all work against low-income student success. Her systemic analysis of barriers is one of the most comprehensive pieces of research on this topic demonstrating the multiple ways that institutions unconsciously create barriers for students. She offers a set of recommendations to campus administrators for rethinking a host of policies and practices on campus.

In Chapter 6, Colyar examines the popular strategy of offering bridge programs for low-income students and demonstrates that while the programs have value, they also create stigma by making the students feel different. The chapter examines cultural values often expressed as expectations and assumptions about what it means to be a college student. She also calls on researchers to conduct scholarship on low-income students in a non-deficit way, and to learn about low-income students on their own, without comparison to a middle-class norm. By understanding these students' unique experiences, we can provide support; whereas, by comparing them to middle-income students, we only serve to marginalize them. Colyar presents data from interviews with participants in a summer bridge program. She notes how programs may be enhanced by developing ties to local communities and leveraging the capital located in students' environments. This may require re-structuring programs in terms of location, schedule, or types of activities. Students might also benefit from programs that, rather than executed in the summer months when they may need to be working, are integrated into the regular school year.

In Chapter 7, Levin, Montero-Hernandez, Cerven, and Shaker describe the challenges of low-income populations at community colleges that are on welfare and trying to return to school. They demonstrate how the transition to college and persistence is hampered by state and federal policies that tie institutions' hands. Specifically, the conservative approach to welfare allocates the responsibility of poverty to individuals, requiring them to work first and make education a secondary goal. The authors use a case study of New Visions program at a community college in California to demonstrate how although the program is an official attempt to encourage welfare clients both to formulate and to pursue educational goals, its primary emphasis remains on employment and economic self-sufficiency. Because the work first goal conflicts with many community colleges' underlying mission, many will not offer welfare to work programs at all, closing down access for low-income adults.

Part IV focuses on persistence, success, and graduation. Studies demonstrate that support should be spread out over time as 44 percent of low-income students drop out after the sophomore year (Bowen et al., 2009). Therefore, we emphasize the host of programs needed to continue success until graduation. In this section, we present studies that have taken a slightly different tack. Rather than study institutions with problems serving low-income students, the authors examine campuses that have been particularly successful, and examine the conditions that have led to their success and what lessons there might be for the broader higher education sector. Because traditional higher education has historically evolved to support middle- and upper-class students, it is not surprising that studying non-traditional campuses can serve to identify models for reconstructing traditional campuses. Also, while most of the existing literature focuses on the student "input" characteristics that cannot change, the authors in this volume propose a new research emphasis on factors that institutions can control (their own policies and practices) because what colleges do affects whether their students succeed.

In Chapter 8, Engle and Lynch review major findings from research conducted by Engle and O'Brien (2007), studying public four-year institutions that serve large numbers of low-income students and graduate their students at better-than-expected rates after taking the diverse academic and economic backgrounds of their student bodies into account. By conducting case studies of these institutions, they were able to identify policies and practices that improve overall retention and graduation rates at colleges and universities that serve large populations of low-income students. The institutions they studied had made major changes in the following areas: 1. focus on the first year; 2. monitoring student progress; 3. improving instruction in gatekeeping courses; 4. special programs for under-resourced populations; and 5. creating a culture of success. They also suggest additional changes needed on these exemplary campuses including marketing services, offering services at more convenient times, being attentive to students' work schedules when programming, and removing stigma related to programs. Like Colyar, the authors call on schools to amend programs for low-income students to honor their needs, but do not marginalize them with special labels or set-aside programs. The less delineation amongst the students, the better.

Chapter 9 provides insights from minority serving institutions (MSIs)— Historically Black Colleges and Universities (HBCUs), Hispanic Serving Institutions (HSIs), and Tribal Colleges and Universities (TCUs), which often have large numbers of low-income students. Because MSIs have historically provided postsecondary education opportunities for low-income students, they work in ways that are more intentional and better for low-income students; they can serve as models for other institutions. This chapter highlights practices MSIs have developed historically to overcome some of the barriers facing their low-income students, such as increasing financial literacy, culturally relevant curriculum and learning resources, active and collaborative learning, student-centered support services, and community engagement and outreach. The authors draw on a study called Building Engagement and Attainment for Minority Students (BEAMS) program through which approximately 100 four-year MSIs engaged in data-based institutional change to improve their student support work.

Chapter 10 delves into one of the areas brought up in the BEAMS study as critical for low-income student success—financial literacy. Kezar and Yang draw on a three-year study of Individual Development Accounts (IDAs)—a matched savings account paired with case management and financial education. The chapter describes the importance of financial literacy for low-income student success, helping them break the cycle of poverty. The study demonstrated how traditional college campuses have a bias against offering financial literacy (and potentially other services/programs that assist low-income students). For example, college leaders assume that all college students receive financial knowledge in the home. Kezar and Yang work to remedy the lack of financial education by showcasing ways that campuses can begin to offer financial education: creating a campus-wide team, curricular models, ways to include financial information in first-year seminars and student clubs and activities, and training for academic advisers, faculty and other professionals who interact with low-income students. The study and the chapter recommendations also pay particular attention to TRIO programs that work with low-income youth, offering specific recommendations for revising these programs to better address financial literacy among students.

Part V, the final section, looks at the processes of transfer and moving on to graduate school. This is an area with very little research, and an area we hope will be a focus of scholars in future years. Chapter 11 examines transfer of low-income students from two- and four-year schools and the many institutional barriers that prevent transfer. Dowd proposes that too much emphasis is placed on transfer agreements and other statewide policies. Instead much more attention needs to be paid to campus environments and whether faculty have expectations that students will transfer, and helping faculty be transfer agents who encourage and support transfer. She also proposes that campus staff need to be engaged as researchers and try to identify barriers to low-income students' success, similar to the argument in Chapter 1, as Kezar describes the way administrators can use post-structural analysis to diagnose problems on campus and reconstruct processes and practices.

Chapter 12 looks at graduate school and deconstructs current barriers that exist, as well as revealing ways in which current support mechanisms might be improved. Jun and Paredes-Collins note how the McNair Scholars Program has been extremely important in gaining access and retaining low-income graduate students but it puts the burden on the students to change and it can only serve a small number of students. The authors call for a reconstructing of graduate preparation programs from new orientations, to addressing financial knowledge, to a focus on cultural socialization, and to reconsideration of merit in graduate admissions. Chapter 13 is a final reflection on the book as a whole that reveals common themes and draws broader conclusions from across the chapters.

While there are five parts in the book, there is a common analytic lens of post-structural theory. Each chapter has some common components and alludes to the way that post-structuralism can be used to elucidate the concepts chapter authors describe. Common components in each chapter include:

1. each will note the middle/high-income biases relevant to the issue it is examining;
2. each will describe policies or practices that do not serve low-income students well;
3. each will demonstrate the impact of the policy or practices on low-income students;
4. each will deconstruct the policy or practice; and,
5. each will note a possible new or revised policy or practice.

In summary, the book aims to uncover organizational biases that prevent postsecondary institutions from adequately serving low-income students, and recommends new and/or revised policies and practices that have the potential to make these students thrive. This goal can best be met through the application of post-structural theory that deconstructs existing institutional norms in the service of developing new approaches to organizational practices.

The book makes several major contributions. First, it showcases an issue that has received much less attention in diversity discussions: social class. Second, it highlights organizational policies and practices rather than public policy to help low-income students, as the role of organizational policies and practices has been largely ignored to date. Third, it provides a comprehensive approach to low-income student success, rather than narrowly looking only at access policies, it also examines other policies such as retention and transfer. Fourth, the book offers practical solutions and advice to professionals in higher education. We hope that readers are inspired by the critical analysis to try and shift their own practice and to alter campus policies so that they better serve low-income students.

NOTES

1. Low-income and social class are used interchangeably in many chapters. In Chapter 1, I describe more about our definition of these terms.
2. This section was written by MaryBeth Walpole based on research she conducted for the book: *Economically and educationally challenged students in higher education: Access to outcomes* (2007). For more detail about studies of low-income students, please see her book.

REFERENCES

Adelman, C. (2006). *The toolbox revisited: Paths to degree completion from high school through college.* Washington, DC: U.S. Department of Education.
Akerhielm, K., Berger, J., Hooker, M., & Wise, D. (1998). *Factors related to college enrollment, final report* (Mathematica Publication No. 3360-028). Washington, D.C.: U.S. Department of Education.
Aries, E., & Seider, M. (2007). The role of social class in the formation of identity: A study

of public and elite private college students. *The Journal of Social Psychology, 147*(2), 137–157.

Arzy, M. R., Davies, T. G., & Harbour, C. P. (2006). Low-income students: Their lived university campus experiences pursuing baccalaureate degrees with private foundation scholarship assistance. *College Student Journal, 40*(4), 750–766.

Bailey, T., Jenkins, D., & Leinbach, T. (2005). *Community college low-income and minority student completion study: Descriptive statistics from the 1992 high school cohort.* Community College Research Center Teachers College: Columbia University.

Bedsworth, W., Colby, S., & Doctor, J. (2006). *Reclaiming the American dream.* Report prepared for the Bridgespan Group Inc. Retrieved on March 12, 2007 from: http://www.bridgespangroup.org/kno_articles_americandream.html

Berkner, L., He, S., & Cataldi, E. F. (2002). *Descriptive summary of 1995-96 beginning postsecondary students: Six years later* (NCES Report No. 2003-151). Washington, DC: U.S. Department of Education, National Center for Education Statistics.

Bowen, W., Chingos, M., & McPherson, M. (2009). *Crossing the finish line: Completing college at America's public universities.* Princeton, NJ: Princeton University Press.

Bowen, W. G., Kurzweil, M., & Tobin, E. (2005). *Equity and excellence in American higher education.* Charlottesville: University of Virginia Press.

Cabrera, A. F., Nora, A., & Castaneda, M. B. (1992). The role of finances in the persistence process: A structural model. *Research in Higher Education, 33*(5), 571–593.

Choy, S. P., & Carroll, C. D. (2003). *How families of low- and middle-income undergraduates pay for college: Full-time dependent students in 1999–2000* (NCES Report No. NCES-2003-162). Washington, DC: U.S. Department of Education, National Center for Education Statistics.

Department of Education. (2003). *The condition of education.* Washington, DC: Department of Education.

DesJardins, S. L., Ahlburg, D. A., & McCall, B. P. (2006). An integrated model of application, admission, enrollment, and financial aid. *The Journal of Higher Education, 77*(3), 381–429.

Engle, J., & O'Brien, C. (2007). *Demography is not destiny: Increasing the graduation rates of low-income college students at large public universities.* Washington, DC: The Pell Institute.

Government Accountability Office. (2005). *College textbooks: Enhanced offerings appear to drive recent price increases* (GAO-05-806). Washington, DC: Author.

Heller, D. E., & Rasmussen, C. J. (2002). Merit scholarships and college access: Evidence from Florida and Michigan. In D. E. Heller & P. Marin (Eds), *Who should we help? The negative social consequences of merit scholarships.* Cambridge, MA: The Civil Rights Project at Harvard University.

Horn, L. (2006). *Placing college graduation rates in context: How 4 year college graduation rates vary with selectivity and the size of low-income enrollment* (NCES 2007-161). Washington, DC: U.S. Department of Education, National Center for Education Statistics.

Hurtado, S., Inkelas, K. K., Briggs, C., & Rhee, B. (1997). Differences in college access and choice among racial/ethnic groups: Identifying continuing barriers. *Research in Higher Education, 38*(1), 43–75.

Karabel, J. (2005). *The chosen: The hidden history of admission and exclusion at Harvard, Yale, and Princeton.* New York: Houghton-Mifflin Co.

Paulsen, M. B., & St. John, E. P. (2002). Social class and college costs: Examining the financial nexus between college choice and persistence. *The Journal of Higher Education, 73*(2), 189–236.

Perna, L. W. (2000). Differences in the decision to attend college among African Americans, Hispanics, and Whites. *The Journal of Higher Education, 71*(2), 117–141.

Seider, M. (2008). The dynamics of social reproduction: How class works at a state college and elite private college. *Equity & Excellence in Education, 41*(1), 45–61.

St. John, E. P., Cabrera, A. F., Nora, A., & Asker, E. H. (2000). Economic influences on persistence reconsidered. How can finance research inform the reconceptualization of persistence models? In J. M. Braxton (Ed.), *Reworking the student departure puzzle* (pp. 29–47). Nashville, TN: Vanderbilt University Press.

St. John, E. P., Paulsen, M. B., & Carter, D. F. (2005). Diversity, college costs, and postsecondary opportunity: An examination of the financial nexus between college choice and persistence for African Americans and whites. *The Journal of Higher Education, 76*(5), 545–569.

Steinburg, M. P., Piraino, P., & Haveman, R. (2009). Access to higher education: Exploring the variation in Pell grant prevalence among U.S. colleges and universities. *The Review of Higher Education, 32*(2), 235–270.

Stitt-Gohdes, W. L. (1997). *Career development: Issues of gender, race, and class.* ERIC Clearinghouse on Adult, Career and Vocational Education Information Series, 371. ED 413533.

Teranishi, R. T., Ceja, M., Antonio, A. L., Allen, W. R., & McDonough, P. M. (2004). The college choice process for Asian Pacific Americans: Ethnicity and socioeconomic class in context. *The Review of Higher Education, 27*(4), 527–551.

Tierney, W. G., & Venegas, K. M. (2007). The cultural ecology of financial aid. *Readings on Equal Education, 22,* 1–35.

Tierney, W. G., & Venegas, K. M. (2009). Finding money on the table: Information, financial aid, and access to college. *The Journal of Higher Education, 80*(4), 363–388.

Walpole, M. (2007). *Economically and educationally challenged students in higher education: Access to outcomes* (ASHE Higher Education Report, Vol. 33, No. 3). San Francisco: Jossey-Bass.

Wei, C. C., & Horn, L. (2002). *Persistence and attainment of beginning students with Pell Grants* (NCES 2002-169). Washington, DC: U.S. Department of Education, National Center for Education Statistics.

Wei, C. C., & Horn, L. (2009). *A profile of successful Pell Grant recipients: Time to bachelor's degree and early graduate school enrollment* (NCES 2009–156). Washington, DC: U.S. Department of Education, National Center for Education Statistics.

I
Background and Context

1

RETHINKING POSTSECONDARY INSTITUTIONS FOR LOW-INCOME STUDENT SUCCESS

The Power of Post-Structural Theory

ADRIANNA KEZAR

> Nowadays it's fashionable to talk about race and gender; the uncool subject is class (bell hooks, 2000, p. vii).

We are a country with an ever-widening gap between rich and poor, but as hooks notes, no one wants to acknowledge this fact. While we have begun to make strides in advancing women and creating opportunity for certain ethnic groups (Hispanics more so than African Americans), 38 million people live in poverty and are largely missing from our discussions about access or an ongoing source of programming on college campuses (hooks, 2000; Walpole, 2007). With the difficult and unprecedented economic times ahead, poverty and issues of class will become more important and increasingly significant.[1] hooks (2000) and other commentators worry that we are becoming more and more class segregated, even as we become more racially diverse; "the evils of racism and much later sexism were easier to identify and challenge than the evils of classism" in a capitalist society (p. 5). Infrequently we talk about money, but never about class. In fact, hooks (2000) suggests that "race and gender can be used as screens to deflect attention away from the harsh realities class politics expose" (p. 7).

There are also deeply held and inaccurate notions of a classless society in the United States that discussions of class expose. We live in a capitalist society and live with the meritocratic myth that anyone can be successful (Borrego, 2003; Vigeland, 2008). A capitalist economy reinforces class divisions and sees them as a natural part of creating wealth for elites. In other words, some groups must work in positions that are less well paid and the economy must be stratified in order to generate wealth. As a result of this line of thinking, class is naturalized into the social and economic fiber of the nation. Scholars also suggest that people in the United States generally like to see themselves as middle class even when they are extremely wealthy or in poverty (Vigeland, 2008). The reluctance of people within society to acknowledge their own class position and the ability of class to be hidden (in such a way that race and gender cannot be) obfuscates reality. As a result, social class is a taboo subject and one that has not been integrated into diversity initiatives on most college campuses.

In this chapter, I describe a framework for creating a discussion of class within higher education and for developing an understanding around issues of social class, which in the United States is typically related to income (also see note 1).[2] First, I provide a brief historical overview about opportunities for low-income students in higher education to provide a context for the discussion; my goal in this section is to demonstrate the way the system was created to support middle- and high-income students and make it difficult for low-income students to succeed. Second, I introduce post-structuralism—the analytical framework used within this book—for deconstructing and reconstructing higher education institutions to serve low-income students. Third, I apply post-structuralism to expose some of the ways that middle- and high-income students are privileged on college campuses, and I use post-structuralism to deconstruct underlying and unquestioned assumptions that have become normalized and disadvantage low-income students. Fourth, I provide ideas for reconstructing the system of higher education, with particular focus on the institutional level (which I will demonstrate is the most important level for creating change when analyzing situations through a post-structural analysis), in ways that provide greater opportunities for low-income students. This chapter provides a meta-critique of higher education and its treatment of low-income students that is explored further within the individual chapters in this book. Each chapter will use the framework of post-structuralism by: 1. noting middle- and high-income biases or privileges relevant to the issue they are examining; 2. describing and deconstructing policies or practices that do not serve low-income students well; and, 3. recommending new or revised policies or practices to better serve low-income students.

HISTORICALLY SITUATING THE SYSTEM OR STRUCTURE OF OPPORTUNITY FOR LOW-INCOME STUDENTS

Post-structuralism highlights how all societal structures are shaped by historical factors and historically situated; as history evolves, new possibilities can and have emerged (Bourdieu, 1977; Foucault, 1980). Post-structuralism highlights the trend for elites' interests to be supported by societal and institutional structures and episodic progressive tendencies to support low-income students through novel social and institutional structures such as financial aid. While the history of colleges and universities is complex with respect to providing access to low-income students, today's institutions largely support middle- and high-income students' success, but this twist of fate was not always supported by the philosophy of the times. To comprehend how the current structure that supports wealthy students emerged, a brief overview of the formation of colleges and universities and major shifts over time will help explain the evolving purpose and characteristics of campuses.

During the Renaissance (1300s to 1400s), when universities emerged, there was some philosophical support for the intellectual abilities of all human beings regardless of economic status. Building on Athenian notions of equality and Christian notions that people of all social stations can make a contribution, universities provided scholarships, had low-cost tuition, and sought out students from various social statuses (Lucas, 1994). However, over time, universities became finishing schools for the sons of the gentry or vocational schools for civil bureaucrats (typically middle class). In fact, this trend always overrode more populist movements and efforts to shift the purpose of higher education that emerged from 1300 to present. For much of the following 800 years, colleges and universities became exclusively for the wealthy in Europe (Lucas, 1994). The core structures and culture of higher education, from its beginning, have supported the interests of middle- and high-income students and communities.

As colleges and universities developed in the United States, they were first more open than the class-bound European universities. As Lucas (1994) notes, during the 1600 and 1700s, "unlike class bound Europe, in the environment of the new world where privilege was suspect and individual striving for self-improvement strongly encouraged, opportunities for a poor, but ambitious youth to attend college and thereby advance himself remained open" (p. 108). Colleges were created largely by religious institutions, for the purpose of training clergy and statesman—many of the students at college were the sons or daughters of more humble individuals such as clergymen, shopkeepers, farmers, and even servants. Faculty (typically clergy) remained suspicious of the gentry and their commitment to learning, believing they had little commitment to learning and were just more interested in "carrying themselves handsomely and entering a room genteely" and having a good time with little discipline and academic focus (Lucas, 1994, p. 109). But as the United States grew, by the late 1700s, colleges began to take an elitist and patrician stance. Once again, similar to European universities, American universities restricted access to the well-to-do. Tuition became increasingly expensive, the availability of charity scholarships declined, and opportunities to work through college disappeared, along with other structures that had been created to ensure low-income individuals access (Cohen, 2007; Lucas, 1994). At many institutions, the curriculum began to focus on more generalized liberal education, student life, and activities focused on networking among well-to-do families; rowdiness and frivolity were commonplace.

This is not to say that there have not been movements and efforts over the last thousand years to include the interests of low-income students within colleges and universities, but these efforts have been few and largely failures (Lucas, 1994). A few of these efforts deserve mentioning and they represent structures and approaches that can be drawn upon today. As noted earlier, in the medieval and Renaissance universities, low-income youth that desired to enter the clergy were provided scholarships to enable them to attend university. As colleges emerged in the American colonies, they also provided scholarships for poor youth. Therefore, the concept of scholarships for the poor has a long history. In the early 1800s there was the People's Movement to form colleges as the United States expanded to the west, fueled by Jacksonian ideals of equality. The intent was to train the sons of farmers and expand the purpose of colleges and universities, which had largely become the exclusive domain of the elite by the late 1700s. This movement resulted in the development of special institutions such as Oberlin with a unique mission—"a true people's college committed to teaching the children of the poor to become schoolmasters or rise by their wisdom and merits into stations hitherto occupied by the rich; to fill our pulpits, to sit in our state chambers, and on our seats of justice, and to secure in the best possible way the liberties of our country" (Lucas, 1994, p. 123). This movement also created an effort to develop colleges where students would be employed while attending classes, and pay their way through to graduation (work colleges); the notion of work-study remains a powerful concept today. Many think of work-study as a modern concept, but its roots go back hundreds of years. Unfortunately, work colleges largely fell out of favor and the experiment was not adopted or continued by many schools. Later, this concept of expanding higher education to all classes of society was adopted by Congressman Morrill who proposed the Morrill Acts or land-grant legislation in 1862 and 1890 and the formation of colleges and universities. These new land grant institutions supported agricultural and mechanical arts, research on farming, and focus on regional and local needs, educating *all* citizens of local communities.

In the late 1800s, municipal colleges and universities were formed (now termed urban institutions) that specialized in more industrial and technical training, offered evening courses, created part-time enrollment options, provided retraining for workers, credential programs, and other options beyond degree programs, and were located so that students could commute to college. It was predominantly the low-income students who enrolled in these institutions; in response, these institutions began to recreate policies and practices (e.g. part-time enrollment). They created a host of innovative practices that worked for low-income students and were a departure from the type of institutions formed for middle- and high-income students. Junior and community colleges emerged— particularly rural and urban ones —also modifying their characteristics and structures to be more accessible to low-income populations by offering courses at various hours, remediation, and a technical and more varied curriculum. Some municipal and community colleges remain a model of the types of policies and practices needed across the enterprise of higher education.

The Servicemen's Readjustment Act (or G.I. Bill) provided access to many low-income students who had served in World War II; the bill helped pay for college, a luxury they would not have been able to afford. Most people are aware of the Pell grant that provides aid for students based on financial need—not merit—which was a breakthrough policy for providing access to low-income populations that could not afford college. Pell grants were created in 1965 with the authorization of the Higher Education Act. Pell grants are unique in that they do not require repayment, are awarded based on a "financial need" formula determined by the U.S. Congress. Private scholarships were typically tied to merit and the amount of scholarship money available was quite small.

In the early 1970s, TRIO programs—federal programs to increase access to higher education for low-income students—were developed; these were an important innovation in that people recognized that money was not the only issue that contributed to the success of economically disadvantaged students. Today there are innovations emerging from projects such as the Achieving the Dream Project, which is aimed at institutions investigating their underlying structure and revising policies and practices to better meet student needs such as emergency funds, revised academic advising, new approaches to remediation, and the like.

These are several examples of the way that low-income students gained access to higher education, typically through external intervention and policymaking. But these changes were often short-lived and as external policymakers moved on to other priorities, colleges and universities returned to traditional practices and devolved back to serving middle- and high-income students. These external efforts did not penetrate the underlying logic and assumptions that guide many postsecondary institutions. In some contrast, then, the assumption in this book is that more local, internal, and institutionalized efforts at change can continue to alter the system to better serve low-income students.

Today, we must unravel hundreds of years of instantiated practices that exclude low-income students. But history demonstrates that over time practices have emerged that also can help low-income students. There have been some important developments in the last 200 years that can be built upon such as the ideals within the People's Movement of the 1830s, the Morrill Acts of 1862 and 1890, the new structures and practices of the municipal colleges and rural and suburban community colleges, and the policies such as the Servicemen's Readjustment Act, Pell grants, and TRIO and GEAR UP programs to provide support services for low-income students.

Much of the struggle for equality over the last 50 years has focused on race and gender, which are extremely important to address. However, campuses, as noted in the preface, have spent much less time in the recent past examining their underlying structures related to the way that low-income students are or are not well served. Commentators note a problematic assumption—that programs for first-generation college students always address the needs of low-income students. Not all low-income students are first-generation and not all first-generation are low-income (Borrego, 2008). This brief historical overview is important to demonstrate the long-standing values and assumptions that support middle- and high-income students and which work against low-income student success. Some policies and practices that have emerged over time to support low-income populations may have disappeared or not grown to their potential, but they can be examples for future thinking about ways to disrupt the current norms. History also reminds us that policies and practices can and do change over time, that underlying assumptions are dynamic—not static—and that we can shape and alter structures differently, if we are aware how they have been developed to support a particular interest. Historical review is part of post-structural analysis, described next.

POST-STRUCTURAL ANALYSIS

In this book we argue that campus administrators, faculty, and policy-makers will benefit if they begin to examine colleges differently, through post-structural analysis—gaining knowledge so that they can make and carry out decisions that help low-income students. In this section, I will briefly describe structuralism (which precedes post-structuralism) and post-structuralism. After this brief overview, I explain how an analytical technique that relies upon post-structuralism can be used in a practical fashion—as demonstrated throughout this book (even though it might initially sound abstract and complex). I invoke a post-structuralist perspective[3] for three reasons: 1. structuralism and post-structuralism have been used historically to understand issues of class and socioeconomic status and are a major set of theories in sociology; 2. it makes visible hidden assumptions which prevent progress; and, 3. it offers strategies and perspectives for rethinking institutional policies and practices to serve low-income students. Post-structural theory has been used by feminists and critical race theorists to demonstrate how the underlying structures of colleges and universities (as well as other institutions) privilege men or White people and simultaneously create barriers for women or people of color (McIntosh, 1988; Weedon, 1987). The same arguments and evidence can be helpful in demonstrating the way colleges and universities support the interests of wealthy students and highlighting practices and policies that create barriers for low-income students. I use the phrase "post-structuralist perspective," rather than post-structualist theory as there is no decided upon single theory and post-structuralism is a term used to describe a school of thought or set of assumptions.[4]

In taking this approach, we follow the path taken by other scholars studying low-income populations. Structuralism and post-structuralism are the main theories used to understand low-income students. Walpole (2007) summarized various approaches within structuralism and post structuralism including: status attainment model, human capital theory, financial nexus model, Bourdieu's cultural capital, and critical race theory. I direct you to Walpole's text for further elaboration of specific models and approaches. As Walpole (2007) notes, all these theories emphasize:

> structural forces in society, such as economic forces, families, schools, and communities, (that) shape social class attainment; and how individual choices, also referred to as agency, affect a person's socioeconomic status, or how the two are combined in order to understand outcomes. (pp. 17–18)

She notes how the specific theories and models generally share many basic assumptions. *There has been far greater focus on structuralism than post-structuralism which is a more recent development and the main contribution of this book is to give specific focus to post-structuralism.* Post-structuralism is reflected in Bourdieu's cultural capital theory, for example. Rather than focus on a specific theory or model, we introduce the broader tradition and demonstrate how it can be used to help understand and enhance the success of low-income students.

Post-structuralism is a set of theories developed to understand social or class distinctions among sociologists in France.[5] It builds upon and critiques structuralist theories that emerged in the 1950s to understand and predict class relationships. For example, many label Marxist theories and various Marxist thinkers as structuralists (Lynch & O'Riordan, 1998). An underlying premise of structuralism is to understand the broader hidden or obscured practices and policies (called structures) that become practiced norms that create barriers for certain classes to advance. The focus is on the larger structure or system as determining and shaping human behavior, rather than seeing class distinctions as only a result of individual actions or behavior. At a very basic level, structuralism is about studying phenomena as complex systems of inter-related parts that can be analyzed.[6] It was a reaction to the overly individualistic tendencies in existential philosophy popular in the 1930s to 1950s, and harks back to more structural theories such as Marxism from the late 1800s. People do not remain poor because of individual choices, but because society is set up and reinforces keeping them poor. For so long, people have understood poverty as an individual choice rather than seeing values, habits, policies, or practices that prevent people from changing their socioeconomic status. Structuralism was a decidedly different way of understanding class and caste distinctions.

Many of the current practices to aid low-income students can benefit from the application of structuralism. TRIO programs and Pell grants operate on an assumption that we need to fix or focus on the individual; they do not address changes in the overall system of higher education. While these are essential programs, they rest on a problematic, individualistic assumption: by providing individuals extra support, policy-makers and leaders can fix the issue of access. Structural and systematic changes become largely ignored. The authors in this volume argue that this overarching change in mindset is essential for creating better policies and practices on campuses. Administrators and leaders need to take responsibility for changing policies, practices, cultural norms, and power conditions that shape the system in which low-income students operate and try to be successful. We can no longer be satisfied with allowing the students to either fight with or assimilate to the system.

Why is it problematic to take an individualistic focus on low-income access? It is problematic because it propagates the meritocratic myth in higher education: if individuals try hard enough, they can succeed. For some, the fact that individuals who are poor have made it to college suggests there must be a level playing field and others who do not get in are simply not trying hard enough. Structuralism and post-structuralism clearly critique and demonstrate the fallacy of this myth, which is built into our colleges and universities and the way we structure access.

This book will also provide evidence of the many ways that college and university structures exclude low-income people from an opportunity to participate and be successful in higher education. As noted in the historical record, from time to time, individual leaders have recognized the inherent structural problems and attempted to recreate institutions. However, the majority of European and American history and tradition has been influenced by the belief that individuals are not constrained by the broader society or the institutions within society. Others acknowledge that structures do support middle- and high-income values and sensibilities, but that these values are important for low-income people to assimilate. Structuralism critiques assimilationist perspectives by demonstrating how structures change once low-income populations begin to get access. For example, once low-income students received high school degrees in larger numbers a college degree became required for most middle-income work. Structures evolve to privilege middle- and high-income groups in ways that are problematic, continuing to disadvantage the poor.

Structural institutional analysis focuses on examining the mission (organizational goals, purpose, vision), culture (dominant beliefs, proper behavior, criteria for success, rules of the game), structure (pedagogical approaches, social interaction, communication, activities to accomplish basic tasks, procedures), power relationships (access to hierarchy, openness to issues of class, grassroots participation in key decisions), and resources (materials, people, money, facilities, information) within campuses to understand how campus structures are established to privilege or suppress certain individuals or groups of people (Chesler & Crowfoot, 1989). Structural institutional analysis has been used to help people understand the difference between individual racism and institutional racism, demonstrating the way that inequalities and discrimination become embedded into organizational norms and practices. For example, Chesler and Crowfoot (1989) define both direct and indirect institutional discrimination:

> Direct institutional discrimination is organizationally prescribed or community prescribed actions which have an intentionally differential and negative impact on members and subordinate groups and are carried out routinely by a large number of individuals guided by the rules of a large-scale organization. (p. 441)

Chesler and Crowfoot (1989) use the example of the intentional tracking of minority students into certain colleges, universities, or career paths as an example of institutionalized discrimination. Indirect institutional discrimination is the same activity, but is not carried out with prejudice or intent to harm. They note that, at face value and in intent, the norms and resulting practices appear fair or at least neutral (Chesler & Crowfoot, 1989). These aspects of institutional discrimination only become apparent through deep analysis of embedded institutional characteristics such as resources, culture, and power. At its heart, structural theory emphasizes the need to conduct such analysis (often called deconstruction) of the system and its parts so that they can be reconstructed or rethought. Despite its important contributions, structuralism had analytic weaknesses, which led to post-structuralism and the rise of new ideas. For example, structuralism is ahistorical and merely described structures, which had a tendency of reinforcing these structures as natural/real, not as social constructions. Structuralism does not examine how such structures evolved (Foucault, 1980).

Post-structuralism builds upon some of the important assumptions of structuralism—for example, the focus on the system rather than only the individual. It adds additional theoretical perspectives and insights, largely from interpretive and post-modern ideas prevalent in the 1960s and 1970s. The following are key assumptions of post-structuralism: the existence of agency even in marginalized groups; the historical and social development of structure; the power of language to reveal habits, practices and norms; the importance of local contexts; the mutability and complexity of identity; and the embodiment of power. The characteristics of post-structuralism are summarized in Table 1.1. I review post-structuralist assumptions most relevant for the analysis in this book, but acknowledge that this chart and the overall book will not utilize all the assumptions in post-structuralism.[7] While the assumptions described next may seem overly theoretical and have only modest shifts from structuralism, the new assumptions make visible a few key points that can fine tune our view as we work to refashion and redesign institutions. To make the contributions more tangible, I provide examples for how these assumptions affect the way we understand the lives of low-income students.

A first assumption of post-structuralism is the issue of agency. Foucault and other post-structuralists became concerned that structuralist theories are overly deterministic and do not account for human agency; consequently, the individual becomes lost in the focus on the system. Due to this concern, post-structuralists focus on the way that individuals have agency (even if it is severely constrained) and the way people navigate and resist the larger structures that attempt to limit their progress and create barriers. This allows for more investigation into resistance and tension, which is created when an individual encounters the broader system; a whole array of resistance theories have emerged, for example. Chapters will examine resiliency and ways people have succeeded in spite of the system and what can be learned from their success.

A second major assumption is that people interact and interpret the larger system that is working to prevent their advancement. Post-structuralist thought is influenced by interpretivists' views of epistemology and knowledge construction. Structuralists are typically more influenced by positivist notions that individuals contend with systems which are an objective reality. Because people are complex and make meaning differently, each individual will interact with the larger systems in unique and different ways and their resistance will vary (which is likely to frustrate administrative leaders reading this chapter, but stay with me). It will be difficult to predict, as structuralist theories often attempted to do, ways that the system will impact individuals. For example, assumptions by faculty and staff that students have money for extracurricular activities will impact individual students differently, and it is difficult to make generalized statements about how this norm affects students. For some students, it will lead to attrition, for others it may create tension between working to obtain money for extracurricular activities and academic success, and yet others students may reject this norm and focus on scholastic work exclusively. The book will emphasize the varying agency of individuals, and some chapters will examine the socially constructed ways that students engage the institution. We will emphasize the individual and complex ways the system impacts low-income students, and likewise the student response.

Furthermore, post-structuralists emphasize the importance of language for creating meaning, shaping culture, and reproducing reality. Structuralists envisioned power structures as real and tangible, but post-structuralists see power and oppression embedded in day-to-day practices and habits, accessed through language rather than mission or resources as emphasized in the structural example of Chesler and Crowfoot (1989). Post-structuralists intensely investigate language to capture how the system is operating; by decoding language, we can understand and appreciate hidden assumptions. Language is a way to understand norms, which constrict the possible range of activities and actions that are seen as normal. Through structural analysis we can identify problems, but might miss the nuances of oppression captured in practice. This also differs from structuralism by emphasizing the importance of changing the way people make meaning, not just changing physical structures or policies. You can change a policy, but if people have not changed their language and understanding, then policy change may have much more limited influence. Post-structuralists emphasize that you need to change people's underlying understanding of the policy and the language they use to describe and interpret it. Just because a sexual-harassment policy is in place does not mean that workers understand what a sexually harassing act is or have changed their mindset about women. Post-structuralism attempts to dig deeper at creating change. For example, we can set up book scholarships for low-income students. However, if we have not developed a general understanding among faculty about the burden of the cost of books and the importance of them examining how much the assigned books cost each term, the policy is not likely to meet the intended goals. If we speak to faculty and understand their underlying assumptions about the cost of attendance for school and the role of books through the language they use, we can have a better possibility of altering norms around costs. In this book, we will attempt to be sensitive to deeper solutions that can be developed through an examination of language, underlying assumptions, and meaning.

Post-structuralists also emphasize the impact of local situations or institutions as an important underlying assumption. Marxist theory provided interpretation of conditions across different cultures, time periods, or situations. Post-structural theorists emphasize how power conditions in the system vary depending on these important categories of culture, time period, and situation. Low-income students within higher education are located in different types of institutions, have varying goals, and come from very different family backgrounds. Post-structuralism emphasizes the importance of coming up with local solutions for low-income students within the institutions they attend. GEAR UP represents a program that adopts post-structuralist ideals by creating local partnerships between schools and colleges to address the needs of particular communities. The program challenges and changes schools, rather than attempting to only fix individuals. More policies and programs are needed that take into account the individual circumstances of low-income students. Adult returning low-income students need childcare facilities, centers for working families, and other support systems that are specific to their needs. Differences between Hmong students and Chinese students in cultural backgrounds and experiences will affect their experience and opportunity in colleges.

Related to circumstance and local history is the issue of identity. Post-structuralism conceptualizes individuals as having multiple and dynamic overlapping identities. Gender, race, sexual orientation, geography, and other issues overlap with class background. As Borrego (2008) notes, "there is no single class identity: class is only experienced through multiple lenses" of identity (p. 2). Post-structuralism intentionally engages these various aspects of identity. Structuralism typically foregrounded class and ignored these intersecting aspects that can lead to additional marginalization and individualized or customized solutions. While this book also foregrounds class, each author is aware of and will describe the intersection of race, gender, and class. We also provide some case studies and descriptions of particular campuses because deconstructing campus environments has to occur on a localized level as the norms of each campus are quite different. Each campus serves different low-income students, and the direct and indirect discrimination that is built into the systems will vary.

Power relationships are a decidedly important construct within post-structuralism. Power is no longer a disembodied objective force in the world; instead post-structuralists examine the interactions of individuals to ascertain how power operates. It is in the interactions between people that power becomes embodied and real. Therefore, in addition

Table 1.1 Summary of Assumptions/Characteristics of Post-Structuralism

Post-structuralism	
System rather than individual (also a major assumptions of structuralism)	Class is a result of an overarching social, economic, and political system, not an individual choice or circumstance. These forces become embedded within individual institutions—in this case colleges and universities.
Less deterministic; human agency	People can resist their class position and transcend classes, typically through assimilation. Classes are not impenetrable.
Socially constructed	People conceive of and construct their views of class and socioeconomic status.
Language	We can best access, understand, and change people's views about socioeconomic status and class through an examination of language as a source of understanding meaning. In order to change institutionalized norms, we also have to change meaning, often through language.
Situational	Examining individual institutions is important as overarching forces that work against low-income and privilege high-income students are impacted by local conditions and history.
Identity	Engage multiple aspects of identity that shape lives of low-income students and make their encounters with institutions unique.
Power	Invested in relationships, not just structures; importance of involving marginalized group as part of change process.
Recreating reality	By dissecting and deconstructing structures through analysis of the system, language, interpersonal relationships, local conditions, and individual interpretations, we can work to recreate and build new structures, by exposing problems and providing new approaches.

to examining mission, resources, and other institutional structures that embody power, analysis needs to also focus on inter-personal relationships. A low-income student may seek out advising but finds the adviser treats them with an air of superiority and discounts their questions as foolish. As a result of this personal interaction of power, the student stops seeking help.

Also, post-structuralists see more room for negotiation and believe that individuals that have been conceived of as disempowered in society, such as low-income people, have power, can also oppress others, and have more agency than within structuralist theories. As a result, for post-structuralists low-income people are important to include in the change process. They should be agents of change, not just theorized or acted upon. Change efforts should involve low-income populations in more than analysis, but also in developing solutions and organizing change. Chapter authors will identify the way power operates in the relationships (in addition to structures) between low-income and middle- and high-income students, or between faculty and low-income students. They will also focus on solutions and approaches that involve low-income populations in the deconstruction and reconstruction of the institution.

In sum, post-structuralism adds important analytic approaches that can help create a picture that reflects and supports low-income populations in numerous ways: conducting analysis of the system in ways that focus on human agency; examining the socially constructed nature of individuals within the system; focusing on the power of language to reveal habits, practices, and norms that are often hidden; paying attention to history, situation, and local context; representing the complexity of identity and the overlapping facets; and seeing power as dynamic and embedded in relationships. It is important to note one deviation that will be made in this and other chapters. While post-structuralism tends to emphasize the analysis of interactions and language more so than structures, this book will emphasize both. The post-structuralists' critique adds interactions and language to analysis but it does not discount many of the assumptions of structuralism (e.g., the importance of a systemic examination, structures as embodying hidden assumptions and barriers, the inter-related connections in the system), which we will continue to emphasize in this book.

Post-structural (and structural) analysis in this book entails a three-pronged approach: 1. *revelation*—expose privilege for one group and inequities for another group by revealing practices that disenfranchise another group; 2. *deconstruction*—examine specific institutional policies or practices and investigate the impact of the structure, policy, or practices on low-income students; and, 3. *reconstruction*—provide ideas for new or revised structure, policy, or practice. In the next section, I apply post-structural analysis to assess hidden assumptions in higher education, in order to demonstrate how it can help us to rethink the way our campuses are structured. The subsequent chapters in the book will also follow a similar pattern of analysis.

REVELATION: ASSESSING HIDDEN ASSUMPTIONS AND PRIVILEGE

As Gilbert (2008) notes,

> class privilege is the elephant in the room when it comes to diversity education. Students who willingly wrestle with race, gender, sexual orientation, and religion often balk at exploring class privilege, which threatens the fundamental myth that all people in the United States enjoy equal access to opportunity. (p. 7)

Because of this resistance to engage in discussions about class, faculty, staff, administrators, and students are largely unaware of the way that middle-income and wealthy students are privileged in their experience on campus. Peggy Mcintosh's (1988) work on White privilege has been extremely helpful in assisting people in seeing the ways in which the world is shaped to make the experience of people who are White easier on a daily basis, and make the experience of people of color much more difficult, creating undue stress. In this book, we identify and demonstrate the ways in which middle- and high-income students are privileged on campus and make this information available to faculty, staff, and administrators so that these practitioners recognize the additional burden the low-income students face. The book also addresses some ways that campuses can be changed to alleviate some of these pressures that create strain and level the playing field for low-income students. By describing this privilege, we make the hidden parts of the system that are "normalized" visible. Through their visibility, these practices and policies can be examined and deconstructed so that a more equal higher education system can be developed. These privileges also demonstrate how the system works against low-income students and suggest the need to change the system. Some examples will help to demonstrate this issue. Peggy McIntosh (1988) uses a series of unquestioned assumptions to reveal inequities. I follow her approach with the unquestioned assumptions of middle- and high-income students listed in Table 1.2. These statements make visible what some students take for granted (that they can pay for books) and question this general assumption as something normal. Can

Table 1.2 Unquestioned Assumptions of Middle- and High-Income Students in Postsecondary Education

1. Middle- and high-income students do not worry about paying for college and do not think about dropping out on a daily basis due to finances.*
2. Middle- and high-income students do not worry about paying off or incurring debt because their parents can help them pay off debt and/or they have seen that their parents have succeeded in accumulating and paying off debt.
3. Middle- and high-income students choose colleges based on the quality and fit with their personality; finances are not as significant a factor.
4. Middle- and high-income students have money for books and equipment necessary for studies.
5. Middle- and high-income students have money for extracurricular and co-curricular activities that are considered important to social integration and success in college.
6. Middle- and high-income students can think about and choose among enriching educational experiences such as study abroad, volunteer work, or internships.
7. Middle- and high-income students do not have to think about working 20 or more hours a week (in fact low-income students typically work over 35 hours) to pay for the basics of food and shelter.
8. Middle- and high-income students do not have to send money back to their parents to support them and their siblings.
9. Middle- and high-income students have often been socialized to understand financial basics such as credit, debt, savings, budgeting, and financial planning.
10. Middle- and high-income students do not worry about paying for on-campus housing at schools where living on campus is required.
11. Middle- and high-income students do not have to live with multiple roommates in order to make housing affordable, which can often leads to a loud and busy environment for studying.
12. Middle- and high-income students have been socialized to cultural knowledge about ways to act at social events, food and drink that are part of social activities, and other knowledge that makes social integration easier and relates to less stress.
13. Middle- and high-income students have money for clothes that help them fit into the campus environment, social activities, and community events such as commencement.
14. Middle- and high-income students do not have to worry about the cost of a gown for graduation.
15. Middle- and high-income students have parents who are connected to higher education institutions and are alumni, which provides unparalleled access and attention.
16. Middle- and high-income students rarely attend community colleges with insufficient funding and facilities, and likely attend four-year institutions that are well-funded with elaborate facilities.
17. Middle- and high-income students typically live close to campus or on campus and do not have to commute long distances for affordable housing.
18. Middle- and high-income students believe in competition and individual success; low-income students tend to have stronger group affinity, making competitive situations set up in schools such as grading or debate more difficult for them.
19. Middle- and high-income students attend well-resourced high schools with better opportunities for learning and success.
20. Middle- and high-income students have faculty role models with similar experiences and background.
21. Middle- and high-income students do not have to worry about whether they can enroll in needed classes because it conflicts with their work schedule.
22. Middle- and high-income students see themselves represented in the curriculum; they read authors from their same background and experience.

* While I say "do not," I recognize that this is not true for all middle- and high-income students and that this essentializes this group in order to make the point. Using "often" would likely be the most accurate word, but for rhetorical purposes, I use "do not" as a generalization that can often fit.

all students really pay the extravagant costs for books that can be over $1,000 a semester?

These assumptions also point out challenges that low-income students face that are often invisible to campus staff such as: financial stress, fear of debt, lack of discretionary funding, working long hours, living far from campus, lack of transportation, needing childcare, crowded housing conditions, having to attend low resourced schools because they are convenient, staying close to and helping family, lack of role models for college, lack of knowledge about college, having difficulty understanding FAFSA (Free Application for Federal Student Aid) and college admissions processes, being less likely to feel faculty are approachable or have a similar background to them, feeling like outsiders socially, being unable to find peers, not understanding social etiquette of middle- and high-income, feeling they have to give up their culture to be successful, and feeling pressured to enroll in a major that is lucrative rather than their passion. These many challenges have been empirically documented and are summarized in Walpole (2007). Campus administrators need to make themselves aware and familiar with these unquestioned assumptions that create structural barriers for students.

While these are just a sampling of the many ways that middle- and high-income students are privileged on campus, there are hundreds of other ways in which middle- and high-income students are free from the worry that low-income students experience on a daily basis, which makes it more difficult for them to access and be successful in higher education. One of the outcomes of the "Whiteness Movement" has been to develop much greater awareness among people who are Caucasian of the many privileges that they experience and to help them better understand the stresses that people of color encounter (Borrego, 2008; McIntosh, 1988).

In higher education and society, we need a "Wealth Movement" in which middle-and high-income people recognize the privileges that they experience and are better attuned to the difficulty that low-income people experience as they engage various institutions that are biased against their success, including postsecondary institutions. Campuses can use this more general analysis about hidden assumptions in the system as a place to begin on-campus analysis. With an appreciation of the inherent biases that privilege middle- and high-income students and the barriers for low-income students, campuses can begin to more deeply examine their specific structures and history to understand ways that their own campuses need to be altered to create opportunity—undergoing their own deconstruction.

DECONSTRUCTION AND RECONSTRUCTION—
ANALYZING SPECIFIC CAMPUS ENVIRONMENTS AND
PRACTICES

Higher education staff, administrators, and faculty typically do not ex-amine the way institutions are structured to disadvantage low-income students, and, as hooks (2000) notes, they blame the student for not being good enough and postsecondary staff pride themselves for having pro-vided financial aid, which should be enough. Examining the system and structures through deconstruction can help faculty and administrators dispel the myth that low-income students' success is an individual problem and out of their control. In my research about low-income students, I have often heard the following type of comment: "We gave them financial aid, and they still did not succeed, so what can we do?"

This section aids staff in understanding how to deconstruct current practices that shape low-income student success, usually disadvantaging them, and provides ideas for creating new structures that can better serve low-income students. I provide a few examples (curriculum, housing polices, pedagogical style, and orientation programs) of this process of deconstruction and reconstruction in this chapter, but the other authors will provide more detail about a variety of structures, practices, and processes that can be altered. While these processes can be separated in analysis, I combine the deconstruction and reconstruction process in this chapter.

One example of a structure that needs to be deconstructed is the college curriculum. Low-income students are likely to find themselves invisible in the curriculum. While campuses offer ethnic and women's studies, few campuses offer working-class or poverty studies. General education reform efforts often include an effort to include women and people of color (e.g., their efforts historically, diverse authors, or diverse literature in classes) in core course material. However, there is not a similar effort to include individuals with a low-income background within course materials at most institutions. By examining the curriculum in this way, campuses can initiate efforts to rethink (reconstruct) their general educa-tion requirements and consider whether they should start a working-class studies program or integrate social class into one of the other programs on campus. A post-structural analysis emphasizes certain assumptions that should be taken into account as the reconstruction process is being conducted. For example, as faculty develop poverty or working-class studies programs and choose textbooks, they should include material to help students to develop capacities to examine the complexities of class. It is important that multiple class perspectives are offered so that differ-ent types of working-class students can see themselves. In fact, Purdue

University has an important approach to help students see the connections between local context/history and class development/experience. The students in this general education course on poverty go out into the local community (Cleveland) and learn about and document the local history around poverty. In this way, students see how social class and poverty is historically and culturally situated and experience the phenomenon by talking with and being out in the community—it is not an abstraction. In addition, it is important that class be investigated at multiple levels examining individual attitudes, institutional practices, and cultural norms. Also, material should emphasize the intersection of race, class, and gender so that students develop a sophisticated appreciation of the way these different aspects of identity are overlapping and interlocking.

Housing facilities and policies are another area that may benefit from a post-structural analysis. Campuses often require living on campus and encourage students to live in crowded residence halls. For students who can find no one else from their background (low-income) in such settings, this can be extremely uncomfortable. bell hooks (2000) recalls how she had to see a school psychiatrist at Stanford to be given permission to live off campus (since living on campus was the norm)—certainly a way to make someone feel unwelcome and ostracized. She was adamant about getting off campus because she experienced so much contempt from other classmates because she did not dress or act appropriately. These issues came up more when living in close quarters and are much more likely to cause tension if students live on campus. Also, hooks had nowhere to go on holiday breaks when the dorms closed—all the middle- and high-income students could fly home, a luxury she could not afford. So, it is important to think about the challenges presented by requiring students to live on campus as well as specific housing polices such as holiday breaks. Thinking through a post-structuralist lens, different types of students may experience housing policies in unique ways and different campuses will have varying cultures. Therefore different subgroups of low-income stu dents should be considered when developing policy and campuses should review their history and local culture as they craft housing arrangements. As a result of this rethinking, campus leaders might propose housing as optional, may try to create a housing unit that groups people from similar backgrounds, or link low-income students with staff or faculty mentors to help them better adjust to housing. Accommodations should be made for breaks—keeping them open or providing optional locations, if the cost to keep an entire facility open is too costly.

Another area to deconstruct is pedagogical style. Many higher education courses are taught based on theoretical principles and spend little time connecting theory to practice. Low-income students often come from environments where concrete results and practical knowledge have been the focus, rather than theory or abstract thinking. In order to make students more successful, faculty can make better links between abstract principles they are describing and the way they shape actual problems or circumstances in the world. In her book on *Teaching Working Class*, Linkon (1999) emphasizes the importance of making sure that theoretical work is connected to more relevant examples and connected to work or internship experiences. Low-income students are looking for real-world applications of learning. Grassi, Armon, and Barker (2008) describe a teacher education program specifically designed to retain low-income students by connecting them to schools that are in low-income areas—an issue the students care about. Also, classrooms are often structured in ways that create competition and reward individual effort. Many science courses are graded on a curve where some students must fail. Low-income students often come from communities that value group affiliation over individual success and competition, and thrive more in courses where group activities and collective effort is rewarded. Faculty development can be crafted on campuses to discuss the benefits and disadvantages of different approaches to grading and assignments. Also, because of the power relations that often play out between faculty and students, post-structural analysis would suggest that there needs to be particular emphasis on helping faculty see that students may be intimidated by faculty or their classrooms practices. Also, students from certain ethnic or racial backgrounds will also reinforce cooperative and collective approaches to pedagogy, making this an even stronger value for certain populations of low-income students. While the individual classroom is harder to access and reconstruct, it is important to find avenues for impacting this arena as it has a strong influence on student retention (Cole, 2008).

Orientation programs on campus largely assume that students have a basic understanding about the importance of getting to know faculty members, how to communicate with faculty and staff, how to be successful in class, what can be learned from co-curricular and extracurricular activities, how to meet other students, and other basic information that would be communicated to students who had parents who attended college or lived in communities where people attended college. Low-income students are often afraid to ask questions or demonstrate a lack of knowledge in class for fear that it will expose them as out of place and that they do not belong on campus. However, working-class students often need help transitioning and learning the unwritten rules. More campuses have begun to provide separate orientation for first-generation college students, but these individuals are typically chosen from bridge programs and other programs aimed at racially diverse students, not necessarily low-income students (Borrego, 2008). It is important that orientation programs think more about ways to recruit low-income students (that may not be in racially focused programs) and make the material pertinent to their needs. These are just a few examples of structures that need to be examined and reconstructed on campus. In other chapters, you will read about transfer policies, financial aid, engagement, remediation, and the like.

CONCLUSION

The structures that do not support low-income students are part of a larger system of prestige that supports the garnering of money and privilege in the academy. As hooks (2000) notes: "Much of discussion among faculty is about obtaining money through grants and consulting. Prestige is heaped on people who bring in the most money to the institution. Greed is an overwhelming value and part of the consciousness of academe" (hooks, 2000, p. 61). While this book does not address this broader set of structures in detail, it is important to understand that as structuralism would predict, these systems are inter-related.

Efforts to reveal hidden assumptions, deconstruct structures, and consider new ones will likely evoke these broader systems and entrenched beliefs that support the wealthy at all levels of the institution—administration, faculty, staff, and others. I want to merely end this chapter by reminding readers about this broader system and remark that other chapter authors (see chapters by St. John, Chambers and Deller, and Levin et al., which examine the link between institutional policy and state or federal policy) will also refer to the broader systems that support the wealthy and create an overarching set of structures that complicate the task of making low-income students successful. While for clarity and precision, we focus on low-income students and the structures that impact them most directly, faculty reward structures, professional roles, and other systems may also need further exploration to ensure student success.

NOTES

1. Class and socioeconomic status (ses) or income level are related, but not inter-changeable concepts (Walpole, 2007). Income level/ses is a descriptive category that accounts for the amount of money that certain populations or individuals have. Class is related to income in that people in society are typically divided into different status levels based on wealth. In the United States different classes based on income are lower class, working class, and middle class, for example. But class is a term that refers to stratifications in society but they may be based on income or other characteristics. In the United States, income level typically is used as a mode to stratify people, so class and income overlap strongly within this society. Class may also refer to more than income level and focuses on life experience as a result of income. People can come from a middle-class family and go

     into poverty. They might continue to be privileged from their upbringing as middle class (Linkon, 1999). Also, those in poverty can ascend into the middle class but maintain a working-class perspective.

2. I use the term low-income to refer to a broad class of people referred to by several different terms—low-income, working-class, and low socioeconomic status.

3. Post-structuralism is not a finite theory but is a term used for a variety of thinkers that critiqued structuralism. Few of these individuals actually called their work post-structural. Using the term is somewhat problematic, although it is commonly used to describe a particular set of assumptions embedded across these similar thinkers.

4. Many people confuse post-structuralism and post-modernism. They are related but distinctive. They are not synonymous.

5. Post-structuralism in literature and sociology have different emphasis. In this book, we are using the sociological, not literary approaches to post-structuralism. The approach we adopt is similar to that adopted by women's and ethnic studies and in feminist analysis. We use it to bring class to light rather than race and gender.

6. The following are common assumptions of structuralism —articulated in the sentences in the text, but summarized for clarity: 1. the structure is what determines the position of each element of a whole; 2. structuralists believe that every system has a structure; 3. structuralists are interested in the structural laws that deal with co-existence rather than changes; and 4. structures are real things that lie beneath the surface or the appearance of meaning. Meaning is captured through an analysis of the systems (Weedon, 1987).

7. Given this is a huge body of thought and most people do not engage all aspects of this school of thought, this is an acceptable and logical choice.

REFERENCES

Borrego, S. (2003). *Class matters: Beyond access to inclusion.* Washington, DC: NASPA.

Borrego, S. (2008). Class on campus: Breaking the silence surrounding socioeconomics. *Diversity & Democracy, 11*(3), 1–2. Washington, DC: Association of American Colleges and Universities.

Bourdieu, P. (1977). Cultural reproduction and social reproduction. In J. Karabel & A. Halsey (Eds.), *Power and ideology in education* (pp. 487–511). New York: Oxford University Press.

Chesler, M., & Crowfoot, J. (1989). An organizational analysis of racism in higher education. In M. Peterson (Ed.), *ASHE reader on organization and governance in higher education* (4th ed.). Lexington, MA: Ginn Press.

Cohen, A. (2007). *The shaping of American higher education.* San Francisco: Jossey-Bass.

Cole, D. (2008). Constructive criticism: The role of student-faculty interactions on African American and Hispanic students' educational gains. *Journal of College Student Development, 49*(6), 587–605.

Foucault, M. (1980). Two lectures. In C. Gordon (Ed.), *Michel Foucault: Power/knowledge: Selected writings and other writings 1972–1977 by Michel Foucault.* Hemel Hempstead: Harvester-Wheatsheaf.

Gilbert, R. (2008). Raising awareness of class privilege among students. *Diversity & Democracy, 11*(3), 7–9. Washington, DC: Association of American Colleges and Universities.

Grassi, E., Armon, J., & Barker, B. (2008). Don't lose your working-class students. *Diversity & Democracy, 11*(3), 4–6. Washington, DC: Association of American Colleges and Universities.

hooks, b. (2000). *Where we stand: Class matters.* New York: Routledge.

Linkon, S. (1999). *Teaching working class.* Amherst, MA: University of Massachusetts Press.

Lucas, C. (1994). *American higher education: A history.* New York: St. Martin's Press.

Lynch, K., & O'Riordan, C. (1998). Inequality in higher education: A study of class barriers. *Journal of Sociology of Education, 19*(4), 445–478.

McIntosh, P. (1988). *White privilege and male privilege: A personal account of coming to see correspondences through work in women's studies.* Working Paper No. 189. Wellesley College: Center for Research on Women.

Vigeland, T. (Host). (2008, January 11). What is the middle class? [Audi podcast]. Retrieved from Marketplace.publicradio.org/display/web/2008/01/11/what_is_the_middle_class?

Walpole, M. (2007). *Economically and educationally challenged students in higher education: Access to outcomes* (ASHE Higher Education Report, Vol. 33, No. 3). San Francisco: Jossey-Bass.

Weedon, C. (1987). *Feminist practice and post-structuralist theory.* Oxford: Blackwell.

II
Access to Postsecondary Institutions

2

LESSONS LEARNED FROM INDIANA'S TWENTY-FIRST CENTURY SCHOLARS PROGRAM

Toward a Comprehensive Approach to Improving College Preparation and Access for Low-Income Students

EDWARD P. ST. JOHN

Indiana was the first state to develop a comprehensive approach to improving educational opportunities for low-income students. The Twenty-First Century Scholars Program (TFCS) was modeled after the "I have a dream" program in New York City schools. Any low-income student who took a pledge to prepare for college would receive a promise of financial aid equal to tuition; in addition, programs would be created so that the families of the students could learn how to help them prepare for and succeed in college. Governor Evan Bayh introduced the program into legislation in 1990, but the program was controversial and became an unfunded mandate. The Lilly Endowment began funding the parent component of the program in 1992, and eventually the state funded its grant obligation through the program. TFCS has been treated as a national model (Advisory Committee on Student Financial Assistance, 2002), with features of the program being replicated in programs in other states.

The financial aid guarantee provided by TFCS has certainly been an important part of the Indiana story and the gradual improvements in access in the 1990s compared to other states. However, while the total grant commitment—to fund tuition—was substantial, the actual increase in per-student cost over the state's base grant was modest, because Indiana also funded a generous need-based grant program in the late

1990s and early 2000s. Indiana had also made changes in high school graduation requirements to increase the number of high school students who graduated prepared to go on to college. That the guarantee provided an incentive for academic preparation in an environment that already encouraged and supported it is a part of the story not frequently told (Lumina Foundation, 2008).

Most of the research on TFCS to date has focused on its impact on enrollment (e.g., St. John, Musoba, Simmons, & Chung, 2002). This chapter provides the following:

- Background on the Twenty-First Century Scholars Program, with a focus on the roles of state K-12 education policy, aid guarantees, and support services, which have been the foci of the program.
- Deconstruction of the program highlighting recent research on TFCS indicating that college and university campuses have not provided sufficient academic support for students (Lumina Foundation, 2008).
- Guidance for states and campuses to expand college access using comprehensive, cohesive strategies based on my research on Indiana colleges and universities (St. John & Musoba, in review).

TWENTY-FIRST CENTURY SCHOLARS PROGRAM IN CONTEXT

The Twenty-First Century Scholars Program was implemented in Indiana, a state that was already in the midst of reform. After discussing the program's design in context, I summarize previously published research, examine new findings related to preparation, and provide descriptive information on the students.

Since the late 1990s, the state of Indiana has required all high schools to offer the Core 40 diploma and strongly encouraged them to offer the additional advanced courses for completion of an Honors diploma. The state provides additional funding to schools per student completing a Core 40 or Honors diploma as an incentive for schools to provide these opportunities to more students (Theobald, 2003). The Core 40 comprised of college preparatory courses, including Algebra II, while the Honors diploma included additional language, science, and math courses, along with the alignment of those courses with college admissions. While Indiana has had college preparatory and Honors diploma options for some time, Indiana's SAT (Scholastic Achievement Test) takers had taken fewer advanced courses than those nationally, so it was important to provide incentives for schools to offer and encourage participation in advanced courses.

Another aspect of the pattern of improved access in Indiana has been that outreach, encouragement, and support services have historically been available through the Indiana Career and Postsecondary Assistance Center (ICPAC) (Hossler & Schmit, 1995). This has led to a sustained statewide effort to provide information on education and career options to students in middle and high school. This process of outreach has doubtless contributed to the maintenance of relatively high completion rates in Indiana high schools as compared to the national average, even given an environment of stiffening requirements for graduation.

Still another component of the Indiana story has been the sustained commitment to need-based student financial aid. In a period when many states—Georgia, Louisiana, Michigan, Florida, and New Mexico—have shifted to merit aid as a priority, Indiana has risen among states in its investments in need-based student aid. In 2004, Indiana ranked third behind New York and California on investment in state grants, as measured by the ratio of state spending per full-time student on need-based grants to the weighted average tuition charge in the state. State funding of need-based student financial aid has a strong positive association with college enrollment rates in time-series studies of states (St. John, 2006; St. John, Chung, Musoba, Simmons, Wooden, & Mendez, 2004). In fact, national trends in enrollment rates for high school graduates appear to rise and fall in a pattern consistent with this indicator.

Indiana's Twenty-First Century Scholars Program certainly contributed to the improvement in college enrollment rates in Indiana. Students who qualify for the federal Free and Reduced Lunch Program in the 8th grade are eligible to sign up for TFCS, pledging to take the steps to prepare for college, remain drug and crime free, and apply for college and student financial aid. In return, the state of Indiana guarantees Scholars they will receive grants equaling tuition charges in a public college or university. This grant award, modestly higher than what a high-need student would receive otherwise, provides a guarantee for financial support that eases family concerns about college costs at an early stage in the student's academic career.

The Research Base

To build a research-based understanding of the ways TFCS contributes to expanded educational opportunity in the state, it is important to consider the role of state policy in easing concerns about college costs, enabling preparation, expanding college choice, and enabling degree attainment. TFCS provides a framework to guide research examining the impact of these policies. Logically, there are six different ways policy can influence educational opportunity, which are noted below (and in Table 2.1) along with the ways Indiana's programs address these linkages:

- *Easing family concerns about costs*: If low-income parents no longer fear that college costs will be prohibitive, they are more likely to encourage their children to take the steps to prepare for college (Linkage 1, Table 2.1). The pledge process in the Twenty-First Century Scholars Program provides a mechanism for formalizing this link by committing grant funding as a response to the student's pledge.
- *High school policies that provide opportunities for preparation*: The state of Indiana requires all high schools to offer college preparatory curriculum (Core 40) and Honors diplomas and provides extra funds to high schools based on the number of students who graduate with these advanced diplomas. These policies have the potential to improve opportunities for low-income students to complete preparatory courses (Linkage 2).
- *Encouragement and outreach to improve preparation and college application rates*: Indiana provides information as support for all students and their parents and coordinates regional centers to encourage students to prepare and apply (Linkage 3).
- *State grants coordinated with tuition to make pricing more transparent and improve access*: Twenty-First Century Scholars are guaranteed grants equaling public college tuition which means their aid packages are more likely to meet financial need and increase enrollment opportunity (Linkage 4), a link confirmed by prior research (St. John, Musoba, Simmons, & Chung, 2002).
- *State grants to improve the chances of enrolling in college*: Prior research confirms that Scholars awards improve the odds that low-income students will enroll in both two-year and four-year colleges compared to non-enrollment (Linkage 5) (St. John, Musoba, Simmons, & Chung, 2002; St. John, Musoba, Simmons, Chung, Schmit, & Peng, 2004).
- *State grants, college academic programs and student services to improve attainment*: Once admitted to college, Twenty-First Century Scholars benefit from academic support and student aid like other students, and research indicates Scholars have the same odds of persisting through the first four years of college as Non-Scholars (St. John, Gross, Musoba, & Chung, 2006) despite their low-income status (Linkage 6).

Prior research on the Twenty-First Century Scholars and other policies in Indiana evolved over more than a decade. Initial studies tracked

Table 2.1   Twenty-first Century Scholars: Program Features that Link to Academic Capital Formation for Low-Income Students

Potential Linkage	Program Feature
1. Easing concerns about college costs early on can improve aspirations for low-income families.	Students in the Free and Reduced Lunch Program can take the Scholars Pledge to prepare for college and stay drug free which ensures tuition support if they fulfill their obligations and apply for student aid.
2. Education funding and reforms can improve preparation.	Indiana requires all high schools to offer a college preparatory curriculum and provides supplemental funding to schools based on the number of students who complete advanced high school diplomas.
3. Encouragement and information on academic programs and student aid can improve preparation.	State Students' Assistance Commission of Indiana (SSACI) provides support services to Scholars and their parents, including homework support, campus visits, and parent groups.
4. Coordinated state financing (need-based aid equaling tuition) can ease the burden on campuses to meet the financial needs of low-income students.	Provides grants for Twenty-First Century Scholars equaling tuition in public colleges or a subsidy for students in private colleges. State of Indiana requires that the maximum grant award be no larger than tuition charges.
5. Coordinated state finance policies and institutional grants can improve access and opportunity for prepared low- and middle-income students to enroll in more selective four-year colleges.	Indiana indexes the maximum award for state grants to tuition in public colleges. Additional costs for Scholars are relatively modest.
6. Coordinated state finance policies can improve the odds of persistence and degree attainment by low- and middle-income students.	The State of Indiana has delivered on its commitment to Twenty-First Century Scholars and fully funded state grant programs. In addition, colleges provide support services for Scholars which can improve academic and civic engagement during college and the odds of persistence.

students from high school into college and were used to build a new theory of college student choice focusing on the role of early information (Hossler, Schmit, & Vesper, 1999). In addition, the Indiana Commission for Higher Education (ICHE) has collected student records for years, providing a basis for evaluating the impact of the state's student-grant programs on persistence (St. John, Hu, & Weber, 2000, 2001). The initial study of the impact of the Twenty-First Century Scholars Program's funding found that scholars had the same odds of persisting as other aid recipients (St. John, Musoba, & Simmons, 2003) as noted above. After this study was initially presented at a conference, two program officers from the Lumina Foundation requested another study of the program focusing on enrollment.

The Linkage between Aid Guarantees and Preparation

With financial support from Lumina it was possible to develop a cohort file for a survey of eighth-grade students who graduated from high school and enrolled in college in 1999, examining the effects of taking the Scholars Pledge on preparation, enrollment, and persistence. These studies found that the program substantially improved the odds that low-income students would apply for college and student aid, enroll in college, and enroll in a four-year college (Musoba, 2004; St. John, Musoba, Simmons, Schmit, Chung, & Peng, 2002). A follow-up study found that Twenty-First Century Scholars persisted over four years as well as other aid recipients and other low-income aid recipients (St. John, Gross et al., 2006).

In addition, Lumina funded the development of a 2000 cohort with data from the College Board surveys and ICHE student record systems. The results of studies using this cohort (e.g., St. John, Carter, Chung, & Musoba, 2006) provided an initial assessment of state policies on preparation, access, and student success. This research indicates that the comprehensive reform approach used in Indiana—the combination of high school curriculum reform, coordinated state finance policies, and aid guarantees coupled with support services for low-income students provided by TFCS—contributed to improvements in high school preparation and college enrollment by Indiana high school students.

Comparison of Scholars and Other Low-Income Students

The 2000 cohort of Indiana residents in public colleges, compiled from ICHE databases, provides a database uniquely suited to examining the role of high school context in the preparation of low-income students. A longitudinal file was constructed for this cohort that combined SAT questionnaires and data from the State Student Information System (SIS) used for several studies of academic progress (Musoba, 2004; St. John, Carter et al., 2006; St. John & Musoba, in review).

Pell recipients who were not Scholars[1] provide an appropriate comparison group. Both Scholars and Pell recipients were from mostly low-SES (socioeconomic status) families, and parents' education was similar for the two groups, as were educational aspirations. There were a few differences between these populations (Table 2.2):

- There were more African Americans and fewer Whites among the Scholars than the Non-Scholars.
- The majority of both groups were in the lowest income quartile, but this was more likely among Non-Scholars.

Table 2.2 Comparison of Scholars and Non-Scholars (Other Pell Recipients among Freshmen Indiana Residents)

	Not a Scholar 76.89%	Scholar 23.11%
Composite Gender		
Male	41.45	40.10
Female	58.55	59.90
Composite Ethnicity		
Native American	0.53	0.48
Asian American Pacific Islander	1.88	0.80
African American	12.63	24.78
Hispanic	2.70	5.77
White	76.07	64.55
Other	1.13	2.33
Missing	5.06	1.28
Composite Student Income Level in 2000		
Below $30,000	60.10	52.85
$30,000 to $70,000	38.43	41.54
$70,000 and over	1.35	5.61
Missing	0.12	0.00
Composite Parent Education		
Middle/Jr. High school or Less	2.58	2.97
High school	52.00	51.00
College or beyond	41.18	37.85
Missing	4.24	8.18
SAT Test Taker		
Yes	64.17	66.16
No	35.83	33.84
College Destination		
Community College	23.54	14.84
Four-year Public	68.39	78.19
Four-year Private	8.07	6.98
Locale		
City	24.60	42.10
Suburban and Town	41.42	35.93
Rural	26.29	18.77
Missing	7.69	3.21
Percent minority students in school 1 = greater than 11.4%		
Less than 11.4%	59.52	44.91
Greater than or equal to 11.4%	32.51	49.00
Missing	7.98	6.09
Percent free and reduced lunch		
Less than 15.4%	44.80	31.52
Greater than or equal to 15.4%	45.64	63.19
Missing	9.57	5.29

- A higher percentage of Non-Scholars were enrolled in schools with a high percentage of low-income students.
- Scholars enrolled in four-year colleges of all types at higher rates than Non-Scholars; about 8.7 percentage points more of the Non-Scholars were enrolled in two-year colleges.

About a third of both groups completed regular diplomas, while slightly more scholars completed Core 40 and slightly more Non-Scholars completed Honors diplomas (Table 2.3). Higher rates of African Americans and Native Americans had regular diplomas, while a larger percentage of Asian Americans had Honors diplomas. About one third of students in both low-income and high-minority schools received regular diplomas. In Indiana, students in all types of schools had access to advanced courses, but not all students who enrolled in college had completed college preparatory diplomas.

A recent qualitative study of students who signed up for TFCS (Enersen, Sevaty-Seib, Pistilli, & Koch, 2008) concluded that the services provided by the program enabled students and their parents to make informed choices about high school curriculum and taking the steps to prepare for college. Based on the research, it is evident there was a screening process, including:

- Self-selection into the program, often the result of strong parental encouragement;
- Parents who were actively engaged were more likely to attend focus groups and take their students to events including focus groups; and
- Engaged parents and students had an inner hardiness—a set of personal assets—that enabled them to take advantage of the program to build college knowledge.

When we used logistic regression analyses to examine the effects of being a Scholar on completion of advanced diplomas controlling for variables related to background, aspirations, and school characteristics, we found a significant difference between Scholars and Non-Scholars on completing Core 40 diplomas, but not on completion of an Honors diploma (St. John, Fisher, Lee, Daun-Barnett, & Williams, 2008). The analyses also indicated that for low-income African Americans, being a Scholar was associated with completion of an Honors diploma and completion of calculus. These analyses provide a basis for concluding that the Twenty-First Century Scholars Program improves access to advanced courses during high school.

Table 2.3 Breakdown of Independent Variables by Diploma Type for Scholars and Comparison Group

	N	Honors Row %	Core 40 Row %	Regular Row %
Composite Gender				
Male	2,220	21.13	41.22	37.66
Female	3,177	28.49	41.14	30.37
Composite Ethnicity				
Native American	28	10.71	46.43	42.86
Asian American Pacific Islander	88	47.73	34.09	18.18
African American	833	12.85	44.90	42.26
Hispanic	184	16.30	52.72	30.98
White	3,962	29.48	41.65	28.87
Other	76	30.26	39.47	30.26
Missing	226	0.44	12.39	87.17
Composite Student Income Level in 2000				
Below $30,000	3,153	21.38	40.79	37.84
$30,000 to $70,000	2,113	31.42	42.31	26.27
$70,000 and over	126	27.78	33.33	38.89
Missing	5	20.00		80.00
Composite Parent Education Level				
Middle/Jr High school or Less	144	20.14	36.11	43.75
High school	2,794	25.02	42.30	32.68
College or beyond	2,181	28.43	41.91	29.67
Missing	278	9.35	26.62	64.03
21st Century Scholar				
Not a Scholar	4,150	25.61	40.75	33.64
Scholar	1,247	24.94	42.58	32.48
SAT Test Taker				
Yes	3,488	33.34	46.27	20.38
No	1,909	7.36	36.20	56.44
College Destination				
Community College	1,162	3.79	26.59	69.62
Four year Public	3,813	31.08	46.60	22.32
Four-year Private	422	34.36	32.23	33.41
Locale				
City	1,546	22.06	44.76	33.18
Suburban and Town	2,167	28.43	42.87	28.70
Rural	1,325	29.74	41.06	29.21
Missing	359	6.41	15.88	77.72
Percent minority students in school 1 = greater than 11.4%				
Less than 11.4%	3,030	30.10	45.20	24.70
Greater than or equal to 11.4%	1,960	24.01	41.46	34.53
Missing	407	6.14	20.09	68.68
Percent free and reduced lunch				
Less than 15.4%	2,252	30.10	45.20	24.70
Greater than or equal to 15.4%	2,682	24.01	41.46	34.53
Missing	463	11.23	20.09	68.68
Total	5,397	25.46	41.17	33.37

DECONSTRUCTING: INSUFFICIENT SUPPORT BY COLLEGES AND UNIVERSITIES

Recently Lumina Foundation (2008) summarized qualitative and quantitative studies of the TFCS program. Consistent with the review above, the Foundation found effects on preparation and enrollment, but criticized the colleges and universities in the state for failing to provide support services for the new students who enter as a result of their involvement in the Scholars Program. This critique was based largely on the site visits conducted by the Indiana University-Purdue University Indianapolis (IUPUI) study team (e.g. Smith, Helfenbein, Hughes, Stuckey, & Berumen, 2008). Below I examine trends in minority representation in Indiana colleges and universities before providing a focused critique of higher education in Indiana, building on the conclusions of the Lumina reported informed by analysis of minority representation.

Evidence on Minority Representation

Trends in minority participation provide an indicator of how well the state system is doing in representation of minorities in higher education. Unfortunately, Indiana's programs have not equalized opportunity for enrollment of students of color in public four-year colleges (Figure 2.1). There has been some improvement: between 1992, when the first Scholars cohort entered college, and 2006 the ratio of African American FTE

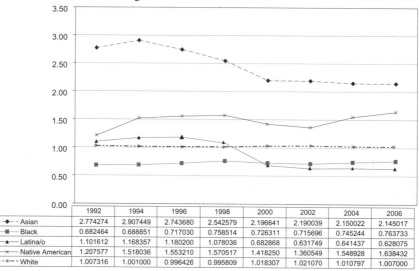

	1992	1994	1996	1998	2000	2002	2004	2006
Asian	2.774274	2.907449	2.743680	2.542579	2.196641	2.190039	2.150022	2.145017
Black	0.682464	0.688851	0.717030	0.758514	0.726311	0.715696	0.745244	0.763733
Latina/o	1.101612	1.168357	1.180200	1.078036	0.682868	0.631749	0.641437	0.628075
Native American	1.207577	1.518036	1.553210	1.570517	1.418250	1.360549	1.548928	1.638432
White	1.007316	1.001000	0.996426	0.995809	1.018307	1.021070	1.010797	1.007000

Figure 2.1 Racial/Ethnic Representation in Indiana Public Four-Year Postsecondary Institutions as a Proportion of the State Population. Data from NCES Integrated Postsecondary Education Data System and U.S. Census Bureau.

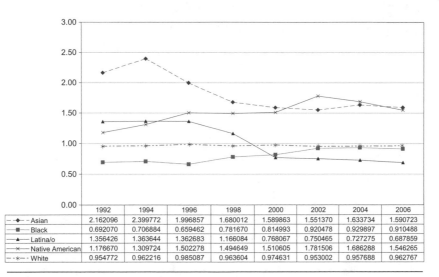

	1992	1994	1996	1998	2000	2002	2004	2006
- - ◆ - - Asian	2.162096	2.399772	1.996857	1.680012	1.589863	1.551370	1.633734	1.590723
■ Black	0.692070	0.706884	0.659462	0.781670	0.814993	0.920478	0.929897	0.910488
▲ Latina/o	1.356426	1.363644	1.362683	1.166084	0.768067	0.750465	0.727275	0.687859
✕ Native American	1.176670	1.309724	1.502278	1.494649	1.510605	1.781506	1.686288	1.546265
- - ✱ - - White	0.954772	0.962216	0.985087	0.963604	0.974631	0.953002	0.957688	0.962767

Figure 2.2 Racial/Ethnic Representation in Indiana Private Nonprofit Postsecondary Institutions as a Proportion of the State Population. Data from NCES Integrated Postsecondary Education Data System and U.S. Census Bureau.

(full-time equivalent students) to total FTE students in public four-year colleges compared to the percentage of African Americans in the state's population rose from 0.68 to 0.76. This represents an improvement possibly attributable to increased access to preparatory curriculum and student aid. However, this is substantially below the national average: nationally the ratio for African American representation in four-year colleges was 0.88 percent in 2006 (St. John, Pineda, & Moronski, in preparation).

In contrast, the ratio of African American representation in private colleges (Figure 2.2) rose more substantially and nearly equaled Whites in 2006. In addition, the gap in enrollment rates for African Americans and Whites in the entire state system (Figure 2.3)—all public and private colleges—had narrowed substantially and nearly equalized. These trends indicate that the combination of policies in Indiana has not enabled equalization of enrollment opportunities in the state's public four-year colleges, although substantial progress was made after implementation of the Twenty-First Century Scholars Program.

The Challenge in Indiana

The underrepresentation of Hispanics is an even more serious problem in Indiana than it is in the rest of the U.S. (St. John et al., in preparation). This challenge is complicated by issues related to immigration to the United States and migration across the United States, along with the same preparation, information, and financial issues that confront other

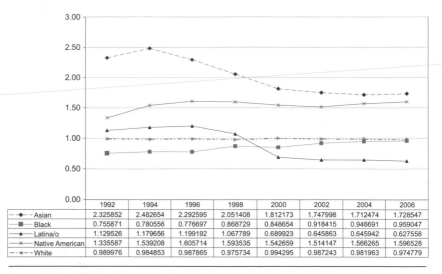

	1992	1994	1996	1998	2000	2002	2004	2006
Asian	2.325852	2.482654	2.292595	2.051408	1.812173	1.747998	1.712474	1.728547
Black	0.755871	0.780556	0.776697	0.868729	0.848654	0.918415	0.946691	0.959047
Latina/o	1.129526	1.179656	1.199192	1.067789	0.689923	0.645863	0.645942	0.627558
Native American	1.335587	1.539208	1.605714	1.593535	1.542659	1.514147	1.566265	1.596528
White	0.989976	0.984853	0.987865	0.975734	0.994295	0.987243	0.981963	0.974779

Figure 2.3 Racial/Ethnic Representation in Indiana Postsecondary Institutions as a Proportion of the State Population. Data from NCES Integrated Postsecondary Education Data System and U.S. Census Bureau.

groups. Indiana has not made progress on confronting this challenge in spite of implementation of the Twenty-First Century Scholars Program. The state of Indiana faces serious problems with respect to minority representation.

Specifically, the problem of unequal access is centered in four-year public colleges and universities, the institutions where African Americans and Hispanics were most seriously underrepresented. Addressing this challenge should be a priority of Indiana's public colleges and universities.

RECONSTRUCTING STRATEGIES

The evidence regarding Indiana's Twenty-First Century Scholars Program illustrates that combining support services with financial aid guarantees enables a higher percentage of low-income students to prepare for and enroll in college. There were gains in enrollment of minority students in Indiana's private colleges and two-year colleges, but the public four-year colleges and universities had not yet responded to the challenge. Public four-year colleges have neither provided the access evident in other types of colleges in the state, nor provided support services needed to retain Scholars who enter with this generous state support (St. John & Musoba, in review).

Linking to Outreach Programs: Access is not Sufficient

Public universities are situated at the intersection of policies and practices that can reinforce access barriers to higher education for low-income students. If colleges use traditional selection methods within state systems that advantage some groups of students (i.e., middle-income, suburban, White) over others (i.e., low-income, urban, minority), then higher education reinforces the discriminatory features of a state's K-12 education system. It is too easy to blame K-12 education and continue with current practices under the assumption they are fair. This elitist position has made it exceedingly easy for public universities to abdicate their responsibility to maintain fair and equitable access for all children in their state.

In states with K-12 systems that are unequal, it is simply unjust for a state university to ignore these underlying inequalities. Universities in the states of California, Washington, Texas, and Michigan have made efforts to address the underlying problems in systemic ways. Universities in these states were obligated to use alternative methods when they could no longer use affirmative action as a partial remedy to inequality. Various models of outreach to high schools and financial aid are being tested and merit further study.

In Indiana there continue to be serious problems with the underrepresentation of minority students in public colleges. A more concerted effort to engage in outreach that builds partnerships with public high schools, possibly coupled with the use of noncognitive variables in the selection of students, would seem warranted. Unfortunately, Indiana's public colleges have not linked their efforts in admissions with outreach to students in the Twenty-First Century Scholars Program, unlike many of the state's private colleges. Instead, the focus in public colleges has been on retention.

Integrating Access with Academic Support

The Indiana Project on Academic Success (IPAS) has recently pioneered a strategy of reform that involves using student records to assess challenges, identify new remedies, and test these approaches (Hossler, Ziskin, & Gross, 2009a, 2009b; St. John & Wilkerson, 2006). Recent evaluations have found that two of the four-year campuses involved in IPAS had improved retention through supplemental instruction, learning communities, and other interventions (Musoba, 2006; Robinson, 2009; Hossler et al., 2009a, 2009b). However, most colleges had not focused on retention of students entering through the Twenty-First Century Scholars Program and overall degree attainment rates remained relatively low in Indiana's public colleges (St. John & Musoba, in review).

Indiana has fallen short of the standard for a comprehensive and cohesive approach to reform. Based on experience using action research to support and inform initiatives in colleges and universities that promote equity in college opportunity (St. John, 2009a, 2009b; St. John & Wilkerson, 2006), it is possible to provide guidance to college administrators and faculty interested in promoting systemic change. Change in universities evolves from strategic initiatives and, therefore, a commitment to remedying inequalities is crucial. The fact that inequalities in K-12 systems render conventional academic strategies ineffective in promoting equity is not well understood by many college faculty members. It is often argued that all students must meet the same standards. But if the standards are unfair as a result of systemic inequalities, it is necessary to rethink this practice and consider balancing what John Rawls (1971) calls "the difference principle," which permits inequalities if they benefit the disadvantaged (i.e., the least advantaged should have the first opportunity) with these conventional arguments.

A comprehensive approach to providing outreach and support is possible, but requires coordination across levels of education. Table 2.4 presents a comprehensive approach to expanding opportunity based on the study of students in Twenty-First Century Scholars, Washington State Achievers, and Gates Millennium Scholars, three programs that combine student aid and support services (St. John, forthcoming). Below is a summary of how well Indiana had met this standard when these studies were completed:

1. *Linking to School Reform*: While the state of Indiana had undertaken curriculum reform in high schools and provided incentives for students to prepare, the public colleges and universities had not built linkages through outreach and partnerships with high schools.
2. *Guarantees for Aid*: The TFCS provided an aid guarantee. Recently, in response to the widely heralded North Carolina Covenant (discussed below), Purdue University and Indiana University have taken steps to make their commitments explicit, but these steps had not been taken during the period studied.
3. *Encouragement and Outreach*: The Twenty-First Century Scholars Program provides a national model for state efforts to provide information, but most public campuses had not built on this base in providing outreach, as illustrated by the relatively low percentage of minorities in public colleges (discussed above).
4. *Admissions*: It is possible to adapt admissions practices to consider noncognitive variables that identify student strengths, an approach used in the Washington State Achievers and Gates Millennium Scholars (Sedlacek, 2004). If Indiana's research universities made adaptations to admissions to consider the strengths like self navigation of educational skills, a noncognitive variable evident among TFCS

students (St. John, forthcoming), it has not been communicated in public forums or other means.

5. *Academic Support:* In recent years, Indiana four-year colleges have made substantial progress with supplemental instruction and other academic support services (St. John & Musoba, in review), but these services had not been explicitly linked with support for students entering through TFCS (Lumina Foundation, 2008).

6. *Student Support:* There are extensive student support services at Indiana's colleges and universities. As is the case for many campuses nationally, a better effort could be made to link these services with students who enter college needing them (Lumina Foundation, 2008).

7. *Communication:* The success of Indiana's TFCS is related to the communication to students and families in middle and high schools. Campus visits help students to develop interest in attending Indiana campuses. More could be done by state colleges and research universities in the state to develop and communicate a commitment to ensuring the success of low-income students (St. John & Musoba, in review).

A Comprehensive Approach is Possible

One excellent national example of a comprehensive approach to providing aid guarantees is the exemplary institutional strategy in the University of North Carolina's Covenant (see www.unc.edu/carolinacovenant/ and www.unc.edu/chan/chancellors/moeser_james/). This program ensures that low-income students (with family incomes indexed to the federal poverty level) will have:

- Grants and work study sufficient to eliminate the need to borrow, a commitment provided to both in-state and out-of-state students who meet the income threshold for the program.
- Outreach and support services including affiliated counselors in North Carolina High Schools.
- Summer programs that provide academic support.
- Counselors and peer advisers to support student transition.
- Work opportunities on campus that further support academic and social engagement.

This program illustrates it is possible for a public university campus to make a transition that moves it toward becoming more equitable in its approach to the recruitment, funding, and support of underrepresented

Table 2.4 Guidance for the Development of Comprehensive and Cohesive Programs (and Financing) to Ensure Equal Access to and Opportunities for Academic Success in Public Universities

Features	Comprehensive	Cohesive
School Reform	• Build partnerships with high-need high schools to support teachers, students, and parents in the preparation and college search processes.	• Coordinate high school partnerships with student aid guarantees, outreach, and selection to ease family concerns about costs and encourage preparation.
Guarantees and Aid	• Communicate criteria for award of need-based aid and packaging strategies to prospective students. • Commit to meeting financial needs, if possible, for all students.	• Link the commitment to supplemental student aid award grants to programs that align with support services. • Coordinate commitments to grant aid with pricing through the annual budgeting process.
Encouragement/ Outreach	• Provide consistent, high quality and trustworthy information on aid packages and grants. • Market programs that build bridges to admission and provide comprehensive support once admitted.	• Build strong partnering organizations to provide academic support for students and teachers. • Design and develop supports for parents (linked to high school partnerships and outreach services).
Selection	• Adapt selection process for fairness in cognitive and noncognitive measures. • Coordinate use of refined selection measures with support services within major academic programs.	• Promote success indicators— the qualities emphasized in noncognitive measures—as part of the marketing strategy. • Build reliable articulation strategies with high schools and junior colleges to ensure diverse pathways.
Academic Support	• Acknowledge tacit contract on admission, indicating services accessible to students to ensure their success. • Target program support— cognitive, noncognitive, and financial—to individual and group needs.	• Integrate opportunities for service learning, engagement in outreach programs, and high school partnerships providing opportunities for give back. • Encourage development of students and professionals.
Student Support	• Provide coaches and peer mentors for students facing difficult transitions, especially first-generation students.	• Align student support services with programs that promote academic achievement and civic engagement.

Features	Comprehensive	Cohesive
Communication	• Emphasize development of human networks that support student development. • Use public relations to emphasize community and diversity based on authentic information.	• Encourage development of mentoring and coaching skills among students, especially upper division and graduate students.

students. The aid commitment made by UNC has been widely replicated,[2] but most campuses have not linked academic support services to this financial commitment. The research evidence on the UNC Covenant indicates that this comprehensive approach has reduced the retention gap for low-income students at the campus (Ort & Williford, 2009; St. John & Musoba, in review).

CONCLUSIONS

States and their public colleges and universities share an interest in expanding college access and equalizing opportunity for enrollment by low-income students. A few states, including Washington and Wisconsin, have adopted the Twenty-First Century Scholars approach. Other states have attended meetings of the National Governors Association featuring TCFS and other programs as models.[3] It is clearly possible to advocate for such state-level programs. However, it is crucial that states also have strategies for improving preparation and encouraging families. A comprehensive and cohesive approach is desirable, and stakeholders must work together toward this end.

Colleges and universities face more serious challenges with respect to equalizing opportunity if they are located in states without grant programs as generous and well targeted as Indiana's Twenty-First Century Scholars Program. It is very difficult for four-year colleges to maintain equal opportunity for enrollment and persistence if they must provide a substantial portion of the need-based grant aid for qualified, low-income students. Without this investment, unequal degree completion rates across income and race groups are virtually unavoidable. Yet making this investment often means higher tuition for students who can pay the price (Hossler, 2006).

In addition to facing the affordability challenges, public colleges are confronted by preparation challenges whether or not they have generous state grant programs. National research indicates low-income students and students of color have more limited access to advanced courses in high school than middle-income students (Adelman, 2005; St. John, 2006). This means that colleges must adjust for the unequal circumstances before college. Precollege programs like Twenty-First Century Scholars can help increase the number of low-income students who prepare. Linking outreach to collegiate support services represents an important step forward often not evident in public institutions.

The problem of inequality in opportunities for persistence represents a serious challenge. The Twenty-First Century Scholars Program fell short of its aims in degree completion; students who participated in the program completed college at about the same rate as other low-income students (St. John et al., 2008). We hope knowledge of this shortfall was taken into consideration when colleges and universities used TFCS as a model. Public colleges and universities must shape their own outreach, admissions, and student aid programs to ensure equal opportunity for students in their states. If a state has a comprehensive state program, it is easier to develop programs that enhance state aid and support services to insure access for underrepresented, low-income students. But whether or not such state programs exist, it is essential that colleges review their programs, consider how well they work, and formulate ways they might be altered to equalize opportunity for low-income students to enroll *and* attain Bachelor's degrees.

NOTES

1. Because of the financial requirements for admission into TFCS, most students who applied were also eligible for Pell grants.
2. Based on email correspondence with Shirley Ort, Associate Provost and Director of Financial Aid at the University of North Carolina. UNC hosted a national meeting on this model and maintains a list of universities that have documented aid commitments similar to UNC's.
3. In 2002, National Governors Association sessions were held with a focus on: "Twenty-First Century Scholars: Indiana's Best Practices for Student Financial Aid" in Indianapolis, Indiana. Sessions in Charleston, West Virginia, focused on "New Directions in Merit-Based Financial Aid."

REFERENCES

Adelman C. (2005). *Moving into town and moving on: The community college in the lives of traditional-age students.* Washington, DC: U.S. Department of Education.

Advisory Committee on Student Financial Assistance. (2002). *Empty promises: The myth of college access in America.* Washington, DC: Author.

Enersen, D. L., Sevaty-Seib, H. L., Pistilli, M. P., & Koch, A. K. (2008). *Twenty-First Century Scholars, their parents and guardians, and the sites that serve them*, Prepared for Lumina Foundation for Education. Layfayette, IN: Purdue University.

Hossler, D. (2006). Student and families as revenue: the impact on institutional behaviors. In D. M. Priest & E. P. St. John (Eds.), *Privatization in public universities: Implications for the public trust.* Bloomington, IN: Indiana University Press.

Hossler, D., & Schmit, J. (1995). The Indiana postsecondary-encouragement experiment. In E. P. St. John (Ed.), *Rethinking tuition and student aid strategies* (pp. 27–39). San Francisco: Jossey-Bass.

Hossler, D., Schmit, J., & Vesper, N. (1999). *Going to college: How social, economic, and educational factors influence the decisions students make.* Baltimore: Johns Hopkins University Press.

Hossler, D., Ziskin, M., & Gross, J. (Eds.). (2009a). *Enhancing institutional and state initiatives to increase student success: Studies of the Indiana Project on Academic Success. Readings on equal education Vol. 24.* York: AMS Press Inc.

Hossler, D., Ziskin, M., & Gross, J. (2009b). Getting serious about institutional performance in student retention: Research-based lessons on effective policies and practice. *About Campus, 13*(6), 2–11.

Lumina Foundation (2008). Results and evaluations: An evaluation report. Indianapolis, IN: Author. (http://www.umich.edu/~mpas/LuminaReport.pdf)

Musoba, G. D. (2004). Postsecondary encouragement for diverse students: A reexamination of the Twenty-First Century Scholars Program. In E. P. St. John (Ed.), *Public policy and college access: Investigating the federal and state roles in equalizing postsecondary opportunity. Readings on equal education, Vol. 19* (pp. 153–180). New York: AMS Press, Inc.

Musoba, G. D. (2006). The impact of school reform on college preparation: A multilevel analysis of the relationship between state policy and student achievement. Unpublished doctoral dissertation. Bloomington, IN: Indiana University.

Ort, S., & Williford, L. (2009). *Carolina Covenant 2000 update.* University of North Carolina, Powerpoint presentation, transmitted by email from Shirley A. Ort to Edward P. St. John 3/25/09.

Rawls, J. (1971). *A theory of justice.* Cambridge, MA: Belknap Press of Harvard University Press.

Robinson, L. J. (2009). Students' use of group mathematics tutoring and its impact on major choice. In D. Hossler, J. P. K. Gross, & M. Ziskin, Enhancing institutional and state initiatives to increase student success: Studies of the Indiana Project on Academic Success. *Readings on equal education, Vol. 24.* New York: AMS Press, Inc.

Sedlacek, W. E. (2004). *Beyond the big test: Noncognitive assessment in higher education.* San Francisco: Jossey-Bass.

Smith, J. H., Heltenbein, R. J., Hughes, R. L., Stuckey, S, M., & Berumen, J. G. (2008). *Twenty-First Century Scholars qualitative study: Higher education report.* Indianapolis: The Center for Urban and Multicultural Education, School of Education, Indiana University-Purdue University-Indianapolis, Indianapolis: IUPUI (http://education.iupui.edu/cume/publications/pdf/century.pdf)

St. John, E. P. (2006). *Education and the public interest: School reform, public finance, and access to higher education.* Dordrecht, The Netherlands: Springer.

St. John, E. P. (2009a). *Action, reflection and social justice: Integrating moral reasoning into professional education.* Cresskill, NJ: Hampton Press.

St. John, E. P. (2009b) *College organization and professional development: Integrating moral reasoning and reflective practice* New York: Routledge-Taylor.

St. John, E. P. (forthcoming). *Breaking through the access barrier: Academic capital formation informing policy in higher education.* New York: Routledge Press

St. John, E. P., Carter, D. F., Chung, C. G., & Musoba, G. D. (2006). Diversity and persistence in Indiana higher education: The impact of preparation, major choices, and student aid. In E. P. St. John (Ed.), *Public policy and educational opportunity: School reforms, postsecondary encouragement, and state policies on higher education, Readings on equal education, Vol. 21* (pp. 341–386). New York: AMS Press, Inc.

St. John, E. P., Chung, C. G., Musoba, G. D., Simmons, A. B., Wooden, O. S., & Mendez, J. (2004). *Expanding college access: The impact of state finance strategies.* Indianapolis, IN: Lumina Foundation for Education.

St. John, E. P., Fisher, A. S., Lee, M., Daun-Barnett, N., & Williams, K. (2008). *Educational opportunity in Indiana: Studies of the Twenty-First Century Scholars Program using state student unit record data systems.* Report prepared for the Lumina Foundation (http://www.umich.edu/~mpas/LuminaReport.pdf).

St. John, E. P., Gross, J. P. K., Musoba, G. D., & Chung, A. S. (2006). Postsecondary encouragement and academic success: Degree attainment by Indiana's Twenty-First Century Scholars. In E. P. St. John (Ed.), *Public policy and equal educational opportunity: School reforms, postsecondary encouragement, and state policies on postsecondary education, Readings on equal education, Vol. 21* (pp. 257–291). New York: AMS Press, Inc.

St. John, E. P., Hu, S., & Weber, J. (2000). Keeping public colleges affordable: A study of persistence in Indiana's public colleges and universities. *Journal of Student Financial Aid, 30*(1), 21–32.

St. John, E. P., Hu, S., & Weber, J. (2001). State policy and the affordability of public higher education: The influence of state grants on persistence in Indiana. *Research in Higher Education, 42,* 401–428.

St. John, E. P., & Musoba, G. D. (in review). *Pathways to academic success: Using research to inform reform: Analyses of Indiana's millennial cohort.* Albany, NY: SUNY Press.

St. John, E. P., Musoba, G. D., & Simmons, A. B. (2003). Keeping the promise: The impact of Indiana's Twenty-First Century Scholars Program. *The Review of Higher Education 27*(1), 103–123.

St. John, E. P., Musoba, G. D., Simmons, A. B., & Chung, C. G. (2002). *Meeting the access challenge: Indiana's Twenty-First Century Scholars Program. New Agenda Series, Vol. 4, No. 4.* Indianapolis: Lumina Foundation for Education.

St. John, E. P., Musoba, G. D., Simmons, A. B., Schmit, J., Chung, C. G., & Peng, C-Y. J. (2002). *Meeting the access challenge: An examination of Indiana's Twenty-First Century Scholars Program.* Bloomington, IN: Indiana Education Policy Center.

St. John, E. P., Musoba, G. D., Simmons, A. B., Chung, C. G., Schmit, J., & Peng, C. J. (2004). Meeting the access challenge: An examination of Indiana's Twenty-First Century Scholars Program. *Research in Higher Education, 45*(8), 829–873.

St. John, E. P., Pineda, D., & Moronski, K. (in preparation). Higher education in the United States: Legal, financial, and educational remedies to racial and income inequality in college access. In E. P. St. John, J. Kim, & L. Yang (Eds.), *Globalization and social justice: Comparative studies of public policy and college access.*

St. John, E. P., & Wilkerson, M. (Eds.). (2006). *Reframing persistence research to support academic success.* New Directions for Institutional Research No. 130. San Francisco: Jossey-Bass.

Theobald, N. (2003). The need for issues-driven school funding reform in urban schools. In L. F. Mirón & E. P. St. John (Eds.), *Reinterpreting urban school reform: Have urban schools failed, or has the reform movement failed urban schools?* (pp. 33–52). Albany, NY: SUNY Press.

3

CHANCES AND CHOICES OF LOW-INCOME STUDENTS IN CANADA AND ENGLAND

A Post-Structuralist Discussion of Early Intervention

TONY CHAMBERS AND FIONA DELLER

Over the last decade or so there has been increasing global awareness of the importance of postsecondary education. Most developed and many developing societies have moved from a mid 20th century idea of postsecondary education as "elite" to a new understanding of "mass" postsecondary education (Trow, 1973), and potentially to a newer view of postsecondary education as universal. The growing consensus is that expanded participation in postsecondary education is important to the knowledge economy, in providing the workers required in the labor market of the 21st century, as well as to an individual's ability to participate fully in the social health of societies.

With the previous description as a basic premise, tensions arise on two fronts. First, in aggregate terms, postsecondary education participation rates among most member countries of the Organization for Economic Cooperation and Development (OECD) are good but may be in danger of becoming increasingly caste-like as many countries build larger and more responsive postsecondary education systems, while other countries stall. Second, in individual terms, not everyone has the same equity of access to postsecondary education within certain international jurisdictions, and therefore large segments of the population in any particular society are being shut out of the pipeline into and through postsecondary education.

Students from families that have limited economic resources are among the most challenged in terms of entry into postsecondary education. Low-income students enter postsecondary education at much lower annual rates than middle- and upper-income students. Governments and education institutions have acknowledged the imperative of creating avenues for low-income youth to participate in postsecondary education. The factors contributing to this dynamic are many and complex; however, the traditional response to complex access issues for low-income students (and other underrepresented students) has been to create new or alter existing financial aid programs. The operating principle behind the traditional response is that if money is made available then access is assured for all. We argue in this chapter that a complex network of interrelated dynamics (including financial need) exist that impact low-income students' access to and success in postsecondary education. We further argue that in order to adequately begin to address these complex dynamics, 1. the components of the dynamic must be identified and modified as needed, 2. an integrated approach needs to be developed that targets the network of components, resisting one-dimensional approaches to multi-dimensional dynamics, and 3. the integrated approach needs to begin well before postsecondary education and continue into postsecondary education. The responsibility for creating and sustaining such approaches needs to be shared between government, institutions, communities, and individuals.

This chapter examines the emergent early intervention approaches that are being implemented in Canada and England. Using a post-structural framework, we deconstruct the notion of early intervention access initiatives as pathways to addressing complex social and educational needs of low-income students. We then provide a reconstruction of the possible pathways for early intervention programs to address emergent circumstances of low-income youth and families. The chapter is organized into four related parts. Part one provides a review of early intervention initiatives, as well as their relationship to access to and success of low-income students in postsecondary education. The literature is mixed on the impact of early intervention programs for low-income students. Some laud the increase in the number of low-income students participating in postsecondary education and others acknowledging the growing gap between low-income and higher-income students especially in universities. In part two we contextualize early intervention efforts within Canadian and English social and educational structures. Within part three we discuss case descriptions of specific early intervention initiatives in the two countries with a critical discussion of the initiatives. In the final part of the chapter we offer a reconstruction of possible institution policy and practice, as well as areas of needed research on early intervention efforts.

FRAMING CONCEPTS

Concepts that are central to our discussion in this chapter include low-income, access, social capital, and habitus. Brief articulation of these concepts will serve as a foundation for subsequent discussions in the chapter. These central concepts provide a deconstructed base to challenge traditional assumptions about the circumstances of individuals labeled as low-income (i.e., What is the meaning of low-income? What are the parameters of access? Can and in what form do low-income youth and families possess social capital? How do one's beliefs about oneself impact their chances and choices in life and postsecondary education?).

Low-Income

Typically, low-income refers to an individual's economic situation with its resultant circumstances. In this chapter, we view "low-income" as being equally about access to opportunities, resources, information, and recognition as it is about the lack of access to money. Thus, "low-income" is more of a social dynamic than a static condition. An individual's financial conditions may change, such as a pay raise or higher paying job, but without greater access to other broader social opportunities, resources and information the dynamic of low-income is likely to persist. From our perspective, low-income is a systemic or structural dynamic impacted by a confluence of factors interacting with certain circumstances/contexts that position individuals and groups of individuals on the margins of progress, sometimes for generations.

Access

As with many social constructs, "access" is often experienced as *limited options, not necessarily total exclusion* from choices. However, the impression given throughout the discourse on access is that either individuals are provided the option to enter postsecondary education, for example, or they are not provided that option. The reality is more complex and nuanced in that the access that is available to individuals is contingent on many factors related to social positionality. Access is rarely the opportunity to choose from all possible options. Access is not an all-or-nothing dynamic, nor is it static—i.e., access now or never. At any given point in time, however, what one has access to is guided by a dialectic between past realities and future possibilities…how one has negotiated and made meaning of life circumstances and what one perceives to be life choices.

Social Capital

The term "social capital" has its roots with two theorists: Pierre Bourdieu and James Coleman. Bourdieu (1986) defined social capital as the aggregate of actual or potential resources linked to possession of a durable network of essentially institutionalized relationships of mutual acquaintance and recognition. He suggested that the volume of social capital possessed by an individual depends on the size of the network that he or she can mobilize and the volume of capital possessed by each person to whom he or she is connected.

Coleman (1990) defined social capital as any aspect of a social structure that creates value and facilitates the actions of the individuals within that social structure. Coleman suggested that social capital is intangible and has three forms: (a) level of trust, as evidenced by obligations and expectations, (b) information channels, and (c) norms and sanctions that promote the common good over self-interest.

While both Bourdieu and Coleman acknowledge the social network characteristic of social capital, Bourdieu views social capital as a tool of reproduction for the dominant class, whereas Coleman views social capital as (positive) social control where trust, information channels, and norms are characteristics of a community. Therefore, it seems that Coleman's work supports the idea that it is the family's (or community's) responsibility to adopt certain norms to advance the life chances and choices of family or community members, whereas Bourdieu's work emphasizes structural constraints and unequal access to institutional resources based on class, gender, and race.

Habitus

Pierre Bourdieu proposed that one's early socialization experiences received through family, peer, relational, and institutional contacts are internalized by individuals who in turn shape one's actions, values, and consciousness of themselves in the world. Bourdieu further postulated that "habitus," or one's internalized early socialization, contributes to the development and perpetuation of opportunity structures for some individuals and groups in society, often in an unjust and inequitable fashion. Regarding the potential effect of habitus on the behaviors and consciousness of low-income students seeking access to postsecondary education, Swartz (1997) suggests that "habitus derives from the predominantly unconscious internationalization of objective chances that are common to members of a social class" (p. 104). Further, to link the habitus of groups or individuals, Swartz goes on to suggest that "the collective basis of habitus, stressing that individuals who internalize similar life chances share the same habitus" (p. 105). There are two important dimensions to habitus that need delineating. First, habitus structures action by defining the limits of that action. Second, habitus produces perceptions, beliefs, and practices that reinforce the early socialization of existing external structures, thereby reproducing stratification.

We think of habitus as a generational mix of factors interacting with a psychology and sociology of accessibility that impacts behaviors, consciousness, and both perceived and actual opportunity structures, with a *psychology of accessibility* being how individuals come to think of themselves over time as "the type of people" for whom social opportunities may or may not be available, and a *sociology of accessibility* being how societal beliefs about certain groups and individuals are so deeply rooted in everyday social values and practices that it becomes accepted truth that certain social opportunities and options may or may not be for certain people. In either case, we support Bourdieu's (2004) notion that opportunities exist for habitus to change as individuals experience unfamiliar encounters.

EARLY INTERVENTION AND LOW-INCOME STUDENTS

Access has become the word that defines much of the postsecondary agenda for governments, institutions, research organizations, and advocacy groups. As participation in postsecondary education becomes the norm and the international knowledge economy requires increasing numbers of educated workers, the question that continues to seek answers is "*who is not going to postsecondary education, and why?*". What becomes apparent when answers emerge is that it is those who have the most difficulty generally in society that also have the most difficulty accessing postsecondary education. Aboriginal and native youth (Mendelson, 2006; R.A. Malatest & Associates Ltd., 2004), youth with disabilities (Chambers, Sukai, & Bolton, forthcoming), low-income youth (Frenette, 2007), and youth whose parents did not attend postsecondary education, commonly referred to as first-generation youth (Berger, Motte, & Parkins, 2007; Finnie, Laporte, & Lascelles, 2004; Prairie Research Associates, 2005) are less likely to attend postsecondary education. Also, youth from some ethnic and racial minority groups seem to be less likely to attend (Abada, Hou, & Ram, 2008), and youth from rural and remote locations are less likely to go to universities (Andres & Looker, 2001).

In some cases the reasons may seem apparent. For rural and remote youth, distance to the nearest university is problematic; for low-income youth the costs of a four-year degree may seem prohibitive. However, there is a growing realization that despite programmatic attempts to address these needs students from traditionally underrepresented backgrounds still have limited access to postsecondary education (Cunningham, Redmond, & Merisotis, 2003; Trow, 2000). One of the reasons for the access gap amongst these populations may be that many of these youth tend to face a network of barriers, not a single simple barrier, and often the direct observable barrier (e.g., academic unpreparedness, lack of finances) is the result of a range of barriers that the youth was unable to negotiate from an early age. For example, first-generation students are more likely to be low-income, but also face lower expectations from their family, less access to informational and motivational supports, and thus are more likely to "select out" of the postsecondary path early, have less self-esteem and focus less on academic preparation for postsecondary education, leading to the observable barrier of academic unpreparedness (Finnie & Mueller, 2008).

When seen in this light, it is apparent why parental education is one of the most powerful determinants of postsecondary participation (Drolet, 2005). A parent's participation in postsecondary education gives a child an early advantage. Youth whose parents attended a college or university are more likely to be expected to attend postsecondary education. Further, these parents are more likely to offer advice about programs and possible institutions that the child might attend in the future, talk about their own educational experience and how it benefited them, help the child figure out how postsecondary can help them achieve their goals, help offspring network with others around postsecondary education choices, and acquire and transmit vital information important to the access process. Parents who did not attend postsecondary education are less likely to offer the same foundation. Lingenfelter (2007) succinctly explains that, "children whose parents have participated in postsecondary education are automatically enrolled in a 'program' that, early in life, exposes them to the advantages of higher education and the path to success. Children whose parents have not succeeded in postsecondary education need another way to get this information" (p. 3).

According to the literature on access, key factors that strongly impact participation in postsecondary education include: 1. parental education, 2. finances, 3. academic achievement/preparedness, 4. information and support, 5. peer group influence, and 6. student's self-confidence/self-esteem.

A number of researchers have warned against putting too much emphasis on financial barriers alone as parental expectations and academic preparedness have much more of a direct observable impact on participation (Berger & Motte, 2007; Frenette, 2007). However, the theme of financial barriers runs throughout most of the youth cohorts who do not attend. It seems to show up not as a financial constraint on entry to postsecondary education (funding is often available for low-income and other underrepresented youth in the form of student financial assistance once the youth has decided to attend), but in the form of an early anti-motivational device that persuades students from certain backgrounds that they are not able to access postsecondary. As an added disincentive, some research suggests that youth from low-income families tend to overestimate the cost of postsecondary education and underestimate the economic benefit associated with attaining a postsecondary education—more so than their middle- and high-income peers (Acumen Research Group, 2007; Ipsos-Reid, 2004; Usher, 2005).

What seems important here is that the network of underlying barriers is probably not separable and attempts to disentangle and address select component parts of the network will not be optimally effective for students or institutions.[1]

Similarly, although it seems a good idea to try to identify when to begin the process of addressing these barriers, it is hard to pin down a moment—that tipping point—when youth make conscious decisions about their participation in postsecondary education. That decision is unique to each individual and requires at least two things: 1. the initial support and momentum that allows the youth to believe it is possible for him or her to participate in postsecondary education, and 2. the ability to follow up on these beliefs.

As we will discuss in the following pages, early intervention programs are attempts to address the network of complex structural barriers early in the educational pipeline in order to alter the future educational trajectory (i.e., graduation from high school and participation in postsecondary education) of low-income and other underrepresented and marginalized youth. Early intervention with elementary and secondary school youth refers to specific sets of activities and services designed to reduce school dropout and increase postsecondary participation rates among socially and economically marginalized students. The following section will briefly discuss early intervention programs and the program components that contribute to successful initiatives.

Early Intervention Programs and Their Components

Despite the growing body of literature on early intervention programs, it is generally agreed that too little is still known about the success of early intervention programs, and how they affect postsecondary participation (Cunningham et al., 2003; Educational Policy Institute, 2001; Gandara, 2001; Gullatt & Jan, 2003). It should be noted that since the United States has a significant lead on other OECD countries with respect to early intervention programs, the majority of literature on the success of early intervention is American and refers to U.S. programs.

One possible explanation for the frustration in identifying "what works" is that it may not be possible to isolate components and test their effectiveness. This is why general program evaluations are so important and difficult. Despite this, there have been some attempts to identify those practices that seem particularly effective by identifying common components in successful programs. Gandara's (2001) overview of early intervention initiatives outlined the components that are usually part of successful programs:

- A primary person who monitors and guides the student over time.
- Good instruction coupled with challenging curriculum that is carefully tailored to the students' learning needs.
- Longer-term interventions. The longer students participate in a program, the more benefits they report.
- Cultural awareness of students' backgrounds. Many programs find that they have more success with some groups than with others.
- Positive peer support. Students are more likely to succeed when a peer group provides academic, social, and emotional support.
- Financial assistance and incentives. For many low-income students who identify postsecondary education as a goal, scholarships and grants may be essential to realizing that goal.

Despite the view that there is a lack of in-depth research into various components, there seems to be a consensus that there has been an aggregate increase in success rates of programs overall. How much of it is due to achieving the right mix of program components is unclear. Some of it may be due to other elements in the environment such as the effect of increased understanding of the importance of postsecondary education, a larger number of peers and role models attending postsecondary education, and/or a greater awareness of the importance of outreach.

Early intervention access efforts have emerged as relatively recent activities internationally. Of particular interest are those efforts that show promise in Canada and England. The next section contextualizes the issues of educational access in Canada and England. For each country we first provide a brief background perspective on low-income student participation in postsecondary education, and then we describe the postsecondary system in the country. We include a discussion of related outcomes for students who participate in the country's postsecondary education system.

EDUCATION AND SOCIAL CONTEXT WITHIN CANADA AND ENGLAND

Canada

Background Perspective. In Canada, education is constitutionally the responsibility of the provincial and territorial governments. Provinces and territories have a direct funding relationship with their public institutions, and as such are responsible both for the basic operating grants and for setting limits on tuition fees. Provinces and territories are also more directly responsible for accessibility issues, and often set aside envelopes of money to encourage institutions to focus access programming on particular underrepresented students such as Aboriginal students or students with disabilities. Each province and territory also has its own provincial student loan program which works in partnership with the federal program.

In general, participation rates for all students have risen dramatically in Canada over the last 20 years and it now has one of the highest overall participation rates in the countries in the OECD. In keeping with the general trend in most OECD countries, low-income students' postsecondary enrollment numbers have increased over the last 20 years in close parallel to their middle- and high-income peers (Berger et al., forthcoming). According to a recent study from Statistics Canada:

> slightly more than one-half (50.2%) of youth from families in the top quartile of the income distribution attend university by age 19, compared to less than a third of youth from families in the bottom quartile (31.0%). Even youth from families in the third income quartile have a considerable advantage in attending university (43 4%) over youth from the bottom income quartile. Youth in the second quartile are only slightly more likely to attend university than youth in the bottom quartile. (Frenette, 2007, p. 5)

Over the last decade or so, a number of Canadian provinces have addressed the issue of equity of access through reviews of their postsecondary education systems. Many provinces have implemented tuition freezes, introduced more robust grant systems for low-income and other underrepresented students, debt reduction mechanisms, increases in grants over loans, and generally worked to increase the number of low-income students attending postsecondary education, particularly in the university sector.

In 1998 the federal government focused on low-income accessibility explicitly by introducing a grant program called the Canada Millennium Scholarship. The scholarship was delivered through an arm's length

Foundation with a mandate to improve access for low-income students. One of the Foundation's contributions to accessibility for low-income students in Canada has been the introduction of an extensive research agenda. Another significant contribution is the work the Foundation has done in introducing early intervention programs, and the philosophy behind them, to Canadian governments.

Canadian Postsecondary Education System. Although there are some similarities amongst the provinces and territories, it is also fair to say that there are 13 unique postsecondary education systems in Canada. In general, there are three types of institutions in Canada: four-year, degree-granting universities (of which there are 82), two-year colleges (of which there are over 150), and a collection of private vocational institutes. For the most part, universities offer graduate programs and have a strong research capacity; many of the larger universities also have professional schools such as law and medicine. Colleges offer certificates and diplomas and have a stronger capacity to offer vocational programs and work directly with their immediate communities. Private vocational institutes tend to be smaller and offer diplomas in strictly vocational areas, or English as a second language.

However, despite these generalities, the differences between provincial and territorial higher education systems are more pronounced than the similarities. For instance, some provinces have hybrid institutions called university-colleges which are in effect undergraduate universities. Some provinces emphasize the transfer between institutions to facilitate students moving easily between college and university, while other provinces have strong college systems with colleges that offer four-year "degrees in applied areas." One province, Quebec, has a unique college system: les collèges d'enseignement général et professionnel (CEGEP). Students finish high school in grade 11 and enter the CEGEP system directly. Students may then either take a terminal college diploma or certificate, or pass through CEGEP to university. Students may not enter university directly from high school in Quebec. These college systems are important as in Canada colleges tend to serve more underrepresented students, including low-income students, than universities. In Quebec, CEGEPs are free; tuition is not charged. The three territories in the north (Nunavut, Northwest Territories, and Yukon) do not have universities. Students either attend a college or travel south to a provincial university. This is noteworthy, as it can be extremely expensive for a northern student to attend a university, thereby impacting their participation in postsecondary education in Canada.

England

Background Perspective.   Prior to the 1900s in England, postsecondary education was committed to sustaining social stratification where male youth from aristocratic families were favored over all others for spaces in institutions (Archer, Hutchings, & Ross, 2003). The passage of the Education Act of 1870 and the Education Act of 1944 marked the movement toward broader educational access for lower- and middle-income individuals. The 1963 Robbins Report brought to light the inequities in postsecondary education and sought systemic changes such as more universities in more locations. However, the Dearing Report of 1997 illustrated another shift in postsecondary access as it placed the responsibility of funding higher education on the individual and family and away from public (tax) support.

Although student enrollment increased over the years of continuous efforts to widen participation in English postsecondary education, the benefits of the increases seemed to escape low-income families. Several studies have suggested that over the past several decades the socioeconomic gap among those attending postsecondary education in England has widened, not closed (Bligh, 1990; Galindo-Rueda, Marcenaro-Gutierrez, & Vignoles, 2004). Throughout the nearly century and half of activity to extend education access to a broader range of socioeconomic groups in England, there still remains considerable disparity of educational opportunities between low- and high-income individuals who seek entry into postsecondary education.

English Postsecondary Education System.   Higher education in England is provided primarily by 90 publically funded higher education universities (the 19 colleges and the institutes within the School of Advanced Studies of the University of London are counted as one university), 133 "Further Education" colleges, and one private university.

Trow (2000) concluded that postsecondary education in England is still partial to those from the private secondary schools that prepare students for university entry. Since students who attend private secondary schools receive the equivalent of the first two years of postsecondary education while in secondary school, they have already gained a significant "leg up" in determining their entry into postsecondary education. This disparity is a major contributor to the lingering socioeconomic gap among entrants to English postsecondary education. The secondary education disparity also serves as a rationale for advancing national and local early intervention access efforts in public secondary schools and earlier in the education pipeline.

CASE DESCRIPTIONS AND DISCUSSION

The national early intervention initiative, *Aimhigher*, is an attempt to provide early preparation for underrepresented populations, specifically low-income youth between the ages of 13 and 19, to participate in English PSE (personal and social education). In Canada, several preliminary early intervention efforts are underway. In this chapter we focus on a prototype initiative, *Future to Discover*, in the provinces of Manitoba and New Brunswick that has demonstrated promising results among low-income youth.

Following are case descriptions of each initiative, their relationships with PSE institutions, and their known impact. Using a post-structural framework we discuss the initiatives and offer suggestions regarding issues that the initiatives might consider as they (or if they) move forward.

Future to Discover *(Canada)*

The *Future to Discover* initiative is primarily a research effort to explore the relative impact of information and financial incentives on secondary persistence and postsecondary participation. The initiative targets students in high school grades 10 through 12 in two Canadian provinces: Manitoba and New Brunswick. The initiative is funded by the Canada Millennium Scholarship Foundation, a private, independent organization created by an act of the Canadian Parliament and an endowment from the federal government to provide low-income students with opportunities to pursue postsecondary education. *Future to Discover* has two components: *Explore Your Horizons* provides information to students to assist with their decision-making process regarding future occupational and postsecondary education choices. *Learning Accounts* (available only to students in New Brunswick) support project participants from low-income backgrounds by providing an incentive of $8,000, deposited to a trust account that can be accessed upon successful completion of high school and enrollment in an accredited postsecondary institution.

The *Explore Your Horizons* component includes four classroom-based interventions:

- *Career Focusing* provides students in grade 10 with opportunities to explore a range of occupational options based on their individual passions.
- *Lasting Gifts* is a series of workshops for parents/guardians and their grade 11 teenagers to work together to explore career options.
- *Future in Focus* is designed to assist grade 12 students build personal resilience by helping them develop support networks, explore the

value of community engagement, and learn how to work through unexpected challenges.
- *Postsecondary Ambassadors* are students who are currently enrolled in provincial postsecondary institutions in the respective provinces who interact with high school participants to share their experiences with the process of participating in postsecondary education.

High school students in the program obtain about 50 hours of workshops over three years focusing on career counseling and the importance of all postsecondary paths—apprenticeships and vocational training as well as college and university. Students who participate in the *Explore Your Horizons* component also have access to a dedicated website and receive bi-annual issues of a specially prepared magazine that offers information and testimonials about postsecondary benefits and opportunities.

Aimhigher *(England)*

Aimhigher is a national program that is about widening participation in postsecondary education, as well as addressing fair access issues such as increasing opportunities for people from underrepresented groups to attend postsecondary education institutions where competition for entry is high, and so are the rates of economic returns upon completion. *Aimhigher* is jointly funded by the Higher Education Funding Council for England (HEFCE) and the Department for Innovation, Universities and Skills (DIUS), and is operated through 44 local area partnerships throughout England.

The key target group for *Aimhigher* is the 13–19 age groups which is consistent with the British government's target for 50 percent of youth in that age cohort to participate in postsecondary education. Most *Aimhigher* activities are developed and delivered at an area level, which allows them to be tailored to the needs of specific communities. Core *Aimhigher* activities that are offered and take place in all areas of the country include:

- *Aimhigher* postsecondary campus visits
- mentoring (face to-face or electronic)
- master classes, including subject enrichment or revision sessions
- student ambassadors from postsecondary institutions
- information, advice, and guidance
- summer schools and other postsecondary, education related, residential experiences
- school- or college-based interventions.

The organizational structure of *Aimhigher* is layered with involvement at the national, local, and postsecondary institution levels. The *Aimhigher* National Advisory Board reviews local-level reports on *Aimhigher* efforts and provides advice to the program funders on future program developments. The Aimhigher Management Group (AMG) consists of representatives from funding, regulatory, community, and institutional agencies and is responsible for monitoring the overall *Aimhigher* program. The AMG reviews progress made and commissions any action needed to support the programme. The Area Partnership Committee (APC) is responsible for area-level planning and allocation of funding. Each of the 44 areas has a lead Higher Education Institutions (HEI) which acts as the banker and treasurer for the APC (see above) and is responsible for ensuring full accountability for funding. The lead HEI is also responsible for convening the APC, and ensuring the broad representation of key institutional and local stakeholders.

DECONSTRUCTING THE CHALLENGES AND POTENTIAL EFFECTS OF EARLY INTERVENTION PROGRAMS

Early intervention programs have shown to be vital to increasing chances and choices for participating in postsecondary education for underrepresented populations. Experience in these programs reinforces the obvious lessons about social capital—exposure and access to information, constructive direct opportunities, resources, positive interactions with broad human networks, and strengthened school, family, and community experiences for youth early and regularly throughout their lives increases life options such as participation and success in postsecondary education. Wealthy families experience these lessons in the flow of their daily lives. In a sense, private early intervention programs are built-in features of their social status. For low-income families, initiatives such as externally driven early intervention programs can provide important opportunities for youth and families to expand their understanding and experience with a broader set of available life options.

However, even with the great social and personal potential offered by early intervention programs, we have concerns regarding the design, intentions, impact, and implementation of early intervention programs that may challenge organizers, supporters, and participants to rethink the fundamental principles and practices undergirding these programs. To start, we question the basic premise upon which early intervention programs are often built. That is, participation in postsecondary education among low-income students (and other underrepresented populations) will increase if certain barriers are removed or reduced at a particular time in a student's life. One concern is that the "barriers" are often externally determined through systematic studies and/or political agendas. This concern strikes at the heart of how and who defines the limitations and needs of low-income populations regarding education. For example, does the programmatic focus on information and money in the *Future to Discover* program suggest that the most salient barriers for low-income student access to postsecondary education are about the lack of money and information? Youth and families should be centrally involved with broad networks of stakeholders from communities, education, government, and other pertinent sectors in constructing approaches to educational access that align with local needs, limitations, and assets. The *Aimhigher* approach seems to understand this point as the program is multi-layered with the implementation occurring at the local level, albeit through a postsecondary institution as the lead member of the network. Implicit in the premise of increased participation when barriers are removed is that if low-income students work hard (meritocracy), and families and youth consciously and intentionally choose postsecondary education as a path (existentialism) then the elimination of current barriers should smooth the way for increased participation among this population. Within early intervention programs little focus is given to the historical, systemic, and extensive dynamics that created and sustained the socioeconomic status of these youth and families, such as generations of underemployment and unemployment, disproportionate and inequitable access to quality and humane healthcare, education and housing, social attitudes and discriminatory behaviors toward many low-income populations, and general and pervasive exclusion from networks of power, privilege, and social advancement. The playing field does not become level after students successfully complete the program requirements or take full advantage of early intervention program offerings. Our position is that the same historical and structure dynamics that existed prior to youths' involvement in the early intervention programs will be present upon their completion of the program. We suggest that in addition to existing foci in early intervention programs, there needs to be an infusion of knowledge, exploration, and support targeted at understanding and addressing the effects of the complex circumstances that many low-income youth and families experience.

Additionally, attention should be given to how internalized belief systems (habitus) of the students and their parents impact students' secondary retention and postsecondary participation. How do youth and families internalize "low-income" and what does that mean in terms of their future life options? For many families with very limited economic means, the option of attending postsecondary education is a novel and daunting prospect. The historical story (habitus) that many low-income and marginalized families are told about themselves, and oftentimes tell about themselves, has an impact on how postsecondary education is viewed as an available option. Efforts should be made to assist families and youth with exploring the limitations and benefits of their habitus and the relationship between their habitus and their possible futures. *Pathways to Excellence* in Canada and *GEAR UP* programs in the United States are two examples of early intervention initiatives that attempt to address low-income youth and family habitus. Both initiatives combine academic, social, and advocacy supports for youth and families with financial support for postsecondary education participation. Through these efforts, youth and families are challenged to reassess the beliefs they hold about the educational and social options available to them and their capacities to succeed in their chosen options.

Regarding the assessment of early intervention programs, a clear sense of what measurable success means is elusive in the Canadian *Future to Discover* and English *Aimhigher* programs that we described earlier. We do not mean to suggest that success will be the same for all participants, but we do believe that in order for the programs to "claim" certain outcomes as programmatic success, there needs to be a set of general and specific parameters of what the programs' terms of success would look like. Otherwise, the goals, processes, and outcomes of the programs will be moving targets with youth and families having little sense of where the programs are going and what to expect from the programs. Additionally, supporters and observers can become suspicious of reported program results if success criteria is unclear or if they consistently fluctuate.

Assessment results will reflect at least two things: 1. the relative impact of the programs on students, and 2. the degree to which students' are able to, in Bourdieu's language, "practice successfully in a particular field." In other words, will students learn the rules of the proverbial social capital game and how best to take advantage of available resources in order to be successful? Both sets of results are important to youth and the programs. Missing from the results is how systems, institutions, and the process of access are impacted by the programs, as well as how the level of awareness about youth and families' socioeconomic or cultural status influences their social choices and chances. The missing results speak to the structural level forces that demand attention if root conditions for low-income youth and families are to be changed so that access to postsecondary education, and other social opportunities, are realized in equitable ways.

We further questioned the role of social capital in the construction of the programs and choices to participate in the programs. Presumably, limited salient social capital qualified students for both programs. We wondered how the programs acknowledged, honored, and built on the social capital that youth and families brought to the programs, such as family relationships, spiritual and religious commitments, and community support. Or, were the forms of social capital experienced by low-income families dismissed and replaced by more favored and socially embraced forms of capital?

One critical program design issue is how students are selected for programs. In the United States, students in early intervention programs are sometimes identified through their eligibility for free lunch programs. Canada does not have a free lunch program, thus it lacks one of the most effective proxies for identifying low-income, high-need students. Another option would be to target entire schools; however, in Canada many high schools, and sometimes middle schools, tend to serve more than one neighborhood and have socioeconomically diverse student bodies. One exception to this rule might be high schools for Aboriginal students on First Nations reserves and some rural or remote community high schools with high nonparticipation rates. The English approach is to establish local level teams to tailor recruitment of youth and delivery of programs and services that take into consideration the circumstances in a particular area of the country. While the basic criteria is that youth and family be from lower socioeconomic groups in society, there is flexibility in considering other important selection criteria, as well as for constructing the suite of programmatic offerings based on circumstances identified by the local area partnerships.

The Educational Policy Institute's (2001) College Board Review noted that about two-thirds of all U.S. programs (66 percent) require students to apply for admission. Sixteen percent of all programs operate on a first come first served basis, and about a third have a competitive admissions process. However, one problem with self-selection or application for a program is that they favor students who have already decided to participate in a process that will hopefully lead to postsecondary education. The programs therefore miss students who are most at risk, those students who have already selected out of the postsecondary pathway. In the Canadian environment where early intervention programs are not well known or universally understood, the chance of high-risk students not selecting into these programs may be particularly high.

Gandara's (2001) summary of the challenges faced by U.S. early intervention programs is particularly instructive for both existing programs and those considering initiating such programs at an institution level. Included among the challenges are:

- *Program attrition*: Few programs either report or know how many students that begin their programs actually complete them. Gandara estimates that between one third and one half of all students who begin programs leave before completion or before high school graduation. Nonetheless, programs commonly report high percentages of participants going on to postsecondary education based on counting only the number of participants in the program graduating class.
- *Smaller number of students affected*: It is estimated that only 5 percent of all U.S. students who might be eligible for an early intervention program are actually served. The two programs profiled in this chapter serve small percentages of eligible students as well. However, this argument has been used to reduce, eliminate, or avoid supporting altogether these programs because it's not worth the cost to contribute to the success of so few. Even more insidious is the rhetoric that funds used to increase participation of underrepresented populations in postsecondary education could be put to better use by those who stand a better chance of succeeding and making a more significant contribution to society.
- *Participant selection*: Few programs are explicit about how students were selected to participate and about the characteristics of the most successful participants. This kind of information is critically important in evaluating who can best benefit from the program.
- *Records on program contact*: Few programs keep records on the amount of contact participants have with the program. Similarly, programs are often vague about what constitutes completion, retention, or success in the program.
- *Academic achievement*: While some programs were able to demonstrate that they doubled college-going rates among participants (compared to controls), evidence that programs are effective in raising academic achievement as measured by grades or test scores is limited.
- *Type of postsecondary institution*: Because overall measured achievement is not generally considered, these programs are most effective at increasing the rate of students going to community colleges and less selective four-year institutions. Limiting the range of postsecondary options impacts life options and can further sustain a relative power and privilege imbalance, prolong the limited degree of one's social capital, and potentially perpetuate historically and socially internalized beliefs and values regarding the options available to low-income individuals. Institutions that implement early intervention programs should be clear with participants about the type of institutions to which students are preparing for access.

- *Long-term outcomes*: Little is known about long-term outcomes for students. Most programs do not have data that show whether they increase the rates at which participants obtain postsecondary degrees when compared to students who have not participated in the programs.
- *Costs*: Little is reported about the costs of these programs. However, both programs that we discussed have limited terms of funding with no commitment to extend until goals are met. In fact the *Future to Discover* project time parameters are tied to the completion of the project as research. Additionally, the funder itself is being discontinued with no sense of potential future support for the initiative beyond the life of the funding agency.

RECONSTRUCTING INSTITUTION POLICY, PRACTICE, AND FUTURE RESEARCH FOR EARLY INTERVENTION PROGRAMS

Drawing on the previous program case descriptions and discussion, as well as the general discussion of early intervention initiatives, we offer the following recommendations regarding the creation, implementation, and study of early intervention programs as efforts to address structural inequities in access to postsecondary education. Early intervention programs should consider:

- *Determining the program goals*: The goals of the program (preparing youth to succeed academically in postsecondary education; motivating youth to enter postsecondary education in a specific region/state/province; ensuring that youth graduate from high school with the resources they need to make choices, etc.) can determine the design of the program. It should also be noted that an evaluation may indicate that a program is successful in a different way than the program goal had initially intended, at which point some choices may need to be made about whether the goal or the program should change.
- *Packaging program interventions*: It is important to understand that a package of interventions will be required to address a network of social and personal dynamics. Program developers and implementers should be flexible about adding and subtracting interventions, but not expect to be able to determine exactly which intervention is addressing exactly which dynamic—students are complex in their responses and motivations.
- *Determining the target student population*: Aboriginal youth, youth with disabilities, low-income youth, rural youth, first-generation

youth, immigrant youth, students from culturally and ethnically diverse backgrounds, etc. may require different packages of interventions, and different sensitivities in relation to parental and community involvement.

- *Deciding upon a student selection process*: How students are selected will impact the effectiveness of the program. Programs where students self-select may seem more successful as they attract students who have already shown some motivation and intention to consider postsecondary education. However, they may not target the most high-risk, high-need students, who may have already selected out of the pathway to postsecondary education and therefore would not sign up for such a program.
- *Establishing evaluation processes*: Where possible, it is important to build in an evaluation process from the beginning with benchmark data so that the success of the program can be determined over time, data about student characteristics so it can be understood which types of students are responding to the program and which might need more help, and qualitative practices for understanding the views of students, parents, practitioners, and administrators who participate in the program.
- *Involving parents and communities in vital and central roles of the program*: The importance of parental and community involvement comes up repeatedly in the research on what makes programs successful. Evaluations of programs implemented in the United States explicitly tied their success to the involvement of parents and communities in the program process from the beginning. Different programs used different strategies for ensuring parental and community involvement; usually these strategies were very much in keeping with the goals and philosophies of the individual programs, as well as the particular circumstances of youth in specific environments.
- *The target age of students and the duration of programs*: A conscious decision needs to be made about when to begin the program, understanding that the earlier the initiative the less intensive it may need to be. On the other hand, the later the initiative the more intense it may need to be as youth become increasingly firm in their choices as they age, and may have begun to act on those choices, for example in relation to academic achievement and financial savings. It is also important to understand that programs that begin particularly early report that interventions need to change over time—what is needed in grade 6 is different from what is needed in grade 9.

SUGGESTED FUTURE RESEARCH

In addition to establishing effective student tracking systems for follow up, and constructing meaningful formative and summative evaluation schemas, we suggest the following research be considered to better understand the factors that influence program participants, the factors that can improve the delivery of programs and services within the programs, and the long-term impact of these programs on individuals, families, and communities. Research suggestions include:

1. Conduct longitudinal assessment of the broad impact of participating in early intervention programs. Explore the impact that youth and family's internalized beliefs (habitus) about their socioeconomic status have on their educational decisions and future outcomes.
2. Examine what combination of program components contribute most to academic performance, student involvement in academically meaningful activities (in secondary and postsecondary institutions), and persistence through graduation.
3. Examine the relative impact early intervention programs have on the host postsecondary institutions and process of access in certain postsecondary environments.
4. Examine the life aspirations of youth and families who participate in early intervention programs and those who do not participate in such programs.
5. Explore the public good and social economic benefit of early intervention programs. Related, study what is at stake for societies if early intervention programs are discontinued.

CONCLUSION

Despite extensive, well-intended efforts to equalize postsecondary education chances and choices for low-income and other underrepresented student populations, enrollment and retention gaps persist between lower- and higher-income groups. The gaps are particularly acute in terms of participation in universities where student spaces are highly competitive and postgraduate social and financial returns are the greatest. It has become clear that persistent (and widening in some cases) gaps exist because a broader network of structural conditions persist and disproportionately, and unjustly, impact the very populations that would benefit most from postsecondary participation. The two early intervention programs reviewed in this chapter address only parts of the structural network of conditions. These complex dynamics are inextricably circular.

Early intervention programs that target youth from underrepresented populations for increased chances and broader choices to participate in postsecondary education are important and vital to interrupt the generational cycle of inequality and marginalization.

Program effectiveness is contingent upon the degree to which the salient networks of challenges facing youth and families are addressed and key efforts are judiciously targeted at impacting tangible conditions (i.e., finances, information, social networks, direct experiences, etc.), as well as attending to the ways in which low-income youth and families oftentimes come to think of their future chances and choices. Additionally, it seems vital for early intervention efforts to intentionally build in ways to acknowledge and honor the assets that low-income youth and families bring to these programs, and not inadvertently view their lives as problems in need of fixing. Our sense is that the more youth and families can view themselves as equally contributing partners in the construction of their future chances and choices, the greater the probability of realizing the kind of social and personal transformation that can and should occur.

NOTE

1. Although it might be argued that this is exactly what student financial assistance programs do, and that these programs do have some effect in addressing the credit constraint of low-income students, the fact is that low-income students still do not attend postsecondary education in the same numbers as their higher-income peers, which points to the notion that there are more complex networks of barriers that must be addressed if low-income student participation is to increase. That being said, it is not known what the participation rate of low-income students would be if financial assistance were not available—although it is assumed it would be much lower—so the actual effect of that program cannot be absolutely measured.

REFERENCES

Abada, T., Hou, F., & Ram, B. (2008). *Group differences in educational attainment among the children of immigrants*. Analytical Studies Branch Research Paper. Ottawa: Statistics Canada.

Acumen Research Group. (2007). *Do perceptions matter regarding the costs and benefits of a post-secondary education? A summary report of the research program development of measures of perceived returns on investment from postsecondary education*. Montreal: Canada Millennium Scholarship Foundation.

Andres, L., & Looker, E. D. (2001). Rurality and capital: Educational expectations and attainments of rural, urban/rural and metropolitan youth. *The Canadian Journal of Higher Education, 31*(2), 1–45.

Archer, L., Hutchings, M., & Ross, A. (2003). *Higher education and social class: Issues of exclusion and inclusion*. New York: RoutledgeFalmer.

Berger, J., & Motte, A. (2007). Mind the access gap: Breaking down barriers to post-secondary education. *Policy Options*, 42–46.

Berger, J., Motte, A., & Parkins, A. (2007). *The price of knowledge*. Montreal: Canada Millennium Scholarship Foundation.

Bligh, D. (1990). *Higher education*. London: Cassell Educational.

Bourdieu, P. (1986). The forms of capital. In G. R. Richardson (Ed.), *Handbook of theory and research for the sociology of education* (pp. 241–258). New York: Greenwood Press.

Bourdieu, P. (2004). *Science of science and reflexivity*. Chicago: University of Chicago Press.

Chambers, T., Sukhai, M., & Bolton, M. (forthcoming). *Assessment of financial barriers affecting students with disabilities in postsecondary education*. Toronto and Montreal: Canada Millennium Scholarship Foundation and the Higher Education Quality Council of Ontario.

Coleman, J. S. (1990). *Equality and achievement in education*. Boulder, CO: Westview Press.

Cunningham, A., Redmond, C., & Merisotis, J. (2003). *Investing early: Intervention programs in selected U.S. states*. Montreal: Canada Millennium Scholarship Foundation.

Drolet, M. (2005). *Participation in post-secondary education in Canada: Has the role of parental income and education changed over the 1990s?* Analytical Studies Branch Research Paper Series. Catalogue No. 11F0019MIE2005243. Ottawa: Statistics Canada.

Educational Policy Institute. (2001). *Outreach program handbook*. Washington, DC: The College Board.

Finnie, R., Laporte, C., & Lascelles, E. (2004). *Family background and access to post-secondary education: What happened over the 1990s?* Analytical Studies Research Paper. Ottawa: Statistics Canada.

Finnie, R., & Mueller, R. E. (2008). *The effects of family income, parental education and other background factors on access to post-secondary education in Canada: Evidence from the YITS*. A MESA Project Research Paper. Toronto: Educational Policy Institute.

Frenettte, M. (2007). *Why are youth from lower-income families less likely to attend university? Evidence from academic abilities, parental influences, and financial constraints*. Ottawa: Statistics Canada.

Galindo-Rueda, F., Marcenaro-Gutierrez, O., & Vignoles, A. (2004). *The widening socio-economic gap in UK higher education*. London: Centre for the Economics of Education, London School of Economics.

Gandara, P. (2001). *Paving the way to understanding education: K-12 intervention programs for underrepresented youth. Report of the national postsecondary education cooperative working group on access to postsecondary education*. Washington, DC: National Postsecondary Education Cooperative.

Gullatt, Y., & Jan, W. (2003). *How do pre-collegiate academic outreach programs impact college going among underrepresented students?* University of California: Pathways to College Network.

Ipsos-Reid Marketing Research. (2004). *Canadian attitudes towards financing postsecondary education: Who should pay and how*. Montreal: Canada Millennium Scholarship Foundation. Retrieved from http://www.millenniumscholarships.ca/images/Publications/factum_en.pdf

Lingenfelter, P. (Ed.). (2007). *More student success: A systemic solution*. Washington, DC: State Higher Education Executive Officers.

Mendelson, M. (2006). *Aboriginal peoples and postsecondary education in Canada*. Ottawa: Caledon Institute.

Prairie Research Associates. (2005). *Survey of secondary school students*. Montreal: Canada Millennium Scholarship Foundation.

R. A. Malatest & Associates Ltd. (2004). *Aboriginal peoples and post-secondary education: What educators have learned*. Montreal: Canada Millennium Scholarship Foundation.

Swartz, D. (1997). *Culture and power: The sociology of Pierre Bourdieu*. Chicago: The University of Chicago Press.

Trow, M. (1973). *Problems in the transition from elite to mass higher education*. Berkeley, CA: Carnegie Commission on Higher Education.

Trow, M. (2000). From mass higher education to universal access: The American advantage. *Minerva, 37*, 1–26.

Usher, A. (2005). *A little knowledge is a dangerous thing: How perceptions of costs and benefits affect access to education*. Toronto: Educational Policy Institute.

4
SHOWING THEM THE MONEY
The Role of Institutional Financial Aid Policies and Communication Strategies in Attracting Low-Income Students[1]

LAURA PERNA, VALERIE LUNDY-WAGNER, APRIL YEE,
LEYKIA BRILL, AND TERAN TADAL

College choice in the United States is stratified by family income. Students with the lowest family incomes are relatively concentrated in private for-profit institutions and public two-year colleges and underrepresented at public and private universities (Baum & Ma, 2007). In 2003–04, students from families with incomes below $20,000 represented 26 percent of dependent students attending private for-profit institutions and 16 percent at public two-year institutions, but only 10 percent of dependent students attending public universities and 10 percent at private universities (Baum & Ma, 2007).

The representation of low-income students is particularly low at many of the nation's most elite colleges and universities (Bowen, Kurzweil, & Tobin, 2005; Hill, Winston, & Boyd, 2005). At 13 of the 39 public universities with the largest endowments in 2006–07, no more than 15 percent of undergraduates received Pell grants (*Chronicle of Higher Education*, 2008). At 28 of the 75 private institutions with the highest endowments, no more than 10 percent of undergraduates received Pell grants (*Chronicle of Higher Education*, 2008). Only 10 percent of undergraduates attending 28 Consortium on the Financing of Higher Education (COFHE) institutions in 2001–02 came from families in the bottom 40 percent of the national income distribution (Hill et al., 2005). The COFHE institutions include many of the nation's most elite institutions (e.g., Amherst, Carleton, Oberlin, Smith, Swarthmore, Vassar, and Williams Colleges, all eight Ivy League universities, and Duke, Georgetown, Johns Hopkins, Northwestern, and Stanford Universities).

Although academic preparation and other forces play a role, the very low representation of students from low-income families at the nation's wealthiest and most selective public and private universities is surprising when considered in light of the investment that these institutions make in student grant aid. In 2007–08, colleges and universities nationwide provided more than $29 billion in student aid to postsecondary education students (College Board, 2008). Colleges and universities are the single largest source of aid in the form of grants to postsecondary education students (both undergraduate and graduate), as 42 percent of all grant aid awarded in 2007–08 was from colleges and universities (College Board, 2008). Private universities are an especially important provider of institutional grant aid. In 2007–08, about half of undergraduates attending private four-year colleges (52 percent) and universities (53 percent) but only one-fourth of undergraduates attending public universities (26 percent) received institutional financial aid (Wei et al., 2009).

Moreover, over the past decade, many of the nation's wealthiest and most selective institutions have expanded the availability of institutional financial aid through programs that eliminate the use of loans for students from low-income families. Princeton University led the way in 2001 by guaranteeing to meet 100 percent of undergraduates' financial need through sources other than loans (Olsen & Lively, 2001). Other institutions, both public and private, have since adopted variations of this "no loan" policy.

The continued stratification of college choice by family income despite the substantial investment in institutional grant aid raises questions about how and why institutional financial aid policies and practices may not be serving students from low-income families. Although other forces (particularly academic preparation and achievement and the availability of resources at the high school attended) also influence students' college choices, this chapter explores how institutional financial aid influences college choices for low-income students. The chapter begins by describing the extent to which institutions use their aid to reduce financial barriers to attendance for students from low-income families. Next, the chapter offers a conceptual framework for understanding how institutional financial aid may directly and indirectly influence students' college choices. Using data collected from a review of institutional websites, the chapter then uses a post-structural perspective (as described by Adrianna Kezar in the introduction to this volume) to deconstruct the ways that selected institutions communicate information about aid to prospective low-income students and their families. Although focusing on a small group of colleges and universities, the examination of how institutional strategies for communicating information about financial aid may fail to reach students from low-income families may have relevance to other colleges and universities. We conclude with recommendations for reconstructing institutional financial aid policies to better serve students from low-income families, as well as recommendations for further research.

THE USE OF INSTITUTIONAL FINANCIAL AID TO REDUCE FINANCIAL BARRIERS TO ATTENDANCE

Although definitions of "need" and "merit" vary across institutions (McPherson & Schapiro, 2006a), available data suggest that many institutions award substantial amounts of aid with the goal of reducing financial barriers to attendance for students from low-income families. In 2007–08, private four-year institutions awarded 70 percent of their institutional aid dollars based on need, while public four-year institutions awarded 44 percent based on need (College Board, 2008).

Despite the magnitude of dollars invested in need-based institutional financial aid (College Board, 2008), however, available institutional resources are insufficient to meet the demonstrated financial need (as calculated by the federal needs analysis formula)[2] of all students at all but the most selective institutions with the highest endowments (Bowen et al., 2005; McPherson & Schapiro, 2006a). In 2006–07, institutional grant aid covered only 44 percent of unmet need for students attending public four-year institutions, 34 percent at higher-priced four-year institutions and 18 percent at lower-priced private four-year institutions (College Board, 2008).

Some institutions respond to shortfalls in available financial aid resources through a strategy known as "gapping," or offering an amount of financial aid that does not meet a student's entire financial need. When available aid does not cover financial need, students must use loans and/ or work to close the gap. For example, because New York University's (NYU) $175 million financial aid budget is insufficient to meet the full financial need of its 19,000 undergraduates, more than half of all students graduate with debt (58 percent with an average of $21,000 in 2007) and 80 percent work at least one job (Masterson, 2009).

Other institutions respond by considering both merit and need in determining how much and what types (i.e., grants, loans, work) of financial aid to award each admitted applicant. For example, Boston University reports meeting the full need (through grants, loans, and work-study) of only 75 percent of the most desirable students admitted for fall 2009 (Pappano, 2009). Using data from the College Board, Reed and Shireman (2008) found that, in 2005–06, 49 percent of institutional grant aid at public, four-year institutions and 25 percent of institutional grant aid at private, non-profit, four-year institutions were awarded "in excess of" students' financial need. But, these same institutions also reported substantial portions of unmet financial need for their first-time, full-time freshmen (35 percent at public four-year institutions and 23 percent at private, non-profit, four-year institutions).

Institutions have long considered both academic merit and financial need when allocating scarce financial aid resources (Bowen et al., 2005; Reed & Shireman, 2008). Like admissions decisions (Killgore, 2009), financial aid award and packaging decisions are influenced by institutional mission, goals, and priorities, including raising the *U.S. News & World Report* ranking and enrolling a diverse class to maximize peer effects on learning (Bowen et al., 2005; Reed & Shireman, 2008; Singell, 2002). Based on data collected through interviews at 17 of the "most selective" colleges and universities in the Northeast, Killgore concluded that these institutions consider students' academic and nonacademic achievements in admissions decisions but that "merit" is defined and redefined based on other institutional needs and priorities, including prestige, financial stability, athletic tradition, and alumni support.

Some research suggests that both public and private institutions are reducing their commitment to allocating student aid based on financial need (McPherson & Schapiro, 2006a). Using data from the National Postsecondary Student Aid Survey (NPSAS), McPherson and Schapiro show that, at both public and private colleges and universities, institutional grant awards increase as a student's ability to pay (as measured by Expected Family Contribution) declines, but also increase with a student's academic merit (as measured by SAT score), even after controlling for race/ethnicity, major field, and institutional type. The analyses also show that, between 1992–93 and 1999–2000, financial need became a less important determinant of institutional grant awards at private colleges and universities while academic merit became more important at public colleges and universities. The payoff for high SAT scores to institutional grant awards also increased over this period at private institutions for students with the lowest financial need (i.e., highest EFC [expected family contribution]) but not for students with lower family incomes.

A decreasing emphasis on financial need disadvantages students from low-income families in at least two ways. First, low-income students are less likely to qualify for financial aid that is awarded based on merit, given their lower average levels of academic achievement (Perna, 2005). For example, both SAT test-taking rates and average SAT scores increase with family income (Bowen et al., 2005; Hill & Winston, 2006; Tebbs & Turner, 2006). Low-income students are less likely to be academically prepared for college in part because the high schools they tend to attend have fewer resources, including fewer rigorous courses (Perna, 2005). Second, any shifting of resources away from need-based aid disproportionately impacts low-income students, as research consistently shows that changes in need-based grant aid have a greater affect on the enrollment of students from low-income than high-income families (Avery & Hoxby, 2004; Heller, 1997; Mundel, 2008). The failure of institutions to meet 100 percent of students' financial need also has important consequences for low-income students, as these students must reduce the intensity of their enrollment, work more hours, and/or use more loans in order to pay the price of attendance. Both shifting to part-time enrollment and working more hours reduces the likelihood of completing a Bachelor's degree within six years (Titus, in press).

One potentially promising trend that counters the national decline in the emphasis of institutional aid on financial need (McPherson & Schapiro, 2006a) is the recent expansion of institutional need-based grant aid by a number of selective public and private colleges and universities. Through "no loan" policies, these institutions promise to meet 100 percent of students' demonstrated financial need through a combination of grants and work-study but without the use of loans.

Only institutions with substantial endowments, academically selective admissions policies, and relatively few low-income students have the resources to meet 100 percent of students' financial need with grants (Hill et al., 2005). Although these elite institutions represent only a small share of U.S. colleges and universities and enroll only a small percentage of all undergraduates, their financial aid practices are worth considering for several reasons (McPherson & Schapiro, 2006b). First, ensuring that students from low-income families have financial access to these institutions is critical to ensuring that these students can realize the many benefits that attending these institutions produces, including entrée to prominent national leadership positions (Bowen et al., 2005; McPherson & Schapiro, 2006b). In addition, these institutions "play a prominent leadership role in American higher education," with other institutions seeking to emulate their example (McPherson & Schapiro, 2006b, p. 10). By demonstrating their commitment to low-income students and their families, these institutions may not only encourage other colleges to follow suit, but also raise high-achieving, low-income students' college aspirations.

HOW INSTITUTIONAL "NO LOAN" POLICIES MAY INFLUENCE STUDENTS' COLLEGE CHOICES

Institutional "no loan" policies may influence an academically-qualified, low-income student's college choice in at least three ways. First, by communicating the availability of institutional grants that meet low-income students' entire financial need, prospective students may decide to include an institution in their choice set. Second, as human capital theory suggests, by increasing available financial resources, institutional financial aid may increase the likelihood that a student will attend an institution to which the student has applied for admission and been admitted. Finally, by eliminating loans from the financial aid package, institutional "no loan" policies may encourage students who are averse to borrowing to enroll.

Traditional Approach to Understanding the Role of Financial Aid: Human Capital Theory

The role of financial aid in college enrollment is typically considered through the lens of human capital theory (Perna, 2006). This theory assumes that students decide to enroll in a particular college or university based on a comparison of the lifetime benefits and costs for all alternatives (Becker, 1993; Paulsen, 2001). Individuals are assumed to act rationally in ways that maximize their utility, given their personal preferences, tastes, and expectations (Becker, 1993).

This perspective predicts that institutional grant aid will increase the supply of resources available to pay for a particular institution and consequently increase the likelihood that a high-ability, low-income student will enroll. This perspective also predicts that an institutional aid policy that replaces loans with grants will increase the likelihood of enrollment for students who are averse to borrowing. Research consistently shows that grants promote college enrollment, especially for students from low-income families (Avery & Hoxby, 2004; Haskins, Holzer, & Lerman, 2009; Heller, 1997; Mundel, 2008). In contrast, while some studies (e.g., Avery & Hoxby, 2004) suggest that an offer of loans is positively related to enrollment net of other variables, others (Haskins et al., 2009; Heller, 2008) have concluded that loans have minimal effect on college access or persistence particularly for low-income and minority students. Using regression discontinuity and difference-in-difference analyses, Linsenmeier, Rosen, and Rouse (2006) found that one institution's decision to eliminate loans from financial aid packages for low-income students increased the likelihood of enrollment for low-income, minority students but was unrelated to the likelihood of enrollment for low-income students overall. The authors speculated that replacing loans with grants had a greater effect on enrollment for minority than nonminority applicants because minority students are more averse to debt than nonminority students.

Indirect Role of Institutional Financial Aid: Expanding College Choices

Before being able to choose to attend an elite college or university, the institution must be in an individual's choice set. Hossler and Gallagher's (1987) three-phase model provides a framework for understanding how students develop the set of choices that are considered in their cost-benefit calculations. Based on their review and synthesis of prior research, Hossler and Gallagher concluded that the three stages of the college process are predisposition, search, and choice. In the first stage, predisposition, students become predisposed toward or interested in attending college as they develop educational and occupational aspirations. In the second stage, students search for information about colleges. In the third stage, students decide to enroll in a particular college or university (Hossler & Gallagher, 1987).

During the search phase, students gather information about particular colleges and universities and decide which institutions to include and exclude from their "choice" or application set. Research suggests that perceptions of college prices and financial aid influence the choice of college, especially for low-income students. Using descriptive analyses of data from the 1987 National Postsecondary Student Aid Survey, Paulsen and St. John (2002) found that 64 percent of low-income undergraduates considered tuition and financial aid to be very important in their choice of college to attend, compared with only 33 percent of upper-income students.

The search phase may be particularly important to understanding the enrollment of high-ability, low-income students at "no loan" colleges and universities. Most low-income students who apply and are admitted to these institutions would be expected to enroll, given the magnitude of the institutional grant aid award and the absence of loans. Supporting this hypothesis, Bowen and colleagues (2005) found little difference in the probabilities of admission and matriculation based on socioeconomic status after controlling for SAT scores for students at 19 selective colleges and universities in 1995.

Nonetheless, the representation of low-income students at no loan schools remains low (Mundel, 2008), suggesting that the number of low-income students with sufficiently high academic ability is inadequate or that high-ability, low-income students are not giving adequate consideration to elite colleges and universities in the search phase of the process (Hill & Winston, 2006). In a test of the former hypothesis, Hill and Winston examined whether the underrepresentation of low-income students at COFHE institutions is attributable to insufficient numbers of low-income, high-ability students. Disproving this hypothesis, their analyses show, if the enrollment rate of low-income students at these elite institutions equaled their representation among low-income students with SAT (ACT equivalent) scores of 1,420 or higher, then the representation of low-income students would increase from 10 percent to 13 percent.

Other research also suggests that, to increase the representation of students from low-income families, colleges and universities must increase prospective students' applications to these institutions. Based on their review of prior research, Bowen et al. (2005) concluded that the probability of applying to a selective institution was lower for low-income, high-ability students than for their higher-income peers. Tebbs and Turner (2006) found that AccessUVA, the no loan program at the University of Virginia, was associated with an increase in admissions and matriculation rates for students attending public high schools serving high percentages of low-income students, but no change in application rates for these students. Avery and colleagues (2006) found that, one year after implementation, Harvard's financial aid initiative was associated with an increased representation of low-income students in the freshmen class and that this increase was attributable to growth in the number of applicants from low-income families. Nonetheless, the authors concluded that the representation of low-income students at Harvard continues to be low, largely because "many apparently qualified students still do not apply" (p. 3).

UNDERSTANDING INSTITUTIONAL STRATEGIES FOR COMMUNICATING FINANCIAL AID INFORMATION TO LOW-INCOME STUDENTS: INSIGHTS FROM OTHER DISCIPLINES

The extent to which students do not apply to elite colleges and universities because they are unaware of institutional financial aid (including no loan aid packages) is unknown. Numerous reports document the absence of accurate knowledge of financial aid among high school students and their families (e.g., Chan & Cochrane, 2008; Horn, Chen, & Chapman, 2003). National surveys consistently show that most adults, parents, and students are uninformed or poorly informed about college prices and financial aid (Horn et al., 2003). Little is also known about how students' perceptions of financial aid are influenced by the content, timing, and/or modes of information delivery (Mundel & Coles, 2004; Perna, 2004).

While education literature emphasizes that students' college choices are influenced by a student's "situated context" including their social class (McDonough, 1997; Paulsen & St. John, 2002; Perna, 2006), literature from psychology, health care, information science, and marketing suggests that students' interpretations of financial aid-related information may be mediated by social class. Although at times portraying lower-income individuals as a monolithic group and not focusing on financial aid-related information per se, several studies suggest variations by social class in the effects of various communication strategies.

For example, from their case studies of 25 15-year-olds in Australia, North, Snyder, and Bulfin (2009) concluded that, while access to "information and communication technologies" (e.g., Internet, mobile phones) did not vary across students, use of these technologies at home and school varied based on social class. Students from higher social classes tended to view technology as a means for acquiring information, whereas students from lower social classes tended to view technology as a source of entertainment.

In a summary of marketing research, Morton (1999) notes that "buying behavior" varies across six social classes that are defined by income and other socioeconomic characteristics and recommends that public relations staff consider the targeted social class when determining communication strategies. As an example, she contends that: "Because they [people in the lower middle class] have many obligations but limited incomes to meet those obligations, they read self-improvement and how-to information" (p. 45).

From a synthesis of 12 research papers and meta-analyses, Willems, De Maesschalck, Derese, and De Maseseneer (2005) concluded that doctor–patient communication styles vary by social class. Compared with individuals of lower social class, individuals of higher social class have active communication styles, as they tend to ask questions, exhibit emotion, and express their own opinions. As a result, patients of higher social class receive more information than patients of lower social class. Physicians may provide less information to patients from lower than higher social class because they underestimate the patients' interest in such information.

Arguing that "an individual's mix of social and economic distinctions affects their place in society, shapes their opportunities, and colors their world" (p. 423), Henry (2000) examined variations by social class and age in six psychological characteristics believed to have relevance for marketing. Using a sample of adults who were working in Sydney, Australia, Henry found differences by social class in terms of degree of future focus, self-motivation for "stand-out success," preference for stability and constancy in their life, preference for avoiding stress and challenge, size of social networks, and tendency toward altruism.

Other research stresses the ways that an individual's social context shapes information-seeking behavior. Using ethnographic and interview data collected from janitors at one university, Chatman (1991) showed that six propositions drawn from gratification theory describe how these individuals view their social worlds and gather information. The six propositions are that people with low incomes: 1. do not actively seek information to improve their social status or engage in long-term planning; 2. have low expectations for their ability to improve their social status and attribute any success to luck; 3. rely on knowledge from trusted sources (e.g., family, friends) and do not share information with others; 4. emphasize the present and recent past over the future; 5. rely on local information to reinforce their worldviews and distrust individuals outside of their social networks; and 6. view television and other mass media as a mechanism for diversion. Chatman concluded that information of most relevance to this group was "accessible, had a firm footing in everyday reality, and responded to some immediate concern" (p. 438). Moreover, in order to seek information, these individuals needed to believe that the "information sought will lend some significant benefit to their situation" (p. 447).

In summary, available data and research suggest that raising the representation of high-ability, low-income students at selective colleges and universities requires greater attention to students' perceptions and understandings of institutional financial aid. Little is known about what students know about institutional aid or how their perceptions are influenced by the content and delivery of financial aid information. Research from other fields suggests that perceptions of aid are mediated by social class and that, therefore, to effectively communicate information about institutional aid, institutions should recognize the ways that social class informs students' perceptions and use of institutional aid.

DECONSTRUCTING NO LOAN POLICIES

As a step toward understanding how institutional aid may promote applications to elite colleges and universities among low-income students, this chapter explores the characteristics of institutions with no loan policies and the ways that these no loan schools communicate information about financial aid to low-income students via their websites. As others have noted (e.g., Lazarus & Lipper, 2005), few studies have examined how high school students use information and computing technologies to acquire college-related information. Given the absence of research in this area, our review of websites was designed to describe, not evaluate, institutional communication strategies.

We focus on institutional communication via the Internet for several reasons. First, according to the 2006 "State of College Admission" report produced by the National Association for College Admission Counseling (NACAC) (Hawkins & Clinedinst, 2007), the Internet is increasingly used by both students and institutions in the college admission process. More than half (58 percent) of applications at institutions participating in

NACAC's survey were submitted online in fall 2006. Internet or email was the most common mechanism that students used to contact participating institutions about admission; about 33 percent of all inquiries were via the Internet or email. Virtually all participating colleges and universities report providing information about financial aid (99 percent) and college prices (97 percent) on their website (Hawkins & Clinedinst, 2007). The Internet may also be an economical mechanism for low-income students to "visit" a campus.

Consistent with a post-structural emphasis on the role of language in creating "reality" and reinforcing prevailing values (as described by Kezar in the introduction to this volume), we reviewed the communication styles presented on the websites of the institutions that we identified as "no loan" schools. We developed the template for this examination based on our review of the literature identifying differences across social class in perceptions of technology (North et al., 2009), effective marketing strategies (Henry, 2000; Morton, 1999), doctor–patient communication styles (Willems et al., 2005), and information-seeking strategies (Chatman, 1991). Members of the project team worked together to determine how to operationalize constructs identified from the research review for the template. Because institutions communicate about financial aid on both their admissions and financial aid websites, we completed the template for the admissions and financial aid websites for each no loan school.[3]

Characteristics of No Loan Schools

One of the most striking findings from our review of institutional websites was how difficult it was for our team of five individuals with a high degree of knowledge of higher education to tell if an institution had a no loan policy. Although decisions to eliminate loans from the financial aid packages of low-income students are disseminated in outlets that reach others in the higher education community (e.g., *Chronicle of Higher Education*, *Inside HigherEd*), information on these policies is often not easily found on the institution's own website. Based on her study of admissions processes at 17 "most selective" colleges and universities, Killgore (2009) contends that institutions that adopt "no loan" policies are rewarded for their social justice efforts with "public legitimacy" even though only very small numbers of students benefit from these policies. When interpreted in light of Killgore's study, the challenges that we experienced identifying "no loan" policies may reflect these institutions' potentially conflicting interests around these policies: although they want credit for providing opportunity, extensively publicizing their aid policies and consequently enrolling larger numbers of low-income students may cause a substantial drain on institutional resources.

For this review, we initially included the public flagship in each state as well as colleges and universities from four annual rankings produced by *U.S. News & World Report*: top 100 "National Universities," 25 "Best Liberal Arts Schools," 50 "Top Public Schools: National Universities," and 50 "Best Values: National Universities."[4] Although problematic in many ways (e.g., Ehrenberg, 2003), we referenced these popular/ubiquitous rankings in an effort to replicate the process by which many students and families seek information about "good" schools.

From our initial website review, we identified only 21 institutions with no loan policies. As some institutions that project team members knew to have no loan policies did not emerge from this initial review, we sought other sources for this information. Because we found no organization that systematically collects information on institutional aid policies, we relied on lists included in articles in the *New York Times* (Leonhardt, 2008), *Inside HigherEd* (Rosenberg, 2009a, 2009b), and Wikipedia (2009).[5] Eliminating overlap among the various lists resulted in 163 institutions.

With this additional information, we identified 51 institutions (see Table 4.1) as offering "no loan" policies. Table 4.2 shows that these institutions include both public (n=17) and private (n=34) institutions.[6] The no loan schools are disproportionately baccalaureate colleges (n=16) and research universities with very high levels of research activity (n=32). No loan schools represented only 13 of 53 top public universities, 32 of 100 top national universities, 15 of 26 top liberal arts colleges, and 25 of 50 "best value" universities, per the *U.S. News & World Report* rankings.[7] The low representation of no loan schools among these "top" institutions is not surprising, given that these rankings do not include explicit attention to the characteristics of institutional aid programs. The absence of measures of institutional aid from these rankings—and the inclusion of student selectivity measures that discourage institutions from admitting low-income students—raises questions about the depth of our societal commitment to improving educational opportunity for students from low-income families (Breneman, 2006).

Consistent with expectations based on prior research (e.g., Hill et al., 2005), Table 4.2 shows that the no loan schools are somewhat more selective than non-no-loan schools, as admissions rates are lower (32 percent versus 58 percent) and yield rates are higher (47 percent versus 36 percent) at the no loan schools. In addition, the no loans schools also have smaller shares of low-income students than non-no-loan schools, as only 12 percent of undergraduates at no loan schools but 18 percent of undergraduates at non-no-loan schools received Pell grants. Reflecting the characteristics of "no loan" policies, recipients of institutional aid at no loan schools average higher amounts of institutional grant aid than recipients at non-no-loan schools ($18,019 versus $10,317). Only

Table 4.1 "No Loan" Colleges and Universities and their Identifying Sources

Institution	Source 1	Source 2
Amherst College	*Inside HigherEd*	*New York Times*
Arizona State University	Wikipedia	
Bowdoin	Wikipedia	*New York Times*
Brown University	Institutional website	*New York Times*
Caltech	Wikipedia	*New York Times*
Claremont McKenna	Institutional website	*New York Times*
Colby College	Institutional website	*New York Times*
College of William and Mary	Wikipedia	*New York Times*
Columbia University	Wikipedia	*New York Times*
Cornell University	Institutional website	*New York Times*
Dartmouth	Institutional website	*New York Times*
Davidson	Institutional website	*New York Times*
Duke	Wikipedia	*New York Times*
Emory	Institutional website	*New York Times*
Georgia Institute of Technology	Institutional website	
Harvard	Institutional website	*New York Times*
Haverford	Wikipedia	*New York Times*
Indiana University at Bloomington		*New York Times*
Lafayette	Wikipedia	*New York Times*
Lehigh	Institutional website	*New York Times*
Michigan State	Institutional website	
Massachusetts Institute of Technology	Wikipedia	*New York Times*
North Carolina State	Wikipedia	
Northern Illinois University	Institutional website	
Northwestern University	Wikipedia	
Pomona College	Wikipedia	*New York Times*
Princeton University	Institutional website	*New York Times*
Rice University	Wikipedia	*New York Times*
Stanford University	*Inside HigherEd*	*New York Times*
Swarthmore College	Institutional website	*New York Times*
Texas A&M University	Institutional website	
Tufts University	Wikipedia	*New York Times*
UNC Chapel Hill	Wikipedia	*New York Times*
University of Chicago	Wikipedia	*New York Times*
University of Florida		*New York Times*
University of Georgia	Institutional website	
University of Illinois	Institutional website	
University of Maryland, College Park	Wikipedia	
University of Michigan	Institutional website	
University of Pennsylvania	Institutional website	*New York Times*
University of Virginia	Wikipedia	*New York Times*
U.S. Military Academy	Institutional website	
U.S. Naval Academy	Institutional website	
Vanderbilt University	Wikipedia	
Vassar	Wikipedia	*New York Times*
Washington and Lee	Wikipedia	
Washington University at St. Louis	Wikipedia	*New York Times*
Wellesley	Wikipedia	*New York Times*
Wesleyan	Wikipedia	*New York Times*
Williams	*Inside HigherEd*	*New York Times*
Yale	*Inside HigherEd*	*New York Times*

Note: "Sources" identifies the sources used to classify a college or university as "no loan." Sources include each institution's own website as well as articles in the *New York Times* (Leonhardt, 2008), *Inside HigherEd* (Rosenberg, 2009a), and Wikipedia (2009).

Table 4.2 Characteristics of Institutions in the Analyses

Characteristic	Total	"No loan"	Non "no loan"
Total no. Institutions	163	51	112
Institutional control			
Public	80	17	63
Private, not-for-profit	83	34	49
Carnegie Classification			
Baccalaureate College	29	16	13
Master's	1	0	1
Doctoral/Research	6	0	6
Research (high research)	42	3	39
Research (very high research)	85	32	53
Ranking			
Top public universities	53	13	40
Top national universities	100	32	68
Top liberal arts colleges	26	15	11
Best value universities	50	25	25
Flagship universities	50	8	42
Average:			
Tuition and fees	$20,669	$26,399	$18,168
Institutional grant aid	$12,661	$18,019	$10,317
Loan aid	$4,842	$4,293	$5,083
Average % receiving:			
Pell grants	16	12	18
Admitted	50	32	58
Yield	40	47	36
Any aid	71	63	75
Federal aid	16	13	18
Institutional aid	51	44	54
Loan aid	41	33	45

Source: Analyses of data obtained from the U.S. Department of Education's Integrated Postsecondary Education Data System and Economic Diversity of Colleges (2009)

33 percent of students at no loan schools, but 45 percent of students at non-no-loan schools received loans. But, only 44 percent of students at no loans schools, compared with 54 percent of students at non-no-loan schools, received institutional aid.

Institutional Practices that May Impede Communication with Low-Income Students

In addition to challenges associated with identifying an institution as "no loan," our review of institutional websites suggests other institutional practices that may limit communication about financial aid to low-income students. In particular, some institutional websites lack specificity about the consideration of financial need in financial aid decisions, actual financial aid awards, and net prices for low-income students. Moreover, although we did not examine the effects of different communication strategies on student outcomes, our review suggests that many institutions may not be giving adequate attention to the ways that social class may mediate students' perceptions and understandings of available aid information. More specifically, our review suggests differences across institutions in six dimensions that the literature suggests may be especially important to low-income students: location of financial aid information; present versus future orientation; recognition of the importance of need-based aid; specificity and degree of "how to" information; effort to build trusting and supportive relationships; and attention to the entertainment dimensions of technology.

Location of Financial Aid Information. The location of financial aid information varies across the 51 "no loan" colleges and universities. For five of the 51 institutions, the admissions and financial aid websites are the same. Four of the 51 institutions include no mention of financial aid on the admissions website. Most "admissions" websites include a direct link to financial aid.

For several institutions, financial, aid-related information is found in multiple locations. While this practice may increase the likelihood that a prospective student will find the necessary information, it may also increase the likelihood of potentially conflicting information. For example, one of the 51 institutions specified different family-income eligibility criteria for its "no loan" program on its admissions and financial aid websites.

Present versus Future Orientation. Of the 51 websites, 33 appear to recognize the tendency of lower-income individuals to stress the present over the future (Chatman, 1991; Morton, 1999) by emphasizing the immediate expense or present sacrifice required to pay for higher education; 23 emphasize the future value of an investment in college and four include attention to both dimensions. For example, one institution acknowledges the immediate expense of paying for college by stating: "We do not want the cost of attending [this institution] to be a barrier... We understand that paying for college is a concern for most families." Another institution emphasizes the future benefits of a college investment by stating: "The lifetime earning potential difference between having a high school diploma and a Bachelor's degree is more than $1 million."

Explicit Recognition of the Importance of Need-Based Aid. The 51 institutions also vary in terms of how they respond to low-income students' likely concerns about the availability of need-based aid (Chatman, 1991) and communicate their consideration of financial need in financial aid decisions. Most (n=36) institutions explicitly state that they award financial aid based on financial need. As an example of how an institution communicates its emphasis on financial need, one institution states, "We are committed to providing a comprehensive need-based financial aid program," and then goes on to explain how financial need is calculated. Six of the 51 institutions describe financial aid that is awarded based on financial need, as well as the availability of merit-based scholarship aid.

Specificity and Degree of "How To" Information. Recognizing the potential importance to low-income students of "how to" information (Morton, 1999), most (n=44) provide basic financial-aid information, including a glossary, Frequently Asked Questions (FAQs), due dates or calendar, and/or application steps. At the other seven institutions, basic financial aid information is difficult to find and/or use. For example, one institution requires prospective students and parents to download PDF documents to obtain financial aid information. Another site requires individuals to "sign in" in order to obtain more specific information. While allowing the institution to track prospective students, this practice may discourage individuals who do not trust others who are outside of their social networks (Chatman, 1991).

These 51 institutions also vary in terms of the specificity of information provided. Examples of straightforward and specific information (present on 33 websites) include: explicit information about costs of tuition and fees, room and board; definitions of how financial need is calculated; and hypothetical student scenarios and financial aid packages.

One of the most striking observations from the websites is how few institutions provide specific information about the average amount of financial aid a student receives. Only 18 of the 51 institutions include a statement along the lines of the following: "A student is typically responsible for $5,500 toward educational expenses." One institution includes a very general—but seemingly meaningless—statement of aid awards: "In 2007–08, awards ranged from $1,200 to over $49,000 for families with annual incomes between $6,000 and $200,000." A small number of institutions state the average grant award or include a table that shows the amount of grant aid that a student with a particular family income typically receives. More typical is to include no specific information, or to report the percentage of students who received aid and/or the total amount of institutional aid awarded. As an example of the latter, one institution reports: "Over half a billion dollars was awarded to 46,000 students, including $17 million in scholarships and $65 million in grants." Another institution states: "Around 40% of [this institution's] students receive financial aid."

Effort to Build Trusting and Supportive Relationships.   Institutions also vary in the extent to which they may be building trust with prospective low-income students and their families. About half (n=26) of the 51 institutions offer encouraging or helpful language, 18 use more neutral or professional language or offer a more cautionary tone, and seven use both. In an example of encouraging language, one institution states: "If you're considering [this institution], don't hesitate to apply because you think your family won't be able to afford the cost of an education [at this institution]." As an example of a cautionary tone, another institution warns: "Read all application instructions... Need-based institutional aid can be guaranteed only to students who meet deadlines." In an example of a mixed approach, one institution uses both encouraging (e.g., "we are happy to work with you to develop a financial aid package that will make it possible for you to afford [this institution])" and professional (e.g., "The student and his or her family have the primary responsibility for college costs, to the extent of their ability") language.

Most (n=33) of the institutional websites attempt to engage students and parents by using second rather than third person to refer to the student and/or using students' and parents' voices. In a typical example of an unengaged presentation, one institution states, "Any student may apply for financial aid." Another institution provides no introductory text to help guide a prospective student through the website. As an example of a more engaged presentation, four institutions offer profiles of how students at the institution have paid the costs of their education. Two institutions write that the primary goal of the financial aid office "is to work with you." Institutions may also engage students and their families through the use of photographs of current students and/or financial aid staff (included on 35 of the websites). Nonetheless, minimal effort appears to be made to address the information needs of non-English-speaking families, as only one of the 51 financial aid websites included a second language option.

As another indicator of efforts to build trust, institutions also vary in the extent to which they seem to invite prospective students to contact the financial aid office. About half (n=25) seem to invite contact, while others passively provide contact information. For example, one institution provides a "meet our staff" webpage with the pictures, emails, and phone numbers of all financial aid staff. Others may encourage contact through such language as: "As you develop your family's individual paying-for-college strategy, contact us for assistance" and "Help is just a phone call away." One institution offers "live chat" with a financial aid adviser.

Attention to the Entertainment Dimensions of Technology.   One way that institutions may appeal to the tendency of low-income students to view technology as entertainment (North et al., 2009) may be to use multi- and interactive media. About half (n=27) of the websites used multi-media tools. Presence of these tools varies, with some institutions including only a financial aid calculator and others offering more sophisticated tools such as videos, online chat, blogs by the director of financial aid, and podcasts. The videos include profiles of how the institution's students pay college prices, how to understand financial aid, and/or how to use the financial aid estimator.

RECONSTRUCTING INSTITUTIONAL AID POLICIES

Institutional financial aid is just one of many forces that contribute to the low representation of low-income students at selective colleges and universities (Breneman, 2006; Perna, 2006). Research consistently shows that lower-income students average lower levels of academic achievement and are less likely to attend well-resourced high schools with a college-going culture (McDonough, 1997; Perna, 2005). Given differences in access to high-quality academic preparation, high school counseling and other resources, simply increasing the availability of need-based institutional grant aid will not eliminate the stratification of students by family income across different types of institutions (Breneman, 2006).

Nonetheless, this chapter's consideration of institutional aid builds on Bowen et al.'s (2005) examination of whether elite colleges and universities serve as "engines of opportunity" or "bastions of privilege." Based on their examination of the 1995 entering cohort at 19 academically selective colleges and universities, Bowen and colleagues concluded that these elite institutions promote opportunity, as the likelihood of admission, matriculation, and graduation does not vary substantially by socioeconomic status for students of high-academic ability, and reinforce stratification, as these institutions enroll only very small numbers of students from low-socioeconomic backgrounds. Similarly, this chapter identifies both strengths and weaknesses of the aid policies at selected institutions. The chapter shows that about one-third of the selected colleges and universities have adopted generous institutional aid strategies that are designed to eliminate financial barriers to attendance for low-income, high-ability students. But, these institutions may also continue to be "bastions of privilege" by failing to adequately communicate information about this aid to prospective low-income students and their families.

Reconstructing institutional aid policies to serve more low-income students has important implications for institutional financial aid expenditures. As others have noted (e.g., McPherson & Schapiro, 2006b), no loan schools can afford their generous institutional aid policies in part because so few low-income students enroll. Increasing the numbers of students who use these policies will necessarily increase institutional costs. Because of institutional resource constraints, efforts to increase institutional, need-based financial aid, reduce students' reliance on loans, and increase prospective students' knowledge of institutional aid often require institutional trade-offs (Breneman, 2006; McPherson & Schapiro, 2006b). In his profile of six colleges and universities, Breneman implies the opportunity costs of increasing resources for institutional aid for other institutional priorities, including faculty salaries. Increasing financial aid for low-income students may also require raising revenue from other sources, including tuition paid by full-paying students (Breneman, 2006).

For institutions that decide that the benefits of raising the representation of low-income students are worth the costs, our review suggests several ways that institutional aid policies may be reconstructed to effectively reach students from low-income families. First, institutions should consider ways to effectively communicate information about financial aid and net prices as well as ways to target these communication efforts to students from lower-income families. Individual colleges and universities should build on the framework used in this study to critique the effectiveness of their current online communication strategies for targeted demographic groups.

The absence of clear and visible information about the availability of these generous institutional financial aid packages likely limits not only students' and their families' efforts to learn about financial aid but also school counselors' efforts to assist low-income students with their college-related decisions. The challenges that limit the ability of high school counselors to provide college and financial aid information are well documented (e.g., McDonough, 2005; Perna, Rowan-Kenyon, Thomas, Bell, Anderson, & Li, 2008). Our research team invested substantial time trying to pin down information about institutional aid policies, a finding that does not bode well for students, families, or counselors who may not have the time or "insider" knowledge to obtain this information.

Those reconstructing institutional aid policies should also consider the extent that strategies beyond websites are required to adequately inform prospective high-achieving, low-income students about the availability of institutional aid. Some no loan institutions have hired additional staff to support low-income students and families with the financial aid process (Fischer, 2008). At the University of Virginia, the AccessUVA program includes efforts to communicate with prospective low-income students about the program, including additional visits to high schools serving high numbers of low-income students, public service announcements describing AccessUVA, and additional assistance from UVA financial aid staff to complete financial aid forms (Tebbs & Turner, 2006). Harvard's Financial Aid Initiative includes outreach from Harvard students, staff, and alumni to low- and moderate-income students (Avery et al., 2006).

Selective colleges and universities may also increase knowledge and usage of institutional grant aid by partnering with pre-college outreach and college-transition programs. Several of the nation's most selective institutions have become partners in *QuestBridge*, a program designed to increase the enrollment of academically talented and self-motivated low-income students into elite colleges and universities. *QuestBridge* solicits applications from students and then identifies a pool of applicants, based on academic and financial criteria, from which partner institutions may select. *QuestBridge* places particular emphasis on the socioeconomic disadvantages that students have faced. The 26 college and university partners provide the students they select with a scholarship covering four years of tuition, fees, room, and board; some partners offer additional scholarships to cover books and supplies, travel expenses, and health insurance as well as enrichment opportunities. More than 900 students (across all academic years) received scholarships from partner institutions in 2007–08 (*QuestBridge*, 2009).

Efforts to reconstruct institutional aid policies to better serve low-income students should also consider the limits of "no loan" policies on raising the number of low-income students on campus. Although the effectiveness of these programs may improve over time, the representation of low income students at most no loan institutions is small (Fischer, 2008; Tebbs & Turner, 2006). Bowen et al. (2005) concluded that putting a "thumb on the scale" for students from low-socioeconomic backgrounds during the admissions process (along the lines of the advantage that is provided to children of alumni, athletes, and underrepresented minorities) would do more to raise the representation of students from low-income families than no loan policies.

Finally, reconstructing institutional aid policies should include attention to how to support the educational success of low-income students who enroll (Breneman, 2006). Although persistence and degree completion rates at selective institutions do not vary by socioeconomic status (Bowen et al., 2005), research and personal essays show that students from lower socioeconomic backgrounds attending selective institutions face such challenges as diminished feelings of belonging, heightened class awareness and identity, experiences with classism, and difficulties in bridging the worlds of campus and home (Aries, 2008; Aries & Seider, 2005, 2007; hooks, 2000; Jan, 2009; Kirn, 2009; Langhout, Rosselli, & Feinsten, 2007; Lara, 1992; Lubrano, 2004; Ostrove & Long, 2007; Rendon, 1992; Rodriguez, 1982).

RECOMMENDATIONS FOR FUTURE RESEARCH

To fully understand how to reconstruct institutional aid policies to best serve students from low-income families, additional research in at least four areas is required. First, future research should build on the rubric developed in this study to test the effectiveness of various web-based strategies for informing students and their families about the availability of institutional financial aid. Little is known about how websites or other mechanisms for disseminating information about financial aid (e.g., financial aid workshops, college and career counseling sessions, or one-on-one counseling sessions with college alumni and others) affect students' and families' knowledge and use of financial aid (Porter, Fossey, Davis, Burnett, Stuhlmann, & Suchy, 2006).

Second, future research should consider the extent to which a "digital divide" limits the effectiveness of Internet-communication strategies for students from low-income families. Although increasingly prevalent, access to personal computers and the Internet continues to vary by social class. Only 45 percent of children between the ages of 7 and 17 living in households with incomes below $15,000 had a personal computer at home in 2003, compared with 96 percent of children with household incomes above $75,000 (Lazarus & Lipper, 2005). Substantially lower shares of children from low-income households than from high-income households had access to the Internet (29 percent versus 93 percent) or broadband (7 percent versus 51 percent) at home or used a computer at home to complete school work (29 percent versus 77 percent) (Lazarus & Lipper, 2005).

Third, future research should also consider the types of support that may be required for different groups of students and families to benefit from the information that is provided by the Internet (Mundel, 2008). Drawing on data collected from six focus groups and a cultural ecological framework, Venegas (2006) identified the challenges that low-income students attending urban high schools experience when using the Internet to complete financial aid applications. For example, students had access to computers and the Internet, but access was often limited by connectivity problems. Lack of consistent access to email accounts, confusion about the required application steps, and lack of knowledge among key individuals (e.g., parents, peers, counselors) also limited students' ability to effectively use the Internet for financial aid applications. Other research shows that information communication technologies may promote student achievement and attendance, but only when combined with highly trained teachers and other supports (Lazarus & Lipper, 2005).

Finally, future research should examine whether and how the effectiveness of various communication strategies varies based on socioeconomic status and other characteristics. Research also should examine variations in the types and effects of communication strategies at a more diverse sample of institutions, including institutions that enroll large percentages of low-income students, minority serving institutions, and less-selective institutions.

NOTES

1. The authors thank Matthew Reed, Program Director at The Institute for College Access & Success, for his helpful feedback on an earlier draft of this manuscript. An earlier version of this manuscript was presented at the College Board's National Forum in New York, October 23, 2009.
2. Eligibility for federal need-based financial aid (e.g., Pell grants) is determined by the federal need analysis formula (U.S. Department of Education, 2008). This formula determines a student's Expected Family Contribution (EFC) based on family income, assets, and living expenses. Financial need is the difference between the institutional cost of attendance and the EFC. While eligibility for some federal financial aid (e.g., Pell grants) is determined by the need analysis, institutions have discretion in awarding other types of federal aid (e.g., campus-based aid) as well as their own institutional aid (Singell, 2002).
3. A copy of the template is available from the authors on request.
4. *U.S. News & World Reports* ranks national universities and liberal arts schools based on indicators in seven categories: peer assessment, student retention, faculty resources, student selectivity, financial resources, alumni giving, and graduation rate performance (Morse & Flanigan, 2008). Indicators considered for the ranking of "best value schools" measure: the ratio of "quality to price" (i.e., total price of attendance relative to the net cost for students receiving the average amount of need-based grants); the share of undergraduates receiving need-based grant aid; and the average discount rate (*U.S. News & World Report*, 2008).
5. Just prior to publication of this chapter, we learned of two other lists of colleges and universities with initiatives to reduce students' use of loans. These lists were compiled by The Project on Student Debt (http://www.projectonstudentdebt.org/pc_institution. php) and the University of North Carolina at Chapel Hill (http://www.unc.edu/inclusion/ initiatives.pdf). Although these lists overlap with our final list, there are a few differences. The Project on Student Debt lists seven institutions with no loan policies that are not on our list: Appalachian State University, Connecticut and Oberlin Colleges, and the Universities of Arizona, California, Louisville, and Tennessee. These discrepancies underscore the challenges of identifying no loans schools.
6. The Project on Student Debt identifies 18 public and 34 private institutions.
7. We used data from the Integrated Postsecondary Education Data System (IPEDS) to create a file describing the institutional characteristics of the 163 institutions. We obtained data describing the percentage of undergraduates receiving Pell grants from Economic Diversity of Colleges (2009). We then ran descriptive statistics to compare the characteristics of no loan and non no-loan schools.

REFERENCES

Aries, E. (2008). *Race and class matters at an elite college*. Philadelphia: Temple University Press.

Aries, E., & Seider, M. (2005). The interactive relationships between class identity and the college experience: The case of lower income students. *Qualitative Sociology, 28*(4), 419–443.

Aries, E., & Seider, M. (2007). The role of social class in the formation of identity: A study of public and elite private college students. *Journal of Social Psychology, 147*(2), 137–158.

Avery, C., & Hoxby, C. M. (2004). Do and should financial aid packages affect students' college choices? In C. M. Hoxby (Ed.), *College choices: The economics of where to go, when to go, and how to pay for it* (pp. 239–302). Chicago: University of Chicago Press.

Avery, C., Hoxby, C., Jackson, C., Burek, K., Pope, G., & Raman, M. (2006). *Cost should be no barrier: An evaluation of the first year of Harvard's financial aid initiative*. Washington, DC: National Bureau of Economic Research.

Baum, S., & Ma, J. (2007). *Education pays 2007*. Washington, DC: College Board.

Becker, G. S. (1993). *Human capital: A theoretical and empirical analysis with special reference to education* (3rd ed.). Chicago: University of Chicago Press.

Bowen, W. G., Kurzweil, M. A., & Tobin, E. M. (2005). *Equity and excellence in American higher education*. Charlottesville, VA: University of Virginia Press.

Breneman, D. (2006). Six institutional perspectives on socioeconomic diversity. In M. S. McPherson & M. O. Schapiro (Eds.), *College access: Opportunity or privilege?* (pp. 117–129). New York: College Board.

Chan, D., & Cochrane, D. F. (2008). *Paving the way: How financial aid awareness affects college access and success*. Institute for College Access and Success. Retrieved December 5, 2008 from http://projectonstudentdebt.org/fckfiles/Paving_the_Way.pdf

Chatman, E. A. (1991). Life in a small world: Applicability of gratification theory to information-seeking behavior. *Journal of the American Society for Information Science and Technology, 42*(6), 438–449.

Chronicle of Higher Education. (2008). Enrolling needy students: How the wealthiest colleges rate. *Chronicle of Higher Education, 54*(34), p. A19.

College Board. (2008). *Trends in student aid 2008*. Washington, DC: Author.

Economic Diversity of Colleges. (2009). *Economic diversity of colleges: College-level data for researchers and the public*. Retrieved June 10, 2009 from http://www.economicdiversity.org/

Ehrenberg, R. (2003). Reaching for the brass ring: The *U.S. News & World Report* rankings and competition. *Review of Higher Education, 26*(2), 145–162.

Fischer, K. (2008, April 24). Wealthy colleges show drop in enrollments of needy students. *Chronicle of Higher Education, Today's News.*

Haskins, R., Holzer, H., & Lerman, R. (2009). *Promoting economic mobility by increasing postsecondary education*. Economic Mobility Project, Pew Charitable Trusts. Retrieved May 20, 2009 from http://www.pewtrusts.org/uploadedFiles/wwwpewtrustsorg/Reports/Economic_Mobility/PEW_EM_Haskins%207.pdf

Hawkins, D. A., & Clinedinst, M. E. (2007, August). *State of college admission*. Washington, DC: National Association for College Admission Counseling.

Heller, D. E. (1997). Student price response in higher education: An update to Leslie and Brinkman. *Journal of Higher Education, 68*(6), 624–659.

Heller, D. E. (2008). The impact of student loans on college access. In S. Baum, M. McPherson, & P. Steele (Eds.), *The effectiveness of student aid policies: What the research tells us* (pp. 39–68). Washington, DC: College Board.

Henry, P. (2000). Modes of thought that vary systematically with both social class and age. *Psychology and Marketing, 17*(5), 421–440.

Hill, C. B., & Winston, G. C. (2006). How scarce are high-ability, low-income students? In M. S. McPherson & M. O. Schapiro (Eds.), *College access: Opportunity or privilege?* (pp. 75–102). New York: College Board.

Hill, C. B., Winston, G. C., & Boyd, S. A. (2005). Affordability: Family incomes and net prices at highly selective private colleges and universities. *Journal of Human Resources, 40*(4), 769–790.

hooks, b. (2000). *Where we stand: class matters*. New York: Routledge.

Horn, L. J., Chen, X., & Chapman, C. (2003). *Getting ready to pay for college: What students and their parents know about the cost of college tuition and what they are doing to find out*. Washington, DC: U.S. Department of Education, Institute of Education Sciences.

Hossler, D., & Gallagher, K. S. (1987). Studying college choice: A three-phase model and the implications for policy-makers. *College and University, 62*(3), 207–221.

Jan, T. (2009, May 12). The Harvard disadvantage: Despite outreach, the needy face socioeconomic gulf. *Boston Globe*. Retrieved May 12, 2009 from http://www.boston.com/news/education/higher/articles/2009/05/12/the_harvard_disadvantage/?s_campaign=8315

Killgore, L. (2009). Merit and competition in selective college admissions. *Review of Higher Education, 32*(4), 469–488.

Kirn, W. (2009). *Lost in the meritocracy: The undereducation of an over-achiever*. New York: Doubleday.

Langhout, R. D., Rosselli, F., & Feinsten, J. (2007). Assessing classism in academic settings. *The Review of Higher Education, 30*(2), 145–184.

Lara, J. (1992). Reflections: Bridging cultures. In L. S. Zwerling & H. B. London (Eds.), *First generation college students: confronting the cultural issues*. San Francisco: Jossey-Bass.

Lazarus, W., & Lipper, L. (2005). *Measuring digital opportunity for America's children: Where we stand and where we go from here*. Santa Monica, CA: The Children's Partnership.

Leonhardt, D. (2008). The (yes) low cost of higher ed, *New York Times*. Retrieved June 1, 2009 from http://www.nytimes.com/2008/04/20/education/edlife/essay.html?pagewanted=1&_ r=1&sq=April%2020,%202008%20no%20loan%20schools&st=cse&scp=2

Linsenmeier, D. M., Rosen, H. S., & Rouse, C. E. (2006). Financial aid packages and college enrollment decisions: An econometric case. *Review of Economics and Statistics, 88*(1), 126–145.

Lubrano, A. (2004). *Limbo: Blue collar roots, white collar dreams*. Hoboken, NJ: Wiley Press.

Masterson, K. (2009, May 1). NYU gets aggressive about discussing debt. *Chronicle of Higher Education*, A18.

McDonough, P. M. (1997). *Choosing colleges: How social class and schools structure opportunity*. Albany: State University of New York Press.

McDonough, P. M. (2005). Counseling and college counseling in America's high schools. In D. A. Hawkins & J. Lautz (Eds.), *State of college admission* (pp. 107–121). Washington, DC: National Association for College Admission Counseling.

McPherson, M. S., & Schapiro, M. O. (2006a). Watch what we do (and not what we say): How student aid awards vary with financial need and academic merit. In M. S. McPherson and M. O. Schapiro (Eds.), *College access: Opportunity or privilege?* (pp. 49–73). New York: College Board.

McPherson, M. S., & Schapiro, M. O. (2006b). Introduction. In M. S. McPherson and M. O. Schapiro (Eds.), *College access: Opportunity or privilege?* (pp. 3–15). New York: College Board.

Morse, R., & Flanigan, S. (2008, August 21). Best colleges: How we calculate the rankings. *U.S. News & World Reports*. Retrieved June 12, 2009 from http://www.usnews.com/articles/ education/best-colleges/2008/08/21/how-we-calculate-the-rankings.html

Morton, L. P. (1999). Segmenting publics by social classes. *Public Relations Quarterly, 44*(2), 45–46.

Mundel, D. (2008). What do we know about the impact of grants to college students? In S. Baum, M. McPherson, & P. Steele (Eds.), *The effectiveness of student aid policies: What the research tells us* (pp. 9–38). Washington, DC: The College Board.

Mundel, D. S., & Coles, A. S. (2004). *Summary project report: An exploration of what we know about the formation and impact of perceptions of college prices, student aid, and the affordability of college-going and a prospectus for future research*. Boston, MA: TERI.

North, S., Snyder, I., & Bulfin, S. (2009). Digital tastes: Social class and young people's technology use. *Information, Communication & Society, 11*(7), 895–911.

Olsen, F., & Lively, K. (2001, February 9). Princeton increases endowment spending to replace students' loans with grants. *Chronicle of Higher Education*, p. A32.

Ostrove, J. M., & Long, S. M. (2007). Social class and belonging: Implications for college adjustment. *The Review of Higher Education, 30*(4), 363–389.

Pappano, L. (2009, April 19). The office: Behind closed doors as aid officers decide just how much they want to say yes. *New York Times, Education Life*, 24–26.

Paulsen, M. B. (2001). The economics of human capital and investment in higher education. In M. B. Paulsen & J. C. Smart (Eds.), *The finance of higher education: Theory, research, policy, and practice* (pp. 55–94). New York: Agathon Press.

Paulsen, M. B., & St. John, E. P. (2002). Social class and college costs: Examining the financial nexus between college choice and persistence. *Journal of Higher Education, 73*(2), 189–236.

Perna, L. W. (2004). *Impact of student aid program design, operations, and marketing on the formation of family college-going plans and resulting college-going behaviors of potential students.* Boston, MA: The Education Resources Institute, Inc. (TERI).

Perna, L. W. (2005). The key to college access: A college preparatory curriculum. In W. G. Tierney, Z. B. Corwin, & J. E. Colyar (Eds.), *Preparing for college: nine elements of effective outreach* (pp. 113–134). Albany, NY: State University of New York Press.

Perna, L. W. (2006). Studying college choice: A proposed conceptual model. In J. C. Smart (Ed.), *Higher education: Handbook of theory and research, Vol. XXI* (pp. 99–157). The Netherlands: Springer.

Perna, L. W., Rowan-Kenyon, H., Thomas, S. L., Bell, A., Anderson, R., & Li, C. (2008). The role of college counseling in shaping college opportunity: Variations across high schools. *Review of Higher Education, 31*(2), 131–160.

Porter, J. Y., Fossey, W. R., Davis, W. E., Burnett, M. F., Stuhlmann, J., & Suchy, P. A. (2006). Students' perceptions of factors that affect college funding decisions. *Journal of Student Financial Aid, 36*(1), 25–33.

QuestBridge (2009). *Welcome to QuestBridge.* Retrieved June 12, 2009 from http://www.questbridge.org/index.html

Reed, M., & Shireman, R. (2008). *Time to reexamine institutional cooperation on financial aid.* Washington, DC: The Institute for College Access & Success.

Rendon, L. I. (1992). From the barrio to the academy: Revelations of a Mexican American "scholarship girl." In L. S. Zwerling & H. B. London (Eds.), *First generation college students: confronting the cultural issues.* San Francisco: Jossey-Bass Publishers.

Rodriguez, R. (1982). *Hunger of memory: The education of Richard Rodriguez—an autobiography.* Boston: Godine.

Rosenberg, B. (2009a, May 12). To lend or not to lend? *Inside HigherEd.* Retrieved June 1, 2009 from http://www.insidehighered.com/views/2009/05/12/rosenberg

Rosenberg, B. (2009b, June 1). Personal communication.

Singell Jr., L. D. (2002). Merit, need, and student self selection: Is there discretion in the packaging of aid at a large public university? *Economics of Education Review, 21*(5), 445–454.

Tebbs, J., & Turner, S. (2006). The challenge of improving the representation of low-income students at flagship universities: AccessUVA and the University of Virginia. In M. S. McPherson and M. O. Schapiro (Eds.), *College access: Opportunity or privilege?* (pp. 105–115). New York: College Board.

Titus, M. (in press). Understanding the relationship between working while in college and future salaries. In L. W. Perna (Ed.), *Understanding the meaning of "work" for today's undergraduates.* Herndon, VA: Stylus Publishers LLC.

U.S. Department of Education (2008). *Student Financial Aid Handbook, Vol. 3.* Washington, DC: Author. Retrieved June 22, 2009 from http://ifap.ed.gov/sfahandbooks/attachments/0809FSAHbkVol3Ch3Oct14.pdf

U.S. News & World Report (2008). Methodology: Best values. Retrieved June 12, 2009 from http://www.usnews.com/articles/education/best-colleges/2008/08/21/methodology-best-values.html

Venegas, K. (2006). Low-income urban high school students' use of the Internet to access financial aid. *Journal of Student Financial Aid, 36*(3), 4–16.

Wei, C. C., Berkner, L., He, S., Lew, S., Cominole, M., Siegel, P., & Griffith, J. (2009). *2007–08 National Postsecondary Student Aid Study (NPSAS:08), Student financial aid estimates for 2007–08: First look.* Washington, DC: U.S. Department of Education, National Center for Education Statistics (NCES 2009-166).

Wikipedia (2009). *Student financial aid.* Retrieved June 1, 2009 from http://en.wikipedia.org/wiki/Financial_aid

Willems, S., De Maesschalck, S., Derese, A., & De Maseseneer, J. (2005). Socio-economic status of the patient and doctor–patient communication: Does it make a difference. *Patient Education & Counseling, 56*(2), 139–146.

III
Entering and Transitioning to College

5

ACADEMICS, CAMPUS ADMINISTRATION, AND SOCIAL INTERACTION

Examining Campus Structures Using Post-Structural Theory

MARYBETH WALPOLE

As discussed in previous chapters, low-income students are less likely to obtain their Bachelor's degrees, in part, because they disproportionately attend community colleges and less selective four-year institutions, attend part time, and delay their entry after high school. Many educators believe that enrolling more low-income students in four-year colleges, particularly more selective colleges, encouraging them to attend directly from high school, and encouraging them to attend full time, often by improving financial aid availability, would substantially increase their Bachelor degree attainment rates. Educators believe this because four-year colleges, particularly selective four-year institutions, have higher graduation rates than community colleges and the less selective four-years. These selective, and particularly highly selective, colleges not only have high graduation rates, they are uniquely structured to facilitate high-status employment positions and graduate school admissions for their students. These institutions offer significant structural support to facilitate students' success, and although they are less likely to enroll low-SES (socioeconomic status) students, when those students do enroll, they should benefit from structures that facilitate success as well. One would assume that low-SES students who attend such institutions should be in a position to fulfill the ideal of upward mobility.

Yet, research has not investigated how the structures of these institutions affect the low-income students who do attend them, whether these structures facilitate similar levels of success for low-income students, and whether encouraging low-income students to attend them would increase their attainment. Thus, we know little about the effects these institutional structures have on students from low-income, low-SES families. In response, this chapter explores structures at four selective and highly selective institutions, including policies, requirements, and traditions and investigates how such structures shape low-income students' experiences. Using interview data and a post-structural lens (Kezar, Chapter 1), I illuminate the ways that structures on selective and highly selective campuses privilege high-income students and disadvantage low-income students[1] and suggest approaches for creating a more equitable system. The structures specifically include admissions, GPA (grade point average) requirements for particular majors and other academic experiences, residential pricing structures, financial aid, and social organizations and traditions.

In the following sections of this chapter, I first review the literature relevant to the chapter and then present an overview of the study. Following that, I present data from interviews with 31 students and 27 administrators on four campuses, two highly selective, and two selective, along with discussion that illuminates and deconstructs their campus structures. I then suggest reconstructing those structures in order to support low-income students and conclude the chapter with final thoughts on ways to make campuses more equitable for all students.

WHY FOCUS ON SELECTIVE COLLEGES?

Because low-income students and structures within selective and highly selective institutions are the focus of this chapter, the literature in this section focuses on both highly selective colleges and the structural features that shape students' lives. Low-income, low-SES, first-generation, and working-class students usually attend different types of institutions than their higher-income, higher-SES, non-first-generation, and more upper-class peers (Anderson & Hearn, 1992; Astin, 1993, 1999; Astin & Oseguera, 2004; Bowen, Kurzweil, & Tobin, 2005; Carnevale & Rose, 2004; Hearn, 1984, 1990, 1991; Karabel, 2005; Martin, Karabel, & Jaquez, 2005; McDonough, 1997; Terenzini, Cabrera, & Bernal, 2001; Tinto, 2006; Titus, 2006). Low-income, low-SES students are more likely to attend less selective and public institutions, and they are less likely to attend more selective colleges or universities than other students (Anderson &

Hearn, 1992; Astin, 1993, 1999; Astin & Oseguera, 2004; Bowen et al., 2005; Carnevale & Rose, 2004; Hearn, 1984, 1990, 1991; Karabel, 2005; Martin et al., 2005; McDonough, 1997; Terenzini et al., 2001; Tinto, 2006). However, attending selective and highly selective institutions is beneficial because higher selectivity is associated with higher persistence and graduation rates (Astin, 1993, 1999; Astin & Oseguera, 2004; Bowen & Bok, 1998; Bowen et al., 2005; Carnevale & Rose, 2004; Karabel, 2005; Tinto, 2006; Titus, 2006). Commentators also note that access to more selective institutions leads to graduate admissions and access to high-status career tracks (Carnevale & Rose, 2004; Domhoff, 1983; Katchadourian & Boli, 1994; Useem & Karabel, 1986, 1990; Youn, Arnold, & Salkever, 1999; Zweigenhaft, 1993). These outcomes are in part because these institutions structure students' educations differently than their less selective peers.

The education that selective and highly selective institutions provide is structured differently in several ways. These institutions typically have more resources than less selective institutions. They are more likely to be four-year colleges, to be residential, to have low faculty to student ratios that afford more opportunities for faculty and student involvement, and to offer a wide variety of opportunities in clubs and groups (Astin, 1993; Hoffnung & Sack, 1981; Kingston & Lewis, 1990), institutional features associated with high persistence, and educational aspirations (Astin, 1975, 1993, 1999; Astin & Oseguera, 2004; Carnevale & Rose, 2004; Carter, 1999; Tinto, 1993; Titus, 2006). These colleges are also more likely to foster traits compatible with high-status occupational positions and graduate school attendance because the structure of prestigious institutions encourages leadership, independent learning, and problem-solving skills valued in high-status, high paying occupations (Bowles & Gintis, 1976, 2002; Hoffnung & Sack, 1981). These selective institutions also structure students' academic experiences, with students being more likely to major in liberal arts rather than vocational majors and thus being more likely to attend graduate school (Goyette & Mullen, 2006).

Because these institutions are uniquely positioned to foster upward mobility, this chapter focuses on students' experiences at four selective or highly selective, residential, liberal arts colleges. Understanding these institutions' structures, and how they facilitate or hinder students' experiences and outcomes is critical (Walpole, 2007). In this chapter, I utilize a post-structural conceptual framework to deconstruct ways in which taken for granted policies, procedures, and traditions in these institutions disadvantage low-income and low-SES students and advantage their wealthier peers, and I suggest reconstructions that increase equity (Kezar, Chapter 1).

OVERVIEW OF THE STUDY

This study used data from a larger project focused on how social class and campus context shaped students' experiences. The data for this chapter came from interviews with 31 students from low socioeconomic backgrounds, including 22 White, eight African American students, and one Latina student, as well as from interviews with 27 administrators who held similar student affairs and academic administrative positions on each campus. All of the students were traditionally aged women who had begun their studies on these campuses four years earlier, so almost all of them were preparing to graduate. I defined students' SES using their parents' information supplied by the institutions. The low-SES students' parents had educational attainment of less than a college degree, had occupations that were skilled or semiskilled laborers, clerical, or sales positions, and family incomes under $100,000, and with the exception of two students, under $75,000. The interview data from both the students and the administrators were analyzed to focus on the campus structures, such as policies, procedures, or simply campus customs that aided or hindered low-SES students' experiences on these campuses while privileging the high-SES peers.

All four campuses were nationally ranked, predominately White, highly residential, and focused on undergraduate education. One college was a public institution, the rest were private. Although all four campuses were within about a one-hour drive from a large city, they were situated in small towns and had secluded, protected atmospheres and campuses. All four enrolled fewer than 5,000 full-time undergraduates. Two of the private campuses were similar in that they were two of the most selective institutions in the country, with average entering SAT scores well above 1,200 out of a possible total of 1,600. Both of these campuses were founded as men's colleges and have admitted female students for approximately 40 years. The other two campuses were also quite selective, but had a more regional rather than a national draw, and average entering SAT scores between 1,100 and 1,200, again out of 1,600.

Data collection focused on capturing the effects of social class on the students' experiences in college and their decisions regarding their lives following graduation. I asked students how they made decisions within the college environment regarding friends, work, major field, housing, and activities, and how they made or were making decisions regarding plans for the future. Each student was also asked what her life would be like in 5, 10, and 20 years; how she understood social class; and how she believed it affected her college experience. I asked the administrators to describe their colleges, their students, how social class affected campus life, and their expectations of students while in school and in the future.

All interviews averaged between one and one and a half hours in length, were taped, and transcribed.

Data for this study were analyzed inductively, by reviewing the individual transcripts for themes related to structures on campuses that affected low-SES students' progress (Bogdan & Biklen, 2003). Themes emerged regarding admissions; students' choices of classes, academic activities, or particular majors; their interactions with financial aid; their residential choices; and the choices and situations they faced in the campuses' social milieu. I first deconstruct campus structures related to these themes. Following that, I deconstruct two structures or policies students and administrators discussed that colleges intended to increase students' success rates. These areas were summer bridge programs and direct provision of resources. I then focus the chapter on reconstructing campus policies, procedures, and traditions in ways that reduce the disadvantage low-income students face.

DECONSTRUCTING CAMPUS STRUCTURES

Admission Policies

The first set of campus structures that favored middle- and upper-class students were the admission policies. All four of these campuses were quite selective and that selectivity, based on high achievement in high school, privileged students from more highly educated and wealthier families. Additionally, many people at the two highly selective institutions spoke about the self-selectivity that also occurred in admissions and the difficulty of attracting some types of students. The Director of Admissions on one campus said:

> [the campus] has a very self-selective student body...90 or more percent of our parents have college degrees or higher. [The college] is very well known. This is something we fight all the time in trying to diversify the campus... Typically [the students are] very bright. Typically they've been on the top of the heap in their high school.

The Director of Career Services at one of the highly selective campuses saw a connection between the price of tuition and the self-selection, telling me "students and their families may not necessarily always think of the very selective, highly prestigious institution as being financially within their reach." A student also saw the connection between the self-selection process and tuition, saying most students were "generally from like the upper and upper middle class levels," and then adding "[the college] can do what it wants to try to drive people up from other backgrounds, but people still see the price tag...and don't want to apply."

The two campuses that were selective, but not highly selective, were both conscious of the ways their student bodies were changing based on campus needs and institutional directions, all of which privileged higher-income students. The Dean of Enrollment Management explained that his public campus recruited:

> academically talented students…[who] meet our academic expectations. That is, a student who has achieved in high school…we look at a student that has taken the right courses in high school, honors, AP, strong college prep curriculum. We look at the high school that they come from. Beyond that we look at ACT scores or SAT scores.

The Dean of Students at the same campus said his campus had been "attracting a little bit higher socioeconomic status, but average SAT is around 1,100, 1,120 or so. High school ranks is up there…I know it's been actually increasing." At the private selective campus, financial needs had been increasing the number of wealthier students. The Dean of the College told me:

> Until recently…the vast majority of the students [received] financial assistance. A majority I would say, 80 percent…[but] partially because of I guess of financial needs and partially because of maybe the admissions office…that number of full pays…increased…I think it has to do with looking for more students who can pay a bigger part of their bill.

Academic Expectations and Structures

Once students enrolled on these campuses, they began classes, and in many instances the academic expectations of college were quite different from those of high school. These differences disproportionately affected the low-SES students who have consistently reported lower GPAs in college (Terenzini et al., 2001; Walpole, 2003, 2008). Many campuses had policies tied to students' GPAs, such as GPA requirements for major courses or for graduation, as well as for eligibility to study abroad or to apply for some internships or campus job fairs. Furthermore, on some campuses students had to apply for admission to particular majors, and acceptance was based on their grade point averages. These requirements shaped students' major choices and the choices they made about other academic pursuits on all four campuses.

Three students discussed application processes for particular majors. One told me: "When I was a freshman, you had to apply. [I applied as a] freshman, sophomore…and I finally got in…[a faculty member in the major] basically helped me out a lot… I didn't think I was going to get into the program." A second student also discussed applying for her major, saying: "it is like competitive, it is the only major that you have to apply to get into, and it is hard to get into." A third student discussed a student she knew who "wanted to be a business major but he couldn't get into the department because his grades—they're good but not good enough. It's a competitive department."

Several students discussed having to change their majors due to academic difficulty. One explained that she felt the academic experience "was difficult all four years…[and] the reason why I didn't major in bio is because…I got…two D's, so I didn't want those to be on my major [GPA]." Another student became a history major when she encountered difficulty in economics. She told me: "I thought about economics because I really liked that in high school but…when I got here I didn't do well [in] like basic economics courses." Another described her path to becoming "a civil engineer…I started out as chemical engineer, went through the introductory course of chemistry, started orgo [organic chemistry], made it through the first semester, second semester…it was just torture. It was so hard." One student also discussed how a lack of understanding shaped her college major. She wanted to be pre-med, but was doing poorly in two of her classes. She said:

> I wanted to drop [them] but I thought I'm here on scholarships and grants and full aid and I have to maintain…full time [status], which is at least three courses. And I thought if I dropped…I would lose my funding so I figured I just better swallow the F. It turns out later that so long as you're enrolled for full time you're allowed to drop. But I didn't know that and my [adviser] said I'd just have to find a history major… So I failed both of them. But it was [a] lack of knowledge of the rules.

The Associate Dean of Student Life on one campus also recognized the difficulty some students experienced, telling me:

> There's a lot of students who come from disadvantaged backgrounds who want to be doctors…or engineers. And it's very hard to come in…and pursue either of those tracks and not be prepared. So we do see a lot of students end up dropping engineering or dropping premed when they find out that it's just too demanding.

One student also discussed her study abroad process, commenting that she had to appeal her desire to study abroad because of her GPA, primarily because of a difficult freshman transition. She worked with the Dean who was her adviser on both issues.

> I met with [the Dean] my freshman year about the fact that I was failing my chemistry class and that I was just having problems in general and…if it weren't for her I wouldn't have gotten into the study abroad program…just because my GPA was low due to my freshman year.

Financial Aid Availability

Financial aid availability, yet another set of structures, also shaped students' academic experiences. One student who was graduating the December following the interview explained her delayed graduation, telling me:

> the right thing to do is take four classes each semester [but] I only took three every semester…because of the money…I already had too much loans out and plus the grants and everything they gave me wouldn't cover the 16 credits.

A second student on another campus told me that she had had a consistent difficulty with financial aid:

> just in terms of keeping everything straight, loans and payments and… money coming in from scholarships…the start of every year brings a whole 'nother mess of things…and every…August I'm…being told that I can't go to classes, or whatever, because this isn't straight.

Administrators also saw the effects finances and financial aid had on students' academic experiences. One Associate Dean explained: "We had students who were not taking fine arts courses because the expense was so astronomical." The Executive Associate Dean of Student Life on one campus explained:

> The first week of classes when students are purchasing their books, you will have students…in the bookstore and…[their] parents are there and they're buying the books for them… [Then there is] that student who has to make some real decisions about, okay, this class requires three books and this class requires two books…but I only have enough money to maybe buy one of each, okay? So you can see that tension initially in the first week in terms of class.

Residential Structures

Another area affected by campus structures that shaped students' experiences was where they lived while attending college. This area also intersected with finances and financial aid. In several cases students discussed facing choices to live at home or in cheaper options on campus to save money on these highly residential campuses. The on-campus options resulted from the differential pricing that many campuses utilize for housing, charging students higher prices to live in newer or more desirable housing. Students on all four campuses discussed these choices. One student moved on and off campus, cycling back to living at home, which was about a half hour away, as finances changed. She told me:

> I lived on campus the first semester that I was here. And then I went home the second semester...I couldn't afford to stay on campus... I lived here my sophomore year [Fall] and...then my junior year was actually the first full year I spent on campus. And then the last year, which was my senior, I lived at home because of finances... It's like seven thousand dollars to stay on campus for the two semesters...financial aid paid most of my tuition. But...if I stayed on campus I would have to come up with about seven thousand, like, out of my pocket. If I went home I wouldn't have to come up with any money.

In terms of choosing cheaper options on campus, each of the campuses had apartments or residence halls that included kitchens, thus students could forego meal plans and save money, but these choices also had some cost. One said: "[The campus apartment complex] is cheaper because you don't have to— you have your own kitchen. That's the only place on campus you can live and not be on the meal plan...[but] you're a little bit removed from the social scene." A second student on another campus mentioned that living in campus apartments was partly in response to not having enough financial aid to cover all of her tuition. She said: "It's much cheaper now because I'm living in the apartments, whereas in the dorm I had to take the meal plan and that costs like a thousand dollars, which I could have used for [tuition] credits." Additionally, the Director of Housing on one campus told me about a situation with a student. She said: "The way the financial aid package is put together supposedly everybody is provided with [enough]. And she [the student] said to me, 'if I can get down to [the apartments] I'd have a little more money, but right now I don't have the money to buy [a basic personal necessity.]'"

The fact that these students had to make choices based on constrained financial structures also meant that they inevitably missed some social opportunities, whether those were not being involved in activities because they were not living on campus, or simply missing some of the informal social interaction that occurred in campus dining areas.

Social Activities and Structures

The ways in which students' social activities and options were constrained by their economic situation was another broad area of results. Students on all four campuses mentioned a host of activities that they did not participate in based on finances. One student mentioned: "There was one point actually that I almost did join a sorority because my friend…was joining. And basically what it boiled down to was I didn't have the money to…it's a lot of money." Another student on a different campus, when I asked her what she did for fun on weekends, talked about having friends visit, or going to a nearby city, but then said: "Then there's always that one week when…you don't have money so you just have to sit in your room and suck it up."

There were also activities that students clearly described as particularly expensive and difficult. A student mentioned not being able to test for her black belt, which is the pinnacle of her sport, because of the cost. She explained:

> I can test for my black belt at the end of this semester. But it's really expensive…so it's sort of iffy if I'll be able to test…it's not like the other club sports on campus that are like run by the physical education department. They have like an individual teacher come in and teach you. So he's the one who charges all these fees and stuff…the black belt test is $600. So it's a lot of money…I don't know if I'll be able to afford it. Right now it doesn't look like I'll be able to afford it.

Another explained that she had been unable to come for a freshman orientation program because she had to work. She said:

> In the beginning there's [an orientation program and freshmen] come like a week ahead of time and they…become very closely connected with the individuals who are part of [the program]. And I was invited, but I really could not afford to take a week off ahead of time. So I said no. I said I couldn't attend and…like once you have that week…you've become that closely bonded to other individuals… And I was not in the position where I felt comfortable when I first came here to try to [make friends]—because it was already like a formed group almost. I didn't feel comfortable really.

Moreover, a student on one of the campuses represented what several students on that campus told me about joining social clubs on that campus that were quasi-sororities. In speaking about why she decided not to join such clubs, she said: "I would never regret being a member there, and if I could, I would definitely be a member… But like, it is a lot of money." These clubs were a prime campus mechanism for students' socializing, and several of the students who did not join or joined briefly mentioned the cost as an issue. While not having any money and having to "suck it up" once a month may seem an unproblematic aspect of being a college student, missing out on a major socializing structure like orientation or the social clubs clearly had more long reaching consequences. These low-SES students, again, were missing some aspects of campus life that their peers who were better off financially did not have to sacrifice.

So, clearly, there were multiple policies and traditions on campuses that structured students' experiences in ways that privileged high-income students and disadvantaged low-SES students. While all four campuses had structures that disadvantaged low-SES students, at the same time, all four campuses also had policies and structures that were put in place to assist low-SES students in being successful and engaged on campus. The next section deconstructs the structures that campuses intended to support low-SES students.

DECONSTRUCTING PROGRAMS TARGETED TOWARD LOW-INCOME STUDENTS

The structures campuses had implemented to assist students included summer programs, often based on family income, and programs to directly assist students in meeting expenses. While both can be used to assist students, caution must be exercised in utilizing either of these approaches. In this section, I present data from students and administrators on both types of structures and through deconstruction illustrate why caution is necessary.

Several students mentioned their participation in summer bridge programs during the interviews. One student explained how her bridge program assisted her, telling me:

> You have to take um, a basic writing and reading class. And then there's a math class. And...you have an actual class with a professor... It's very structured...I had more discipline than I ever received before, so it was very shocking for me. But it was helpful...freshman year... I feel like I learned a lot...definitely.

When I asked another student to describe the summer bridge program, she replied: "I'll sum it up real quick for you. Boot camp. But...I [would] do that again...because it really helped me first semester in college." A third student on another campus described the summer program as: "a head start by offering us two classes...that are counted for credit... It's a good head start... It also allows you to pick the two classes you like, because once you're in...you don't get very many choices." An Associate Dean of Student Life explained the program's inception and goals, saying:

We had kids from all sorts of socioeconomic groups. Some are better prepared than others. And I think the university is finally coming around to realizing that, …[and] they put together this new program called the…Summer Institute and that is really an attempt to help students who may not be as well prepared academically but who…[have] certainly shown the ability to persevere…[The program allows them] to get a little bit ahead, to become familiar with the library, the resources of the library, how to study, and get some academic credit.

An additional mechanism for assisting students that administrators at the two highly selective, and not coincidentally well-endowed, colleges discussed was having additional sources of funding, sometimes directly subsidizing individual students and sometimes structured as grants students could apply for, to fund some activities and needs not directly covered by financial aid. The direct subsidies took several forms. One administrator explained that they tried to be creative for students who could not afford activities. She said:

So I see a lot of pressure on students, so those students who are work study, working two and three jobs trying to burn the midnight oil studying, getting up early, students who don't necessarily have the kind of clothing to attend some of the events and have to borrow something from another student…those are just some of the challenges, and what are some creative ways [as a campus we can institute] so that students don't feel bad? It's a hand out for them to meet some of the social and class issues here on campus. And for everything there's a charge here generally. And it's difficult.

A Dean of the College on one of the campuses explained that the campus he worked on tried to provide "opportunities for students regardless of means. [We don't want students to say] I like to go with my friends but I can't afford it. So either it's subsidized for everyone [or] the cost [is very minimal]." A second Dean of the College on another campus explained that while there were ways to assist, there were also limits:

We have some additional funds that we can draw on—if you've got a student who's coming from California and has literally no winter clothes, we have the capacity to supply money to make that reality different. But you can't make different the reality that there may be a roommate whose family is jetting off to ski for the break. That you can't change.

A second strategy for providing needed aid to students was through grants and two administrators discussed grants for which students could apply. A Director of Career Services told me about an interaction she had with a low-income student who had studied abroad:

> I said, "Well how did you manage to pay for that?" [The student said] "Well, I got a grant. I applied to the colleges for studying abroad." I wasn't aware that some of the complexities involved with…study abroad. I find it interesting that they get that kind of assistance…and there's support…let's not make a student's individual personal needs get in the way. So for the students that can't afford to do it but would like to, someone here seems to find a way to make it happen.

An Associate Dean of Student Life described the

> [m]any, many opportunities that you don't get elsewhere with respect to funding for a thesis research. There are students who have come from humble means, I'm pleased to say, have gone off…to do research because [the college] has allowed them the opportunity financially.

Clearly these administrators recognize that students' resources are differentially distributed, and genuinely want to ameliorate the situation. Direct handouts, however, require caution because students first of all must be willing to ask for such assistance, which some, out of a sense of pride, may not be able to do. Secondly, simply giving funds directly to students does little to empower students and has the potential to reinforce students' sense of difference, as Colyar finds in Chapter 6 in this volume. Additionally, on these campuses, these efforts seemed isolated and episodic rather than systematic and consistent. Even on the campus that the Dean above mentioned which had either free or subsidized activities, students mentioned difficulties in participating in activities related to finances. However, the idea of a grant for which anyone can apply is appealing because it does not single out the low-income students as long as information regarding the grant's existence and application requirements and process are readily and equitably available to all students.

Yet, both the bridge programs and the direct assistance, while well intentioned, operate from a deficit model; that is they provide low-income students with assistance because the administrators see the students as lacking preparation and resources. As Colyar discusses in Chapter 6, the bridge programs can be helpful in some ways, but they also often cut students off from external support systems and mark them as different from their peers. In order to further ensure these bridge programs' success, campuses should seek to improve the programs as suggested by Colyar. Moreover, providing direct assistance for students to participate in social opportunities allows administrators to ignore the ways in which campus social structures privilege middle- and high-income students. In providing assistance for low-income students, administrators can believe that students have equitable opportunities and do not have to acknowledge or confront the privilege that they facilitate as part of their administrative roles.

RECONSTRUCTING CAMPUS STRUCTURES

Having deconstructed the campus structures students and administrators found problematic, I now examine ways to reconstruct these policies, procedures, and traditions to make the effects more equitable. The first area I examine is admissions and academic policies. I then turn to financial aid and residential policies, and then to social structures. Finally, I offer a potential mechanism for assisting students.

Admissions and Academic Policies

Admissions and academic policies were both tied to academic achievement. As illustrated in the data, admissions' decisions at these institutions were based on students' academic records in high school. Selection criteria included high school courses, grades, test scores, as well as activities, teacher recommendations, and other criteria such as essays, writing samples, or other documentation. Similarly, campuses had GPA requirements for being admitted into a major, for major courses, for graduation, and for study abroad. Yet these have been the criteria that have been consistently shown to privilege high-income, high-SES students and to disadvantage low-SES students (Adelman, 2006; Akerhielm, Berger, Hooker, & Wise, 1998; Cabrera & La Nasa, 2000; Martin et al., 2005; Oakes, 1985; Perna, 2000; Terenzini et al., 2001; Walpole, 2003, 2008).

The selective colleges, as opposed to the highly selective colleges, were focused on maintaining or increasing their selectivity through admitting students with higher credentials, or on fulfilling the financial needs of the institution by admitting more students who could pay the full tuition without the benefit of financial aid. Only one administrator among all four campuses mentioned the difficulty in recruiting diverse students because of admissions policies, and then she attributed that difficulty to students' self-selection. Thus, the admission structures were not problematized, and because they were not problematized, there was no incentive or motivation to try and examine ways to admit students that did not privilege some at the expense of others. Rather than recognizing the admissions policies as historically and socially developed (Kezar, Chapter 1) with exclusionary intentions (Levine, 2008), the policies were seen as the norm for college admission, and their assumptions went unquestioned (Kezar, Chapter 1).

One way to make these admissions' policies more equitable is to examine the grades and test scores students really need to have to be successful at a particular institution or in a particular major. High school academic profiles and test scores have risen tremendously in the last few decades (McDonough, 1997; Schwartz, 1999), and institutional administrators must ask themselves why high school academic records and standardized test scores that provided the colleges with successful students in previous decades are no longer acceptable. Additionally, administrators should examine student and alumni outcomes and determine the relationship between admissions data and success during and after college. Then based on real data, administrators may be able to make not only more equitable admissions decisions, but also can revisit campus policies tied to GPA.

The data on the admissions' structures also illuminated a specific aspect of post-structuralism, that of language (Kezar, Chapter 1), particularly the phrase "self-selective." This phrase implied that students chose these colleges while the colleges themselves were passive entities. In reality, students did choose these colleges, but their selections were made based on the admission criteria colleges expected; the colleges were not passive entities. Thus, the language used in discussing admissions obfuscated the reality of who selected whom and based on what criteria, a fact the post-structuralist perspective illuminates.

Additionally, the admissions and academic policies illustrate the use of power, another key component of post-structuralism (Kezar, Chapter 1). Campus officials had the power, through campus policies and expectations related to employability or graduate school admission following graduation, to structure students' academic experiences. Students' choices of classes and majors were constrained by these policies and expectations, and those constrictions will have lifelong repercussions. Moreover, the GPA requirements and the resulting student responses to them also illuminate the underlying power system of academia. This power system continues to accumulate privilege through undergraduate education to graduate education for higher-income, higher-SES students by utilizing criteria that have been shown to privilege such students, including grades, access to more rigorous coursework, and test scores (Adelman, 2006; Akerhielm et al., 1998; Cabrera & La Nasa, 2000; Martin et al., 2005; Oakes, 1985; Perna, 2000; Terenzini et al., 2001; Walpole, 2007). This systemic accumulation of advantage and disadvantage has been compared to a funnel, funneling students in particular directions based on social class (Aronson, 2008). Once administrators realize this accumulative effect, they can then examine the data to determine what standards are really necessary for successful student outcomes, can also become more aware of their language and the power that can surrounds it, and can begin to create more equitable structures.

Financial Aid and Residential Policies

The next area I reconstruct is financial aid and differential residence hall pricing. Financial aid budgets are constructed to meet students' needs; however, because of equity concerns, the financial aid budget is the same for everyone, regardless of circumstances. Students, of course, have differing needs, yet simply giving students additional funds is not the solution. However, the financial aid budgets need to be reasonable and their structure and content need to be communicated to students. Students need to understand the consequences of forgoing a loan, such as taking fewer credits as a result, and then graduating a semester late, delaying their entry to the job market as did one student in this study. Campuses also need to rethink their differential pricing policies for campus residences. Because these policies charge higher prices for more desirable and newer housing than for older and less desirable housing, such policies help create and maintain social class division on campuses. It also puts low-income students in difficult positions of needing to make decisions about their meal options, which can result in students' lack of integration into the campus social milieu, and can result in less than optimal nutrition since cheaper, more filling foods are often the least nutritional.

These students' choices to live in less expensive options on or off campus also displayed their agency in response to less than optimal financial choices, which is also an aspect of post-structuralism. They were able to respond, make choices, and in some cases negotiate living arrangements that eased their financial burdens. And in some ways, because all of the students lived on campus for at least part of their college careers, they may have been in a more privileged position than some low-income students who never had the opportunity to live on campus (Astin, 1993). However, low-income students were also forced to make choices their privileged peers did not have to make, including perhaps forgoing some social opportunities, and administrators can, through financial aid, financial education, and eliminating differential housing prices, reduce the need for these choices.

Social Activities and Structures

Reconstructing campus social structures can be difficult, as these cultures, especially if student led, are often intractable, yet low-income students are clearly disadvantaged on campuses with social structures that require additional expenditures. Campus activities that are not student led, such as the martial arts class or the orientation activity in this study, may be easier to change than student-led ones, but that does not mean they will be easy to change. These activities are often set up without considering the cost involved, and are viewed as opportunities to become acquainted with campus early in the orientation case, or to study a martial art, in the other case. Administrators on these campuses likely would have been surprised and concerned to learn about the situations these students faced because they had not considered the costs in offering these opportunities. Although they were certainly well intentioned in providing opportunities, because they did not examine their underlying assumption that all students who wished to could participate, they did not create alternatives for students who did wish to participate but could not afford to. In the case of orientation programs, perhaps administrators could consider additional financial aid or in cases of campuses that do not require extensive travel to attend orientation, administrators could think of scheduling that would alleviate the need to forgo summer earnings. Moreover, when contracting for specific activities, such as martial arts classes, administrators could inquire about additional fees and about structures the contractor may have in place to assist students who want to participate but cannot because of financial reasons.

Campuses with activities for which there is a charge or with structures that require additional fees, such as the fraternities, sororities, and social clubs on the campuses in this study, simply reduce the opportunities available to low-SES students. As I pointed out above, providing students the resources to participate is not the solution. Administrators must instead create alternate social structures that do not require a significant student financial investment or need to create mechanisms within current structures that deemphasize the monetary investment students are required to make. This, I realize, will be extraordinarily challenging on some campuses.

Many administrators, as did several in this study, recognize the disadvantages low-income, low-SES students face, and there is no doubt that many feel badly about students' disadvantages and sincerely want to help them as the administrators in this study did. There was a sense of frustration and resignation in one administrator's comment: "I feel, you know, we're doing our very best for students, but I'm sure we can do more, you know? And I'm challenged to do more." However, that assistance often does not come because they do not recognize that there are any changes needed on the part of campuses; they simply view the student as deficient in terms of resources (Green, 2006). If administrators were to acknowledge the privilege and resulting disadvantage, they may feel compelled to work to create a more equitable environment for all students. Yet because the need for structural change goes unrecognized, the high-SES students' privilege also goes unrecognized, and is thus normalized. As a result, necessary systemic structural changes that would allow low-SES students to become more fully members of their campus communities are invisible and are rarely considered.

Reconstructing Assistance

There is one mechanism I believe may have the most positive potential for assisting low-SES students, and it is one tied to employment. Although scholars have cautioned against too many hours working because it may be tied to poor academic performance and attrition (Astin, 1993; King, 2003), work-study programs or work on campuses has had a positive effect on students (Astin, 1993; Chen & DesJardins, 2008). In reality, most students are working, and the low-income, low-SES students in this study were no exception. These students routinely described working two and three jobs and more than 20 hours a week in order to afford their college education and its attendant costs. But students also discussed working because they valued it in ways that were not financial. One told me: "I think it's good to work, you know…it gives you a little more value to life. You appreciate things more, and I know what my parents went through, you know." Another on a second campus explained: "I love working. I enjoy my jobs a lot, but you ask me to write a paper and I'm like, no, I'll slit my wrists first."

Finally, another student discussed a community partnership scholarship for low-income students she received that was tied to her working in the summers. She explained:

> They would give you money to go to school, to meet your financial aid needs. So, anyway, I applied for the scholarship…and I got it…I could work over the summers…the summer program they established was…you work at…[a] hospital. You'll rotate around the hospital. And we'll get paid for it. And that's the part I was just like, "Oh, I thought it was volunteer work." But this is even better.

Providing students with well-paid opportunities can reinforce their sense of self as capable and hardworking. Of course, students working too many hours can be counterproductive (Astin, 1993; King, 2003), as can putting students in employment situations that marginalize or other them. For example, large numbers of low-income students working in the dining facilities, serving or cleaning up after their nonworking peers, may result in creating or emphasizing a sense of difference, rather than reinforcing a positive self-image. However, because students value work in its own right, facilitating low-SES students' campus employment may be an important mechanism for involving them on campus, thus increasing retention and graduation rates (Astin, 1993), while at the same time empowering them and contributing to their sense of self-worth. If campuses examined their work-study and non-work-study employment and creatively considered the ways in which students could benefit most from it, students may be able to focus their work on campus rather than utilizing options off campus, which scholars have agreed is less optimal (Astin, 1993; Chen & DesJardins, 2008).

Furthermore, working gives students the opportunity to exercise agency, an important consideration in a post-structural framework. In this study, students not only exercised agency in working, they exercised that agency by deciding to enroll in these colleges and by negotiating their way throughout their experience. These students made decisions, albeit within constrained circumstances, to major in some subjects and not others, to work, and to reside in particular locations. They oftentimes consulted with faculty and administrators in their negotiation of obstacles, and sometimes that negotiation was successful in securing them an exception to a particular policy or practice that hindered them. They also worked; clearly, that was a necessity for them, but they also worked because they valued working (Bozick, 2007). They worked multiple jobs and long hours and were often quite creative in securing positions that allowed them to study or that were scheduled in ways that did not interfere with classes and activities. And so in these ways, students demonstrated agency in reacting to and negotiating the campus structures they encountered.

FINAL THOUGHTS

Clearly, throughout the data, the low-SES students contended with campus policies, procedures, and traditions that disadvantaged them. These structures did not affect simply one or two areas; they affected students' experiences in all areas from academic experiences to social experiences, from admission to residential policies, to graduation requirements. Moreover, these structures systematically disadvantaged low-income, low-SES students while privileging their higher-income, higher-SES peers. And although the campuses in this study were selective and highly selective in terms of admissions, many similar policies and procedures exist on almost every campus. Thus administrators on most campuses can use the suggestions in this chapter for reconstructing their campuses in ways that create more equitable experiences for all students.

Additionally, administrators must be particularly mindful of issues around language and power and of providing opportunities that empower students and allow them to exercise agency. The success of low-income, low-SES students is a critical necessity. Rather than viewing them through a deficit lens (Colyar, Chapter 6; Green, 2006; Kezar, Chapter 1), I believe they have much to offer our campuses as demonstrated by the students in this study. The resiliency of these students was astounding. They had been able to surmount multiple obstacles, and most of them were preparing to graduate from one of four excellent colleges. They were hardworking and creative problem-solvers. They will no doubt continue to be resilient, hardworking, and creative; will be successful in their chosen fields after graduation; and will represent these colleges well as alumni. This leads to me to ask why these institutions would not want more of these students? All four of these colleges would say they did want additional students like the ones interviewed in this study, however, there was a distinct lack of systemic dialog about what changes needed to be made to recruit and support them as students. If we truly want to offer all students an opportunity to be successful, we must, as educators, begin to recognize, deconstruct, and reconstruct campus structures, such as policies, practices, and traditions that disadvantage low-income, low-SES students. We must shift the discourse from a focus on deficiencies to a focus on the ways in which campuses privilege some students at the expense of others. The work will not be easy, but begin it must, and sustained systemic dialog is key.

NOTE

1. Although recognizing the distinctions and the arguments regarding the definitions of these groups (Walpole, 2007), this study utilizes the terms low-income and low-SES students, and conversely high-income and high-SES students, interchangeably.

REFERENCES

Adelman, C. (2006). *The toolbox revisited: Paths to degree completion from high school through college*. Washington, DC: U.S. Department of Education.

Akerhielm, K., Berger, J., Hooker, M., & Wise, D. (1998). *Factors related to college enrollment, final report* (Mathematica Publication No. 3360-028). Washington, DC: U.S. Department of Education.

Anderson, M. S., & Hearn, J. C. (1992). Equity issues in higher education outcomes. In W. E. Becker & D. R. Lewis (Eds.), *The economics of American higher education* (pp. 301–334). Boston: Kluwer Academic Publishers.

Aronson, P. (2008). Breaking barriers or locked out? Class-based perceptions and experiences of postsecondary education. In J. T. Mortimer (Ed.), *Social class and transitions to adulthood. New Directions for Child and Adolescent Development, 119*, 41–54.

Astin, A. W. (1975). *Preventing students from dropping out*. San Francisco: Jossey-Bass.

Astin, A. W. (1993). *What matters in college? Four critical years revisited*. San Francisco: Jossey-Bass.

Astin, A. W. (1999). How the liberal arts college affects students. *Daedalus: Journal of the American Academy of Arts and Sciences. Distinctly American: The Residential Liberal Arts College, 128*(1), 77–100.

Astin, A. W., & Oseguera, L. (2004). The declining "equity" of American higher education. *The Review of Higher Education, 27*(3), 321–341.

Bogdan, R., & Biklen, S. (2003). *Qualitative research for education* (4th ed.). Boston, MA: Allyn and Bacon Press.

Bowen, W. G., & Bok, D. (1998). *The shape of the river: Long-term consequences of considering race in college and university admissions.* Princeton, NJ: Princeton University Press.

Bowen, W. G., Kurzweil, M., & Tobin, E. (2005). *Equity and excellence in American higher education.* Charlottesville: University of Virginia Press.

Bowles, S., & Gintis, H. (1976). *Schooling in capitalist America.* New York: Basic Books.

Bowles, S., & Gintis, H. (2002). The inheritance of inequality. *The Journal of Economic Perspectives, 16*(3), 3–30.

Bozick, R. (2007). The role of students' economic resources, employment, and living arrangements. *Sociology of Education, 80*(3), 261–284.

Cabrera, A. F., & La Nasa, S. M. (2000). Understanding the college choice process. In A. F. Cabrera & S. M. La Nasa (Eds.), *Understanding the college choice process of disadvantaged students. New Directions for Institutional Research, 107,* 5–22. San Francisco: Jossey-Bass.

Carnevale, A. P., & Rose, S. J. (2004). Socioeconomic status, race/ethnicity, & selective college admissions. In R. D. Kahlenberg (Ed.), *America's untapped resource; low-income students in higher education* (pp. 101–156). New York: The Century Foundation Press.

Carter, D. J. (1999). The impact of institutional choice and environments on African American and White students' degree expectations. *Research in Higher Education, 40*(1), 17–41.

Chen, R., & DesJardins, S. (2008). Exploring the effects of financial aid on the gap in student dropout risks by income level. *Research in Higher Education, 49*(1), 1–18.

Colyar, J. (forthcoming). Strangers in a strange land: Low-income students and the transition to college. In A. Kezar (Ed.), *Recognizing and serving low-income students in higher education: An examination of institutional policies, practices, and culture.* New York: Routledge.

Domhoff, G. W. (1983). *Who rules America now?* New York: Simon & Schuster, Inc.

Goyette, K. A., & Mullen, A. L. (2006). Who studies the arts and sciences? Social background and the choice and consequences of undergraduate field of study. *The Journal of Higher Education, 77*(3), 497–538.

Green, D. (2006). Historically underserved students: What we know, what we still need to know. *New Directions for Community Colleges, 135,* 21–28.

Hearn, J. C. (1984). The relative roles of academic, ascribed, and socioeconomic characteristics in college destinations. *Sociology of Education, 57*(1), 22–30.

Hearn, J. C. (1990). Pathways to attendance at the elite colleges. In P. W. Kingston & L. S. Lewis (Eds.), *The high status track: Studies of elite schools and stratification* (pp. 121–141). New York: SUNY Press.

Hearn, J. C. (1991). Academic and nonacademic influences on the college destinations of 1980 high school graduates. *Sociology of Education, 63*(1), 158–171.

Hoffnung, R. J., & Sack, A. L. (1981). *Does higher education reduce or reproduce social class differences? Schooling at Yale University, University of Connecticut, and University of New Haven, and student attitudes and expectations regarding future work.* Paper presented at the Annual Meeting of the Eastern Psychological Association, New York.

Karabel, J. (2005). *The chosen: The hidden history of admission and exclusion at Harvard, Yale, and Princeton.* New York: Houghton-Mifflin Co.

Katchadourian, H., & Boli, J. (1994). *Cream of the crop: The impact of elite education in the decade after college.* New York: Basic Books.

King, J. E. (2003). Nontraditional attendance and persistence: The cost of students' choices. *New Directions in Higher Education, 121,* 69–83.

Kingston, P. W., & Lewis, L. S. (1990). Undergraduates at elite institutions: The best, the brightest, and the richest. In P. W. Kingston & L. S. Lewis (Eds.), *The high status track: Studies of elite schools and stratification.* New York: State University of New York Press.

Levine, D. O. (2008). Discrimination in college admissions. In H. S. Wechsler, L. F. Goodchild, & L. Eisenmann (Eds.), *ASHE Reader on The History of Higher Education* (3rd ed., pp. 457–473). Boston: Pearson Publishing.

Martin, I., Karabel, J., & Jaquez, S. W. (2005). High school segregation and access to the University of California. *Educational Policy, 19*(2), 308–330.

McDonough, P. M. (1997). *Choosing colleges: How social class and schools structure opportunity.* New York: State University of New York Press.

Oakes, J. (1985). *Keeping track: How schools structure inequality.* New Haven, CT: Yale University Press.

Perna, L. W. (2000). Differences in the decision to attend college among African Americans, Hispanics, and Whites. *The Journal of Higher Education, 71*(2), 117–141.

Schwartz, T. (1999). The test under stress. *The New York Times Magazine.* January 10, 1999: 30–35, 51, 56, 63.

Terenzini, P. T., Cabrera, A. F., & Bernal, E. M. (2001). *Swimming against the tide: The poor in American higher education.* New York: The College Board.

Tinto, V. (1993). *Leaving college: Rethinking the causes and cures of student attrition* (2nd ed.). Chicago: University of Chicago Press.

Tinto, V. (2006). Research and practice of student retention, what's next? *Journal of College Student Retention, 8*(1), 1–19.

Titus, M. A. (2006). Understanding college degree completion of students with low socioeconomic status: The influence of the institutional financial context. *Research in Higher Education, 47*(4), 371–398.

Useem, M., & Karabel, J. (1986). Pathways to top corporate management. *American Sociological Review, 51*, 184–200.

Useem, M., & Karabel, J. (1990). Pathways to top corporate management. In P. W. Kingston & L. S. Lewis (Eds.), *The high status track: Studies of elite schools and stratification.* New York: State University of New York Press.

Walpole, M. (2003). Social mobility and college: Low SES students' experiences and outcomes of college. *The Review of Higher Education, 27*(1), 45–73.

Walpole, M. (2007). *Economically and educationally challenged students in higher education: Access to outcomes. ASHE-ERIC Higher Education Report* (Vol. 33, Issue 3). San Francisco: Jossey-Bass.

Walpole, M. (2008). Emerging from the pipeline: African American students, socioeconomic status, and college experiences and outcomes. *Research in Higher Education, 49*(3), 237–255.

Youn, T. I. K., Arnold, K. D., & Salkever, K. (1999). *Pathways to prominence: The effects of social origins and education on career achievements of American Rhodes Scholars.* Paper presented at the annual meeting of The Association for the Study of Higher Education, San Antonio, TX.

Zweigenhaft, R. (1993). Prep school and public school graduates of Harvard: A longitudinal study of the accumulation of social and cultural capital. *The Journal of Higher Education, 64*(2), 211–225.

6

STRANGERS IN A STRANGE LAND

Low-Income Students and the Transition to College

JULIA COLYAR

Emily and I sit in the common area of the student union, trying to hear over the sounds of the busy mid-day crowd. We have both brought a brown-bag lunch; Emily opens a blue Tupperware to reveal a rice dish she has made in her residence hall kitchen, and I have a bagel with cheese. She looks out the large window and points to a picnic table on an outside patio: "That's where I studied during the summer program. I wanted to be outside all the time, in our study hours. That was the best part." We are meeting to talk about her experiences in a summer bridge program, a three-week intensive program aimed at preparing low-income students for college life. "It was like boot camp," Emily continues. "That's why I went outside after classes and everything, to try to relax."

Emily is one of six young women who participated in a study about low-income students and the transition to college. Over the course of their first year at university, I met and talked with Emily, Lilian, Teresa, Anna, Jennifer, and Brenda in a series of interviews. All of the young women are considered "at-risk" as college students; they are first-generation college goers from low-income backgrounds. At the same time, they are "typical" college freshmen. They worry about making friends, chemistry assignments, and choosing a major. "At-risk" is a term they would never use to describe themselves. "Math is my favorite class," Emily tells me. She is doing well in all of her classes.

In this chapter, I explore the experiences of these six young women as they navigate their transition to college. In particular, I talked with

121

these young women about their pre-college experiences, their arrivals on campus, and their first-year courses. And while it is important that Emily is doing well in her courses, the typical outcome measures used to describe student experiences—grades or credits completed, for example—are not my focus. Instead, I explore their subjective experiences in the college preparation process; I am interested in the ways students describe and understand the structured summer program that is aimed at easing their movement into college. Using a post-structural lens, I explore the ways a bridge program can be disenfranchising even as it seeks to support students' matriculation into the college environment. I also situate the summer program within the scholarly dialogue related to low-income students, and I argue that bridge programs derive from a larger conversation that privileges middle- and upper-income students.

As with the other chapters in this text, I focus on revelation, deconstruction, and reconstruction. In the first section, I outline some of the scholarship associated with summer bridge programs and low-income students. This section also aims at revelation: scholarship focused on low-income students helps researchers and practitioners understand low-income students, but it also serves to privilege those from higher-income backgrounds.

REVELATION: RE-CONSIDERING SCHOLARSHIP

One of the ways in which privilege is hidden in higher education is in one of the most valued and valuable aspects of higher education work: scholarship. As the introduction to this book notes, American colleges and universities were established and developed for specific kinds of students, namely those from affluent backgrounds. Scholarship focused on low-income students has emerged over the last generation, but much of this literature has re-privileged "traditional students" even as it presents the experiences of low-income undergraduates. In this section, I provide briefly background information related to summer bridge programs. I then discuss two characteristics of the scholarship on low-income students: the ways in which scholarship re-centers "traditional" student experiences, and a theoretical framework often used to conceptualize research related to low-income students.

Locating Summer Bridge

One of the most popular programs available to low-income or under-represented students in the transition to college is the summer bridge program (Gandara, 2001; Myers & Shirm, 1999). Typically, programs are structured anywhere from three to six weeks, and are housed on college campuses. Some programs target specific groups, such as engineering or ESL (English as a Second Language) students. Many programs offer housing for students, while others provide coursework during the day. Though specific curricula varies across programs, most include an intensive academic component—often with remedial courses in writing, mathematics, or science—and supplemental courses in time management, computer skills, or career planning (Villapando & Solorzano, 2005). As Villapando and Solorzano (2005) point out, most programs target academic and social preparation, with little emphasis on students' cultural identities or engagement with local contexts.

Despite the popularity and widespread use of summer bridge programs, little empirical research on programs has been completed (Kezar, 2000; Santa Rita & Bacote, 1996). Much of the available literature includes specific program descriptions or evaluations (cf. Gancarz, Lowry, McIntyre, & Moss, 1998; Gold, 1992). The empirical research that has been conducted shows mixed results: some studies indicate that participation in a summer program can improve academic performance and retention rates for participants (Ackermann, 1990; Garcia, 1991; Walpole, Simmerman, Mack, Mills, Scales, & Albano, 2008); other research indicates that program outcomes are more social than academic (Myers & Shirm, 1999). Some studies show that while bridge programs are helpful as students move into college settings, they do not necessarily aid in retaining students over the long run (York & Tross, 1994).

The small amount of literature related to summer bridge programs is consistent in reporting the goals of programs: to support students in the transition to college, and to assist students that may be academically underprepared for college work. These goals are related to other scholarship focused on student retention and achievement. Summer bridge programs are intended to address important preparation and achievement gaps that are evident in research. Some students, low-income students among them, do not succeed at the same rates as others. In this way, bridge programs are designed by deficit—that is, programs seek to provide the social and academic knowledge and skills that some students "lack." In the next section, I discuss the research related to low-income students. This literature provides the context for the development of bridge programs. I argue that, in describing low-income student attributes, researchers also re-center "traditional" students and reify privilege.

Re-centering Traditional

Much of the research related to low-income students has reported attainment and objective outcomes such as GPA (grade point average), credit hours completed, and time to degree, the external markers that are used to signify success for college attendees (Aronson, 2008). These outcome measures, however, are most meaningful when compared across groups. For example, low-income students' graduation rates are reported in comparison to rates for their higher-income peers. Comparisons across groups, however, articulate and highlight difference, and have the result of re-centering higher-income student experiences as normative or "traditional." Such comparisons for low-income students are measured before they even start their college careers. For example, in terms of pre-college experiences, low-income students are more likely to be academically underprepared for postsecondary enrollment than their middle-income peers; this is evident in lower scores on standardized entrance exams (Corrigan, 2003; Walpole, 2003). Corrigan (2003) notes that while 35 percent of middle- and upper-income students complete at least a "moderately rigorous" high school curriculum, fewer than 20 percent of low-income students do; more low-income students also complete an alternative to a high school diploma, and far more low-income students delay entry into postsecondary education (87 percent, compared to 24 percent of middle- and upper-income students). Each of these elements points to risk factors associated with lower persistence and graduation rates (Adelman, 1999). Each also embodies a series of disadvantages that begin early and cumulate over time (Walpole, 2003). Parent engagement in secondary (or elementary) education, school location and structure, and parental aspirations contextualize each of these risk factors. For example, many low-income families may define "success" in terms of securing a full-time job after graduation from high school. For middle-class parents, "success" is more likely "tied to four years of college attendance, particularly attendance at a 'good' college" (Walpole, 2003, p. 48). Given these statistics, it is clear why summer bridge programs are implemented on college campuses.

Comparisons to middle- and upper-income peers continue in the literature, particularly with respect to enrollment and attainment patterns. Low-income students are more likely to enroll at two-year schools and institutions "positioned lower in the stratified higher education system" (Walpole, 2003, p. 48); they are also more likely to attend part-time and with more stop-outs than their peers (Cabrera, Burkum, & La Nasa, 2003; Chen & Carroll, 2005; Goldrick-Rab, 2006). Because low-income students tend to stop-out of college more often, they also tend to take longer to complete their Bachelor's degrees—if they complete a degree at all (Bozick & DeLuca, 2005). Overall, research indicates that low-income students have lower aspiration and graduation rates (Choy, 2000; Lumina Foundation, 2004). While only 6 percent of students in the lowest income quartile earn Bachelor's degrees, students in the highest income level complete degrees at the rate of 40 percent (Lumina Foundation, 2004).

Comparisons to higher-income peers also include study behaviors, work habits, and campus engagement. Again, in such comparisons, higher-income student behaviors and habits act as the norms against which low-income students are compared. In this way, low-income students are re-articulated as "at risk," "non-traditional," or "other." Researchers, for example, note that students from low-income backgrounds study less, work more hours, and report lower GPAs (Aronson, 2008; Goldrick-Rab, 2006; Horn, Neville, & Griffith, 2006; Walpole, 2003). In addition to lower grades, low-income students are more likely to enroll in remedial (often noncredit bearing) classes, drop courses, and repeat enrollment in order to earn higher grades (Chen & Carroll, 2005). As a result, they complete fewer credits during the semesters they are enrolled. Two longitudinal studies (Berger & Milem, 1999; Walpole, 2003) indicated that low-income students are less socially and academically engaged on campus. For Tinto (1993), lowered involvement is related to diminished commitment to the institution and graduation goals. Ultimately, low-income students require more time to complete the college degree, which delays their entrance into the workforce (Elman & O'Rand, 2004) and can result in lowered lifetime earnings.

All of this research is important in understanding low-income students' experiences and preparation for college. Indeed, outcome measures such as graduation rates are difficult to evaluate in a vacuum, without reference to a goal or standard. However, it is also important to note the ways in which middle- and upper-income student experiences serve as the normative measuring stick. When "traditional" students' experiences serve as the norm, these experiences are further reified as traditional. Privileged students are then further privileged.

My intent in the above discussion is twofold: to outline the existing literature regarding low-income students, and also to present one aspect of institutionalized privilege. Even as scholars talk and write about low-income students, we often also re-privilege the groups that are already considered privileged. I do not intend here to discount any of the important research conducted over the past generation, nor do I question the important work of summer bridge programs; low-income student experiences are enhanced when we know more about their experiences and challenges. Instead, I suggest that a privileging of "traditional," middle- and upper-income students is built into our scholarly work and in the discourses we use to talk about them. Even the descriptive terms used to indicate student status—low- or higher-income—suggest comparisons, hierarchy, and difference.

One reason "low-income" experiences are defined and articulated with reference to higher-income students may be because of the difficulty (and discomfort) of defining social class in the U.S. context. Both "upper class" and "lower class" have been variously defined, with a variety of criteria and in different locations. Class is often conflated with race and ethnicity (Walpole, 2007), and it is often expanded to include values and worldview. Walpole (2007) notes "working class and upper class are terms researchers use to describe specific sections of the class structure, as well as class-specific lifestyles, attitudes, beliefs and values—in other words, class cultures" (p. 3). The various ways class has been operationalized mirrors the variety of theoretical approaches scholars have used to understand low-income student experiences. One of the most influential is Pierre Bourdieu's work on social and cultural capital (1977, 1994). In the next section, I discuss the ways in which Bourdieu's work has been used to re-privilege middle- and upper-income students.

Defining Deficit

Pierre Bourdieu's concepts of capital and habitus have been important constructs for social science researchers over the last generation, particularly as scholars have examined questions of equity in education. A great deal of the research on underrepresented students uses Bourdieu's concepts of cultural and social capital (1977, 1994) as a means of analyzing gaps in students' knowledge and attainment (Villapando & Solorzano, 2005). McDonough (1997), for example, discusses the cultural capital most valuable for making decisions about what college to attend. Perna (2000) looked at enrollment at four-year schools for African American, Latino, and White students, and observed that enrollment rates for African American and Latino students can be described with reference to lower levels of the social and cultural capital necessary for college enrollment. Horvat and Antonio (1999) use Bourdieu's habitus to examine how class and race intersect and influence the educational experiences of African American students as they prepare for the transition to college. And as Villapando and Solorzano point out (2005), many summer bridge programs use a cultural and social capital framework in designing program elements, activities, and curriculum.

For Walpole (2007), the terms "social capital," "cultural capital," and "habitus" are "almost ubiquitous" in the literature associated with underrepresented students (p. 24). Briefly, capital is a form of power for a specific context (Bourdieu, 1987). Social capital can be considered a set of connections or networks that can be useful as individuals navigate the social world. Cultural capital can be seen as a set of mannerisms, skills, and practices that have high status; in addition, cultural capital can refer to high-status knowledge about art or music. While capital concepts help describe structures of privilege and opportunity, the concept of habitus can be used to understand individual agency. Habitus refers to the internalization of an individual's objective situation and includes perceptions and responses related to opportunity. While habitus can be evident in lowered aspirations for some students, it may also lead students to work toward new perceptions, new forms of habitus (Walpole, 2003, 2007). These new forms may lead to more school success and upward mobility. Bourdieu's framework, then, integrates structure and individual agency. Low-income students are not merely adrift in educational systems, but also serve as agents in their own successes.

Bourdieu's work has been important not only in describing various forms of capital that may be useful to students, but also as it describes the ways in which educational institutions help reproduce inequalities (Walpole, 2007). Cultural capital—"specialized or insider knowledge which is not taught in schools" (Walpole, 2003, p. 49)—helps structure educational outcomes via the way it is accumulated and transmitted in schools: higher-income students, who possess more cultural capital to begin with, accumulate more cultural capital through their successes in school as their existing assets are valued, developed, and further rewarded. In this way, Bourdieu argues that educational attainment is not simply a matter of individual effort, but also a result of the educational system's privileging of particular behaviors, values, and preferences. These values and behaviors are associated with the middle and upper classes (Lamont & Lareau, 1988). Low-income students, researchers have argued, struggle more in college because they lack the cultural capital necessary to succeed.

Many other researchers have used a Bourdieuian framework to explore the experiences of underrepresented students, including those from low-income backgrounds (cf. Bergerson, 2007; McDonough, 1997; Perna, 2000; Walpole, 2003). Bergerson's (2007) study, however, shifts the focus from student capital to institutional structures and policies, the ways in which educational institutions "function to reproduce social arrangements in which working class students are offered less opportunity to succeed" (p. 104). Bergerson further suggests that practitioners and scholars should not dwell on changes low-income students need to make in order to succeed. With a focus on the knowledge and values low-income students "lack," little attention is paid to the institutional practices and policies that exclude some students, and any agency individual low-income students possess is overlooked.

The importance of Bourdieu's work in theorizing social inequality and reproduction cannot be overstated. The intersection of structure and individual agency Bourdieu emphasizes provides an important framework for pursuing topics such as college access in complex ways. It is important to note that Bourdieu's framework is not intended as a "deficit" model. It does not explicitly hierarchize the forms of capital or habitus possessed by different groups; a hierarchy is constructed and maintained by social institutions and the actors that work within them. However, Bourdieu's model has often been interpreted as a means of describing and defining the values, practices, and contextual attributes some students possess, and that other students lack. In this way, Bourdieu's model is often deficit-based in application, if not in theory. Despite an attention to agency, and despite the number of scholars who have used his framework, Walpole notes that Bourdieu's concepts have been criticized as "deterministic and for privileging the cultural capital possessed by elite social groups over that possessed by non-elite groups" (2007, p. 24). When researchers rely on this framework, low-income students are often positioned, again, as outsiders, as students that need a "bridge" to college. Bourdieu's framework does not articulate social and cultural capital as something that can be dispensed in programs, handed out like textbooks or pencils. Many programs, however, are designed around the goal of "building" students' capital. When capital is imagined in this way, the characteristics and values of middle- and upper-income students are re-privileged as the norm towards which lower-income students must aspire.

In this section, my goal has been to examine the literature on low-income students with an eye toward post-structural "revelation." What I hope to reveal is the way in which the scholarship related to low-income students has helped to define them as underprivileged. Low-income student experiences are too often framed by the norms and expectations of traditional, middle- and upper-income students. In the next sections, I bring low-income students themselves into the text—their voices and experiences, without the backdrop of deficit or traditional norms. My intent is to present students like Emily as individuals with a great deal of agency and resilience—not simply with a label of "low-income." Following the post-structural approach, I turn to "deconstruction," an examination of the policies and practices that disenfranchise low-income students. In particular, I focus on student experiences in a bridge program aimed at assisting students as they begin their undergraduate careers. Before moving to deconstruction, I offer a brief discussion of the participants.

Participants

The young women in this study were enrolled in their first year of college at a large, urban public university. They come from a range of racial and ethnic backgrounds, and they are pursuing a variety of different majors. Each of the young women participated in the same three-week summer bridge program at their university. Students in the program also receive financial support and academic advisement throughout their undergraduate careers. As indicated in the data reported below, some of their first-year classes were "transition" sections—that is, the classes were exclusively populated with students in the transition program. The young women knew each other because of their participation in the program, but they did not attend the same high schools and did not have any current courses in common.

When **Emily** was in high school, she wanted to be a detective, "like on *Law & Order*." But she started college as an undeclared major and is now thinking about studying medicine. She is tall, with olive skin and dark eyes. During the fall semester, she spent most weekends looking for a local church, trying to find a congregation she felt at home with. In addition to cooking her mother's recipes in her residence hall kitchen, she also spends her time working at one of the libraries on campus.

Lilian arrived in the United States when she was 8 years old. Her family moved from Vietnam in order to secure better educational opportunities for Lilian and her two younger brothers. She lives at home and rides the bus to campus each day, more than an hour and a half coming and going. Her long, dark hair falls across her eyes, and she smiles constantly. But despite her gentle demeanor, she believes college "is a competition," and she wants to win. She is undecided about her major.

Both **Anna** and **Jennifer** are dancers—Jennifer with the cheer team on campus, and Anna with one of the dance clubs. These days, Anna finds little time to perform with her group; her nursing major keeps her very busy. On weekends, she works as a medical assistant at a nursing home, so she does not often visit her family. She is African American, and the first in her family to attend college. Jennifer is a petite, White woman, and she is thinking about studying political science. Though she describes herself as shy, she is active on the cheer team and attends most football and basketball games; the team practices several days a week. She grew up in a city about three hours from campus, and stays connected with her mother via cell phone. They talk at least three times a day.

Teresa was the valedictorian of her high school graduating class. Though she attends college in the same city where she grew up, she does not visit home very often, just often enough to cut and style her cousin's hair. Teresa is quiet and studious; she reads even while she is working at her on-campus job in one of the student lounges. Her aunt, with whom she has lived for the past five years, is Teresa's role model, and she talks often of her influence. Teresa is African American.

For **Brenda**, preparation for college is more than academic, it's "mental and spiritual." Her family is from Ghana, where both of her parents went to college, and where Brenda hopes to travel next summer. When she boarded the bus to travel across the state to come to school, Brenda had only a suitcase and a backpack. But she enjoys being far from home. She believes she is developing her independence and her "spirit." She is currently undecided about her major.

DECONSTRUCTING: RE-EXAMINING SUMMER BRIDGE

In this section, I describe the experiences of Emily, Lilian, Jennifer, Anna, Teresa, and Brenda in a summer support program designed to help smooth their transition to college and bolster their academic skills in preparation for college-level work. I focus on this program as one example of an institutional policy and practice which disenfranchises students even as it offers guidance. A post-structural lens is helpful in this examination as it emphasizes structures and locations of power, as well as their interconnections.

Summer Bridge: Structured for Success

Like many transitional programs, the version Emily and her peers participated in includes an intensive academic component as well as classes in time management, computer and research skills, and individualized counseling. This program is structured over the course of three weeks, during which time students are required to live on campus—even through the weekends. Students are not permitted to leave campus during the program, and opportunities for contact with their families are very limited. Each day is highly structured in terms of class time, meals, tutorial sessions, and mandatory study hours. Students are not permitted to bring electronics—televisions or iPods—when they move into their summer residence halls.

Each of the young women in this study expressed complicated responses to their summer bridge experience. Each recognized the value of the experience, particularly with respect to meeting new friends and acquainting them with the campus. Their comments resonate with the literature that emphasizes the positive social effects of bridge programs. Emily, for example, was relieved when the regular term started and she already knew her way around campus. Other new students asked her for assistance finding buildings and classrooms; she felt "comfortable" even on the first day of the fall term. Lilian "fell in love with" the program. For the first time, she lived away from home and did not have to worry about family responsibilities.

The young women also talked about the program in negative terms. For these students, "support" and "control" were closely aligned. Anna put it most bluntly, describing the three-week program as "like being in jail." She continued: "they had curfews. Curfews! Can you believe it? All I kept think about during those three weeks was 'I want to go home, I want to go home.'" Lilian called it "stress upon stress," and Teresa commented: "That program made me cry every day." Both students and program administrators describe the three-week session as a kind of "boot camp," intended to prepare students for the rigors of college classes and collegiate living.

As the young women talked further about the program, some additional characteristics became clearer. While the program's structure was intended to mirror the rigors of college life, students also experienced powerlessness and a loss of community and family. For Emily, a loss of agency came before the program began, when she learned it would be "required." She had planned a trip to the Dominican Republic to visit family over the summer. "Then [the program] was my only choice. I had to go," she notes. "I was not happy at all. The first week I was like, I want to go home, I am going home." Jennifer talked about losing her summer job because of the program: "There was no way I'd get that time off," she laughed. The sense of a loss of agency or choice was not confined to the simple fact of required attendance. Emily and Teresa both commented on the highly structured days, which offered no time for individual decisions around meal times, study patterns, or what time they would go to bed. Teresa commented further, noting that the program emphasized time management, but "[students] don't plan their own time." She wondered: "how can I learn how to manage my time if I don't manage my own time? I don't know...I'm still working on that part." Lilian realized during the second week that she missed her family. She remembered:

> I had my up and down with the program. But I realized I need to go home. I have three siblings at home that I need to take care of sometimes. I have responsibility at home, so I have to be there. But I couldn't.

Again, each of the young women interviewed for this study recognized the value of the experience. But along the way, they struggled with a sense of powerlessness, homesickness, and disconnection. Brenda admitted: "I felt so alone, like, even with all these other kids."

The summer bridge experience is the centerpiece of a program that provides important support for students at risk of being overwhelmed by the academic and social requirements of college. And as indicated above, research has validated the importance of such transitional programs. It is also important, however, to examine the program with respect to questions of agency and disenfranchisement. As these students indicated, the program contributes to a sense of powerlessness that may already be present as students from low-income backgrounds head to college. Interestingly, the young women recognized that the program bore little resemblance to actual college life. "The time management thing," Lilian commented, "that's huge, that's the thing. But my schedule is nothing like those three weeks. I think it is easier now." College life is, for these young women, highly unstructured, most decidedly unlike their summer boot camp. All of the young women work, some at off-campus jobs. Trying to manage their courses, jobs, and relationships is still a challenge, as it is for so many undergraduates. Each of the young women also expressed regret about the ways in which their families were not part of their summer process. Phone calls were hard to schedule, and even those who lived nearby were not allowed to leave campus during the program. They were cut off from an important source of support, and their families were unable to participate in their daughters' progress.

The young women in this study also recognized that their participation in the summer bridge program marks them as "different." When Anna walks across campus these days, she sees "kids from the program," and though they are not friends, they "recognize" one another. "What does 'recognize' mean?" I asked her. "You know," she said, "we've been through it, we're different." Anna and the other young women know that they were selected to participate in the program because they come from "lower-class" schools and families, as Teresa described it. Teresa, who was valedictorian of her graduating class, admitted, "I guess I was not prepared for college, not at all. My school, it was bad, you've probably heard of it. But I could have learned a lot more. I didn't know how to learn on my own." In her comment, Teresa takes on the responsibility for her underpreparation, despite the fact that she knows her high school did not offer many opportunities.

The unintended messages communicated in a summer program are important to explore. Students receive the message, before they begin their first semester, that they are different, already behind their non-low-income peers. They are subtly told that they need remediation, that success at a four-year college is via a bridge. Given these messages, it is not surprising that Jennifer is confused by her academic success. She told me "sometimes I wonder if I am missing something, because I'm like 'I get it, I understand.' I wonder if it should be harder." When a program like this is separated from the regular school year, unattached to credit hours and tuition, an institution sends a mixed signal: You are a college student, but not quite. In addition, students may receive messages about the role of families and other community supports in their education. All of these young women talked about the support offered by their families and extended families, but they saw no role for them as they transitioned into the college setting. Lilian remembered: "My dad dropped me off with a bunch of water bottles, and that was it."

Fall Courses, Special Sections

During their summer program, the students were advised regarding their fall schedules. For the young women profiled here, their courses were a mixture of general education, composition courses, freshman seminars, and occasionally an introductory course in their major. Jennifer was surprised to learn that some of her general education courses were "reserved" for summer bridge students. Jennifer's Western Civ course is restricted to student participants in the support program. Emily is also enrolled in one of these special sections. The course book is provided for students, and tutoring is available. But Emily was surprised at the course content; it seemed "too easy." She told me: "I was like, I asked people: If you are in [this program] do you get easier classes? Because in high school, I expected that it would be harder." Emily does not want to complain about doing well in her course, but, like Jennifer, she finds success confusing. "Sometimes I wonder why I'm in this course," she explained. Anna's description of the special sections is more critical:

> [The program] makes people look at you like you are less of a person, because it is for people who are financially and academically disabled or however you want to put it, so they look at us like: "oh, you're in [the program] so you're poor." I think people shouldn't look at you funny if you are in [the program] …people are like "oh, you have to take that class because you are stupid."

In this situation, students' class backgrounds are not made visible by clothes or computer equipment or cars. Instead, class background is visible because of enrollment pattern; Anna feels stigmatized by her section of Western Civ. Emily and Jennifer wonder why they are taking "easier" classes; Teresa comments that she wishes she could take courses with other students, not just students in the program. The intention of these special sections is certainly clear: the goal is to develop small learning communities wherein students are supported and can pursue their coursework in familiar environments. At the same time, these young women and their peers are literally placed outside the mainstream; they are academic outsiders, even as they complete courses required of all students.

RECONSTRUCTION: BUILDING NEW BRIDGES

A post-structural lens focuses researchers on hidden assumptions and privileges that exist in structures; it asks scholars to examine how power operates and how individuals assert agency. A summer bridge program is a complicated initiative; its complexity is certainly evident in the young women's descriptions and responses. The summer program these young women participated in is a convenient site in which to examine structures—indeed, the program's highly structured schedule is one of the defining features. A summer bridge program of this kind also reflects a deficit approach; the three-week program is designed to provide academic and social enrichment experiences that low-income students have lacked, and which they need in order to succeed in college. The support program during the regular school year, including enrollment in special sections, continues to position students as different, and separate, from their peers. Unfortunately, as Anna notes, "different" is not always interpreted as a positive attribute. In this section, I turn to reconstruction, to taking the lessons learned from revelation and deconstruction and offering suggestions for new scholarship and practices that may support students in ways that engage and enfranchise them.

Renewed Scholarship

To begin, it is important for scholars to examine the work in which we are engaged. Research carries messages beyond data and findings, and if we are to understand how privilege operates in systems, we must also look critically at our own contributions, as well as the overall canon. Scholarship helps construct privilege even as it illuminates it. Researchers can better understand how privilege operates in postsecondary education by also examining how we talk and write about it. The brief review I offer in this chapter is one example of a critical review. When researchers examine the literature related to low-income students, the status of these students and their experiences becomes clearer: low-income students are too often unfavorably compared to their more privileged peers. Rather than framing low-income students' experiences and challenges in comparison to middle- and upper-income students, scholars can work to understand low-income students themselves, as well as the institutional environments and practices that privilege some students and disadvantage others. Such an approach also requires the re-examination of theoretical models such as Bourdieu's and how they are used. Though Bourdieu's model calls attention to institutions and structures, his capital constructs are often applied to individuals, and often in terms of deficit. Rethinking our scholarship can bring privilege into sharper focus.

In addition, scholars can expand the tools and approaches used to explore the experiences of traditionally marginalized groups. For example, additional qualitative research can be added to the existing scholarship related to low-income students. In particular, ethnographic or observation-based research can be useful toward understanding the institutional contexts in which students work. Such studies can extend what we know beyond outcome measures such as GPAs and retention rates. It is also clear that more empirical research is needed with respect to summer bridge programs and how they affect student transitions to college. Again, this additional research should include qualitative projects which focus on the subjective experiences of students in addition to reporting measure of "success."

New Bridges

While summer bridge programs offer important socializing experiences for low-income students, they also draw from a deficit orientation which undervalues the capital students possess as well as the roles of family and community support. As Villapando and Solorzano (2005) suggest, a "cultural wealth" approach recognizes the assets student bring to educational environments; students bring experiences, cultural values, and aspirations that can be leveraged as sources of empowerment and future successes. For example, instead of excluding families in the summer bridge program, they may be included as active members of a student's support network. Instead of sequestering students on campus for long days of coursework and tutoring, programs might also send students into the community so that they can work or complete service learning projects. Tutors, teachers, or mentors in the program could be community members recruited from some of the students' home neighborhoods. In short, a transition program should build bridges to local communities so that students recognize the value of their own social and cultural capital.

Renewed scholarship related to low-income students and bridge programs can also inform new program structures. It is interesting to note that programs across the United States have similar structural characteristics despite differences in students served and geographic location. Low-income students from New York City, for example, bring very different experiences to a program than those from rural California communities. Programs in different states serve students with a variety of community, racial, ethnic, and educational backgrounds. In many ways, however, programs are structured with a "one size" approach, as if low-income students are more the same than different. Programs typically bring students to a campus for an intensive living/learning experience. As suggested above, programs may be enhanced by developing ties to local communities, leveraging the capital located in students' environments; this may require re-structuring programs in terms of location, schedule, or types of activities. Students might also benefit from programs that, rather than executed in the summer months when they may need to be working, are integrated into the regular school year. "Structure" may also need investigation, particularly if structure and control are too closely aligned in student perceptions. If the current structure of programs leaves students without choices and without a sense of individual agency, alternatives need to be explored. For example, time management may be better practiced if students are empowered to manage their *own* time.

Empowering All Students as Insiders

Re-making programs like summer bridge and "transitions" sections of general education courses is certainly not easy; models of support programs that do not have the suggestion of stigma are difficult to conceptualize. At the same time, finding ways to support all students without also pointing toward "difference" is an important step toward balancing privilege across campuses. When bridge programs or special sections are offered for students, an institution can "locate" support in one place; responsibility for ensuring student success then becomes the responsibility of an office or a specific cohort of faculty and staff. It does necessarily extend across campus to include all members of the community. Instead of special sections, students should be able to access assistance as part of an institutional commitment. All students should perceive themselves as insiders, not as disadvantaged, "at-risk," or different.

BEYOND SUMMER BRIDGE

Rethinking a program like summer bridge will not ensure that all students are successful in college. The challenges low-income students experience are complex and connected to larger social issues. Lilian's campus experience is marked by long commutes to and from school, and she feels pressure from her family to do well. Teresa wonders how she will afford another semester of tuition. My aim in this chapter is not simply to suggest that these challenges can be addressed with a different version of summer bridge. Instead, my goal has been to use summer bridge as an example of a common program and set of policies which disenfranchises some students even as it works to support them. The young women in this study are eager for support and assistance; they want to succeed, and they are enthusiastic even in their struggle. Emily and the other young women are moving forward, toward their goals. They will likely need other bridges of support as they continue.

REFERENCES

Ackermann, S. (1990). *The benefits of summer bridge program for underrepresented and low-income students.* Paper presented at the annual meeting of the American Educational Research Association, Boston, MA.

Adelman, C. (1999). *Answers in the toolbox: Academic intensity, attendance patterns, and bachelor's degree attainment.* Washington, DC: U.S. Department of Education, Office of Educational Research and Improvement.

Aronson, P. (2008). Breaking barriers or locked out? Class-based perceptions and experiences of postsecondary education. In J. T. Mortimer (Ed.), *Social class and transitions to adulthood. New Directions for Child and Adolescent Development, 119,* 41–54.

Berger, J. B., & Milem, J. F. (1999). The role of student involvement and perceptions of integration in a causal model of student persistence. *Research in Higher Education, 40*(6), 641–664.

Bergerson, A. A. (2007). Exploring the impact of social class on adjustment to college: Anna's story. *International Journal of Qualitative Studies in Education, 20*(1), 99–119.

Bourdieu, P. (1977). Cultural reproduction and social reproduction. In J. Karabel and A. H. Halsey (Eds.), *Power and ideology in education* (pp. 487–511). New York: Oxford University Press.

Bourdieu, P. (1987). The forms of capital. In J. G. Richardson (Ed.), *Handbook of theory and research for the sociology of education* (pp. 241–258). New York: Greenwood Press.

Bourdieu, P. (1994). Distinction: A social critique. In D. B. Grusky (Ed.), *Social stratification: Class, race, and gender in sociological perspective* (pp. 499–525). Boulder, CO: Westview Press.

Bozick, R., & DeLuca, S. (2005). Better late than never? Delayed enrollment in the higher school to college transition. *Social Forces, 84*(1), 531–554.

Cabrera, A. F., Burkum, K. R., & La Nasa, S. M. (2003). *Pathways to a four-year degree: Determinants of degree completion among socioeconomically disadvantaged students.* Paper presented at the Annual Meeting of the Association for the Study of Higher Education, Portland, Oregon.

Chen, X., & Carroll, C. D. (2005). *First generation students in postsecondary education: A look at their college transcripts.* Washington, DC: U.S. Department of Education, National Center for Education Statistics.

Choy, S. (2000). *Low-income students: Who they are and how they pay for their education.* Washington, DC: U.S. Department of Education, National Center for Education Statistics.

Corrigan, M. (2003). Beyond access: Persistence challenges and the diversity of low-income students. *New Directions for Higher Education, 121,* 25–34.

Elman, C., & O'Rand, A. M. (2004). The race is to the swift: Socioeconomic origins, adult education, and wage attainment. *American Journal of Sociology, 110*(1), 23–60.

Gancarz, C. P., Lowry, A. R., McIntyre, C. W., & Moss, R. W. (1998). Increasing enrollment by preparing underachievers for college. *Journal of College Admission, 160,* 6–13.

Gandara, P. (2001). *Paving the way to postsecondary education: K-12 intervention programs for underrepresented youth* (NCES 2001–205). Washington, DC: U.S. Government Printing Office.

Garcia, P. (1991). Summer bridge: Improving retention rates for underprepared students. *Journal of the Freshman Year Experience, 3*(2), 91–105.

Gold, M. (1992). The bridge: A summer enrichment program to retain African American collegians. *Journal of the Freshman Year Experience, 4*(2), 101–117.

Goldrick-Rab, S. (2006). Following their every move: An investigation of social-class differences in college pathways. *Sociology of Education 79*(1), 61–79.

Horn, L., Neville, S., & Griffith, J. (2006). *Profile of undergraduates in U.S. postsecondary education institutions: 2003–04: With a special analysis of community college students. Statistical Analysis Report.* Washington, DC: National Center for Education Statistics, U.S. Department of Education.

Horvat, E. M., & Antonio, A. L. (1999). "Hey, those shoes are out of uniform:" African American girls in an elite high school and the importance of habitus. *Anthropology and Education Quarterly, 30*(3), 317–342.

Kezar, A. (2000). *Summer bridge programs: Supporting all students* (EDO-HE-2000-3). Washington, DC: Office of Educational Research and Improvement.

Lamont, M., & Lareau, A. (1988). Cultural capital: Allusions, gaps, and glissandos in recent theoretical developments. *Sociological Theory, 6*, 153–168.

Lumina Foundation (2004). Powerful partnerships: Independent colleges share high-impact strategies for low-income students' success. *New Agenda Series, 5*(4).

McDonough, P. (1997). *Choosing colleges: How social class and schools structure opportunity.* Albany, NY: State University of New York Press.

Myers, D., & Shirm, A. (1999). *The impacts of Upward Bound: Final report for phase I of the national evaluation final report* (MPR Reference No. 8046-515). Washington, DC: U.S. Department of Education.

Perna, L. W. (2000). Differences in the decision to attend college among African Americans, Hispanics, and Whites. *Journal of Higher Education, 71*(2), 117–141.

Santa Rita, E., & Bacote, J. B. (1996). *The benefits of college discovery prefreshman's program for minority and low income students* (ERIC Document Reproduction Service No. 394 536). New York: Bronx Community College of the City University of New York.

Tinto, V. (1993). *Leaving college: Rethinking the causes and cures of student attrition* (2nd ed.). Chicago: The University of Chicago Press.

Villapando, O., & Solorzano, D. G. (2005). The role of culture in college preparation programs: A review of the research literature. In W. G. Tierney, Z. B. Corwin, & J. E. Colyar (Eds.), *Preparing for college: Nine elements of effective outreach* (pp. 13–28). Albany, NY: State University of New York Press.

Walpole, M. (2003). Socioeconomic status and college: How SES affects college experiences and outcomes. *The Review of Higher Education, 27*(1), 45–73.

Walpole, M. (2007). *Economically and educationally challenged students in higher education: Access to outcomes. ASHE-ERIC Higher Education Report* (Vol. 33, Issue 3). San Francisco: Jossey-Bass.

Walpole, M., Simmerman, H., Mack, C., Mills, J. T., Scales, M., & Albano, D. (2008). Bridge to success: Insight into summer bridge program students' college transition. *Journal of the First-Year Experience & Students in Transition, 20*(1), 11–30.

York, M., & Tross, S. (1994). *Evaluation of student retention programs: An essential component.* Paper presented at the annual SUCCEED conference on the Improvement of Engineering Education, Raleigh, NC.

7

WELFARE STUDENTS IN COMMUNITY COLLEGES

Policy and Policy Implementation as Barriers to Educational Attainment

JOHN S. LEVIN, VIRGINIA MONTERO-HERNANDEZ, CHRISTINE CERVEN, AND GENEVIEVE SHAKER

POOR PEOPLE'S COLLEGE AND POOR PEOPLE

Community colleges are the postsecondary educational entry point for economically disadvantaged populations (Levin, 2007). Among the most challenged community college students are public assistance recipients whose opportunities of participation in higher education are linked to the nature of institutional programs aimed to help them overcome financial strains, emotional conflicts, and/or disabilities. Specifically, we examine the role of welfare policies of the State and policy implementation in shaping the educational experiences of community college students who are also welfare recipients. The analysis addresses welfare reform policy, how individual and institutional actors implement such policy, and the characteristics of institutional programs aimed to help welfare recipients transition from welfare to work.

As a primary educational service provider for low-income students, community colleges feature a cost structure and a mission to address this group (Levin, 2007). Because of this defining characteristic, community colleges are framed as potentially democratizing agents and alternately chastised for falling short of the mark as dream-makers (Levin & Montero-Hernandez, 2009). As an institution, the community college fills both a structural and legislative role that is either ignored by other institutional types or deemed to be illegitimate to their purposes. Twenty-six percent of community college students are from households in the lowest income quartile in comparison to approximately 20 percent of students at four-year public and private not-for-profit institutions (Horn & Nevill, 2006). Forty-five percent of first-time college students from households in the lowest income quartile attend community colleges, in comparison to less than 30 percent who go to four-year institutions (Bailey, Jenkins, & Leinbach, 2005)

The economic disadvantage is revealed in more stark terms when the population is limited to welfare recipients. In 2008, 4,032,704 people in the United States received federal welfare aid (U.S. Department of Health and Human Services: Office of Family Assistance, 2009). Based on the most recently collected figures for California, in 1999 1,226,362 people received welfare aid, and there were 107,088 welfare recipients within the state's community colleges (Mathur, 2002). The vast majority of welfare recipients are women with children who tend to live in a culture of poverty that hinders their capacity to make long-term plans and to identify education as an activity to pursue. Prone to low levels of self-esteem and self-confidence, these women find their way to community colleges for education and training (Bombach, 2001). Eighty percent of community colleges report programs specifically directed at welfare recipients, but these do not generally include college-level courses applicable to degree requirements (Meléndez, Falcón, & Bivens, 2003). Yet, though the welfare recipient population finds its home at community colleges, they are not always well served.

Community colleges and their approach to welfare recipients are products of institutional history, community context (e.g., interest groups), legal agreements (e.g., collective bargaining agreements and employee contracts), and, perhaps most significantly, the broad student population (Levin, 2007). Community colleges are not autonomous institutions and their functioning has to be understood as the result of a network of policies and regulations at the federal and state levels which, in some cases, contravene the public agenda for the colleges (Cohen & Brawer, 2008). Institutional policies at community colleges often emanate from federal and state laws, such as the American Disabilities Act. Indeed, educational policies at these public institutions can be viewed as an extension of the State (Carnoy, 1984). The State, then, uses the community college as the educational institution for poor people, and this use is particularly evident in the case of welfare recipients in specially constructed college programs for their education and training.

We argue that current federal and state policies, formulated to encourage primarily market interests, hinder the ability of welfare program participants to pursue their educational goals at community colleges at an optimal level. In this chapter, section one concerns post-structuralism, the theoretical orientation underlying this argument and the discussion's guiding premise. In section two, federal welfare reform policy is analyzed through attention to its ideological components, their transmission at the state level, and agency and institutional circumstances and implementation. California and CalWORKs, the California Temporary Assistance for Needy Families (TANF) program, including New Visions Program at Riverside Community College (RCC) arising from CalWORKs, are used as an illustrative case because of the comprehensive and proactive programs linking welfare-to-work programs to community colleges (Meléndez et al., 2003; Shaw, Goldrick-Rab, Mazzeo, & Jacobs, 2006). Section three ties together the theoretical and policy considerations to examine their coalescence in program initiatives and individual action. At the center of this section is the relationship between CalWORKs and New Visions, as an example of a collaborative governmental and institutional effort to assist welfare recipients in reaching self-sufficiency. At the end of the chapter, we point out the necessity of developing a policy framework that supports the design and implementation of institutional programs aimed to understand and respond to the characteristics and demands of welfare recipients. Effective treatment of welfare recipients involves formal and research-based programming to overcome multiple challenges and negotiate the local context. Ultimately, the post-structural framework and the case of CalWORKs and New Visions emphasize that analysis of experiences and practices within the institutional context is imperative if we hope to learn how to work with low-income students and help them move toward higher levels of personal development.

THE ANALYTICAL FRAMEWORK: POST-STRUCTURALISM AND POLICY

Post-structuralism broadens the scope of a structuralist perspective to include analyses of human agency, the sociohistorical and cultural development of structure, language, practices, norms, interaction, power, and the importance of local context (Best & Kellner, 1991; Bloland, 1995; Epstein, 1998; Kezar, Chapter 1). Post-structuralism provides a framework for the examination of: 1. the ideology inherent in welfare policy language, and 2. the way in which power is enacted to implement policy, design institutional programs, and construct interactions among governmental officials, community college actors, and public assistance recipients. Institutional behaviors emanate from two primary sources: 1. from the power and authority of the State; 2. from the implementation of policy at the institutional level. The State is the framer of institutional contexts (Carnoy, 1984; Slaughter, 1990). However, the implementation of policy is largely dependent on the actors residing within these institutions: their frontline behavior either upholds work-first rhetoric in welfare policy or incorporates a more educational and human development approach. We view the functioning of welfare-to-work programs as defined by a system of power relationships where organizational actors negotiate their belief systems with the prescriptions of welfare policy.

According to this perspective, we identify two relevant aspects related to policy implementation, institutional context, and interactions. First, we acknowledge that to understand the nature of welfare reform policy we need to understand the role of the State in policy formulation and dissemination across the nation as well as the ideological perspective encouraged by the State. Second, we reason that policy implementation and its effects upon recipients are mediated by the forms of social behavior and interaction among those organizational members who are granted responsibility to translate policy language and create specific programs related to it. In what follows, we describe the conceptual elements that guide our analysis.

The State as a Source of Structural Power

The State is conceptualized as both autonomous, containing bureaucracies and legislators, and divided, arising from political coalitions (Carnoy, 1984; Goedegebuure, Kaiser, Maassen, & De Weert, 1993; Hartmark & Hines, 1986; Pusser, 2008; Schlager & Blomquist, 1995; Skocpol, 1985; Slaughter, 1990). The State plays an authoritative role over higher education in three key areas: financial support, regulation of actions, and promotion of access (Pusser, 2008). Particularly relevant are contests over access and affordability in higher education as well as the preservation of a meritocratic and stratified postsecondary system. The functioning of the State is intricately tied to the economic system in which a society is embedded. The material conditions of a capitalistic society form the basis of an inherently unequal classed society, with the State representing the interests of the ruling class within that unequal class system (Carnoy, 1984). The influence of the market is apparent in the functioning of not only the State but also higher education. The State's allocation of funds for higher education programs is heavily influenced by the capitalist economy that pervades U.S. society. Moreover, the State, as the arm of a capitalist system, works to represent and preserve the interests of those who benefit from this system, thus affecting not only the allocation of funds but also the creation of policy in higher education. Because profit is a dominant value that permeates capitalist rhetoric and new capitalism (Sennett, 2006), state-funded programs in higher education frequently contain policy that reflects more the value of profit making than that of educational endeavor.

Agency and Organizational Behaviors

The State, however, is only part of the policy process; individual and collective behaviors are also determinants of policy outcomes. New institutional theorists (Scott, 1998; Weick, 1976) acknowledge that the constraining effects of institutional structures, such as the State, can be suspended or modified when people create informal structures and loosely coupled arrays within organizational settings. The notion of agency helps us explain the foundations of informal action and the emergence of loosely coupled arrays in organizational settings. The concept of agency suggests that social actors are capable of intentional behaviors even though they are constrained by regulatory institutional structures (Ortner, 2006). Both agency and discretionary action are concepts relevant to this chapter since these enable us to understand both the formal and informal dynamics of welfare policy implementation in organizational settings and the forms of interaction with welfare recipients. Structures and their underlying ideologies can, however, limit individual agency, and for our welfare students, these shape both the individual and collective actions of students and policy implementers.

THE IDEOLOGY AND IMPLEMENTATION OF FEDERAL AND STATE WELFARE POLICY

To understand the enrollment of low-income people in community college courses, we need to examine the way in which welfare policy is defined and the opportunities for welfare recipients to pursue educational goals that are both permissible and possible. The ideological components, goals, and regulations of welfare policy function as a strategy to comprehend the reasons why public assistance recipients are directed primarily to either work or education/training. The structure of California's welfare program reflects the factors that frame institutional behaviors aimed to respond to low-income people. We note that institutional- and agency-level interpretation and enactment of policy provide a grounded perspective of welfare recipients. This combination of ideology, local- and institutional-level interpretation, and situational enactment leads toward institutional enabling of specific forms of service to welfare recipients through community colleges and welfare departments.

Ideological Components of Federal Welfare Policy

Existing welfare reform policy was enacted through TANF which became effective with the passage of the Personal Responsibility and Work Opportunity Reconciliation Act (PRWORA) under the Clinton administration in 1997. In this legislation, welfare policy offers dual pathways of development for low-income people: work and education/training (Shaw et al., 2006). Yet, the specific policy regulations of the reform exemplify the promotion of the interests of the market and its beneficiaries over that of individuals in poverty; individuals' opportunities for personal development, education, and financial mobility are trumped by capitalistic notions of profiteering. Commonly referred to as "work-first," the policy reduced welfare clients to economic entities that merely need to obtain and hold jobs to achieve economic independence while de-emphasizing the role of education in this process (Shaw et al., 2006). Entry into the productive employment system is expected in the shortest time possible. Indeed, subsequent to passage of the legislation, studies found a decline in the postsecondary enrollments of welfare recipients (Cox & Spriggs, 2002; Jacobs & Winslow, 2003). Within two years, college enrollments for welfare recipients dropped 20 percent relative to other poor individuals. At least 13 percent of this decline was attributed to work-first state policies (Cox & Spriggs, 2002).

Welfare reform is the product of continual ideological negotiation among social groups which advocate for either a work-first or a human capital approach in policy formulation. The liberal approach embraces a skill-building or human capital orientation to alleviate poverty and promote social mobility. The conservative approach allocates the responsibility of poverty to individuals, requiring them to work first (Shaw et al., 2006). The 1998 Workforce Investment Act is an outcome of the latter, and is a strategy designed to funnel clients into employment quickly while minimizing the opportunity and importance of education and training. The work-first emphasis and its influence upon the decline of welfare recipients' enrollment in postsecondary education are related to various symbolic features embedded in U.S. culture (Mazzeo, Rab, & Eachus, 2003). First, U.S. culture rests on an individualistic perspective in which people's financial independence and hard work are central to a productive society. Second is the perspective decrying state subsidies for social groups including undocumented immigrants and women (especially African American poor women), largely stigmatized as lazy, unmotivated, and cheaters of the system (Rose, 2000; Seccombe, James, & Battle Walters, 1998). Although women are the dominant participant group in the nation's welfare program (96.4 percent of the case load), scholars note that the structure and regulations in welfare policy are based on sexist assumptions that tend to reproduce the female-headed family as a stigmatized and disadvantaged social form (Shaw et al., 2006). Welfare policy language is replete with the assumption that two-parent families and employment are the primary paths to self-sufficiency (Schram, 1993).

State Level Welfare: Devolution and Policy Reinterpretation

At the state level, local welfare programs can try to balance the work and education requirements of welfare clients in the development of their specific welfare-to-work program plans (Shaw & Rab, 2003). The autonomy and flexibility granted to states in the implementation of federal policy provide local agencies with the capacity to interpret the ideological elements of the policy language (Jacobs & Winslow, 2003) which has allowed states to develop different approaches to the federal TANF program (Mazzeo et al., 2003; Rose, 2000). States have also established distinctive regulations for permitting work and education/training as allowable "work activities" to shape the structure of welfare clients' personal welfare-to-work plans. The construction and implementation of the CalWORKs program, for example, can be understood as the result of both the work-first ideology embedded in federal policy (TANF) and the second-order devolution strategy (Fording, Soss, & Schram, 2007).

Within welfare policy implementation, states take one of three approaches to education as an allowable work activity (Jacobs & Winslow, 2003): education 1. as a stand-alone activity, or 2. in combination with work, or 3. not an authorized work activity. Within California, the state defines education/training as an allowed activity in combination with work. Arguably, CalWORKs is a state attempt to soften the work-first prescriptions inherent in the TANF program (Shaw et al., 2006). Yet, although the California program is an official attempt to encourage welfare clients both to formulate and to pursue educational goals, its primary emphasis remains on employment and economic self-sufficiency.

As described by the California Department of Social Services (CDSS), CalWORKs is a welfare program approved by the state for implementation in 1998 that gives cash aid and services to eligible, needy families. The CDSS mandates that under CalWORKs welfare recipients must participate in 18–24 months of welfare-to-work activities, followed by work or community service, to remain eligible for up to 60 months of cash aid. CalWORKs encourages the participation of TANF recipients in education and training by offering support and services enabling engagement in work and study activities simultaneously. A participant's welfare-to-work plan may include attendance at a California community college if the county welfare department agrees that it will help lead the participant toward unsubsidized employment, and if the college affirms that the participant is making progress once in the program. Coordination between the entities is necessary. The CalWORKs Community College program involves five components: work-study, job development and job placement, childcare services, curriculum development, and instruction. CalWORKs welfare programs are enacted through institutional agencies such as county welfare departments that seek to establish interorganizational networks to expand choices and services for welfare clients. Employment service counselors first help clients find unsubsidized jobs. The goal is for participants to engage in 20 hours per week in working activities. In phase two, case managers encourage welfare recipients to enroll in education/training programs for an additional 12 hours per week, for a combined total of 32 hours in welfare-to-work sponsored activities.[1]

Organizational Implementation of Welfare Reform

The ideological perspective (i.e., work-first approach) of welfare reform, filtered through state policy, complicates the construction of organizational structures in which integral support programs can be developed to serve low-income people. On the one hand, the market-oriented interests in welfare policy reduce the possibilities of allocating a sufficient budget for welfare departments to provide staff training and integral services for welfare recipients. On the other hand, strict regulations and excessive bureaucratic demands from welfare reform policy discourage the participation of organizations such as community colleges whose functioning is based on a human capital approach and clashes with the work-first approach of welfare policy promulgated by welfare departments at the local level.

Culture and Roles in Welfare Departments. Welfare agencies are responsible for the registration and initial treatment (helping clients find unsubsidized jobs or to enroll in education/training) of public assistance recipients (Lurie, 2001). Departmental structuring influences interactions with welfare clients and program outcomes (Brock & Harknett, 1998). By the end of the 1990s, welfare departments experienced a shift from an eligibility determination to employment-focused, case management culture (Bane & Ellwood, 1994; Johnson, Ketch, Chow, & Austin, 2006; Lens, 2008; Meyers, Glaser, & Donald, 1998). This shift encouraged new role demands. Welfare workers became required to act as case managers whose responsibilities involved: (a) increasing personal contact with clients and empowering client participation in decision making, (b) providing information about services, regulations, and available choices, (c) communicating new behavioral expectations to assist welfare recipients to move toward self-sufficiency, and (d) forming service linkage or the development of interorganizational networks (Johnson et al., 2006; Morgen, 2001; Meyers et al., 1998).

Welfare departments receive a limited budget to train their staff and help them transition into their new working role demands (Brock & Harknett, 1998; Jewell & Glaser, 2006; Johnson et al., 2006; Lurie, 2001; Morgen, 2001). Moreover, welfare departments' acknowledged characteristics include extensive and ambiguous policy manuals, ongoing budget cuts (linked to deficient or nonexistent professional training for staff), excessive caseloads (e.g., 200 cases per case manager) which generate worker stress and ill-served clients, lack of time to implement policy shifts, the maintenance of a factory-like logic in the delivery of services, pressure from an accountability climate along with its performance measures, and a competitive ranking system (Lurie, 2001; Morgen, 2001). As a result, interaction between welfare staff and clients tends to be infrequent and mechanical, leading to incomplete assessments when welfare recipients are directed either to education/training or to unsubsidized jobs (Jewell & Glaser, 2006; Lens, 2008). These organizational conditions of welfare departments enforce eligibility and compliance rather than provide integral attention to clients (Seccombe et al., 1998). Although these departments and their personnel work closely with community colleges to assign and monitor public assistance recipients in specific courses or short-training programs, the collaboration is complicated as caseworkers struggle to perform their role demands properly and organizational conditions hinder interaction with clients (Bloom, Anderson, Wavelet, Gardiner, & Fishman, 2002).

Community Colleges as Welfare Implementers. In the states where public assistance recipients are offered education and training opportunities, the role of community colleges as policy implementation structures is central because these institutions can develop curricular paths for educating and training people who need to acquire workplace skills or join career ladder initiatives. Yet, not in all states do community colleges engage in welfare programs enthusiastically. The market-oriented approach embedded in welfare policy has driven some community colleges to avoid participating because they consider the legislation premise to be a contradiction of their mission and philosophy (Mazzeo et al., 2003; Shaw et al., 2006). Community college personnel report that it becomes difficult to engage in fruitful educational experiences with welfare students enrolled in courses with a pre-established agenda which do not lead toward the Bachelor's degree (Levin & Montero-Hernandez, 2009). Work-first policy with its emphasis on quick job acquisition contradicts the community college mission of access to education and training opportunities as well as student development in cognitive and personal domains (Levin, 2007). However, in serving low-income students through work-first policy, community colleges are constrained as they cannot resort to typical supportive behavior patterns or encourage welfare participants who are students to behave as other students. Thus, welfare participants are not treated equitably and are denied some of the rights and privileges of fellow students, a form of injustice (Levin, 2007).

The programs, services, and aid community colleges do make available to welfare recipients are largely influenced by state policy that allocates funds to community colleges (Greenberg, Ashworth, Cebulla, & Walker, 2005; Meléndez et al., 2003). Some community colleges have found niches of support and ideological agreement within state welfare programs when state programs acknowledge the beneficial effects of education and training upon welfare clients and society. The California Community College (CCC) system, for example, relies upon budgeted dollars to employ CalWORKs coordinators charged with assisting students in reaching self-sufficiency. Even though select states set up their welfare policy to function collaboratively with community colleges—as is the case in California—college personnel are constrained when creating programs for welfare recipients who are unlikely to engage in long-term educational commitments. These constraints include reduced budgets and the lack of acknowledgment and support from some subgroups within the community college itself (McCormick, 2003).

For community colleges to provide services to welfare recipients, they must engage in multiple actions such as finding additional sources of financial support and forming interorganizational networks to overcome their lack of staff and resources all while complying with substantial data reporting requirements and administrative requirements. When community colleges do not receive sufficient state support through budget allocation, for example, it reduces welfare recipients' access to postsecondary education and diminishes the accessibility of credit-bearing higher-education courses—opportunities that could encourage greater long-term benefits for welfare recipients (Shaw et al., 2006). Without appropriate funding and recognition and in light of mission conflict, community college leadership and personnel must be highly motivated to embark on welfare program development under current policy conditions. Likewise, the outcomes and indeed the proclaimed success of programs are influenced by interactions between individuals and between program and policy.

INTERACTION WITH WELFARE RECIPIENTS: DISCRETIONARY ACTION AND PROGRAM DESIGN

The services that welfare recipients use and their opportunities to engage in education, training, or work have depended upon three factors: 1. the ideological components of welfare reform, 2. the organizational conditions under which policy is implemented, and 3. the program initiatives from organizational agents (i.e., community colleges and welfare offices) and the interactions between these and welfare clients. Sections one and two have discussed the first factors. This section completes the argument, examining the interaction structures of welfare agencies and community college programs that either depart from or comply with welfare policy, and noting the implications for welfare clients. Interpretations of policy ideology among organizational agents both in welfare agencies and community colleges and their decisions regarding how to implement policy cause different kinds of interaction with welfare recipients, forms of support, and outcomes. Central is the notion of agency or discretionary action, the freedom and power of organizational members to make decisions given a specific normative and ideological model (Hasenfeld, Ghose, & Larson, 2004; Lens, 2008). The concept of agency enables the understanding of variations in the interactions between organizational agents and welfare clients.

Interaction within Welfare Agencies

In welfare departments, workers' activities are often guided by ethical judgments; welfare staff are active interpreters and promoters of morally tinged rules, continually judging individuals' social worth, the causes of their predicament, and their desired outcomes (Hasenfeld, 2000). Welfare workers' discretion may have both positive and negative effects upon various dimensions of the institutional context: interactions with clients, establishment with other organizations, and use of sanctions (Lens, 2008). The discretionary power in welfare agencies may direct welfare recipients to low-wage, low-skill employment activities that stop their dependence upon welfare cash or they can be exposed to education/training experiences that enable them to expand their educational and career ambitions. For example, welfare workers can approve cash assistance for clients who were not employed and wanted to enroll in a community college (Morgen, 2001).

Studies of negative discretion in welfare departments show that the possibility of a racial bias on the part of welfare workers was associated with a larger use of sanctions among African American recipients (Hasenfeld et al., 2004; Lens, 2008). Studies in Illinois and Massachusetts

(Mazzeo et al., 2003) found that even when states had promoted a liberal ideology that acknowledged a human capital approach to fight poverty, when translated into practice caseworkers chose to communicate only the work-first message. That is, welfare recipients, even when their work requirements were fulfilled, rarely were told that education is an allowable benefit (Shaw et al., 2006). A compelling conclusion from studies on discretionary behavior within welfare departments is that the beliefs and values of frontline workers can become barriers to educational access among welfare clients (Mazzeo et al., 2003).

Programming in Community Colleges

Productive practices to assist public assistance recipients are hardly the result of the straightforward implementation of formal policy but arise from the dedication of relatively few individuals who excel in serving low-income students without the benefits of broad institutional support (Levin, 2007). Indeed, college personnel have overcome structural barriers for welfare recipients by creating and sustaining productive relationships with caseworkers and administrative staff in states' department of human services (Shaw et al., 2006) and at the local county level (Levin, 2007). For welfare-to-work programs, community colleges have engaged in institutional changes aimed to accommodate the demands of TANF participants. Institutional actions have focused on five areas: case management and support services, instruction and academic support services, instructional practices, curricular restructuring (e.g., grouping existing introductory vocational courses with remedial courses in basic education, life management skills, and job readiness), and interorganizational links with social service agencies and industry (Meléndez et al., 2003; Meléndez, Falcón, & Montrichard, 2004). One initiative in a California community college (New Visions) demonstrates how both discretionary action and formal programming are integrated in problematic ways when adapting the work-first ideology and serving public assistance recipients.

Established in the early 20th century, Riverside Community College (RCC) has a diverse student body and a long history in workforce development. Serving low-income students and developing and sustaining partnerships with local agencies and institutions are hallmarks of RCC's recent history. RCC's New Visions initiative is an example of programming created to serve TANF recipients advised to enroll in postsecondary education courses. Run out of its Workforce Development department, New Visions was established in 1998 and continued through 2002. The New Visions program consisted of a series of institutional policies and strategies of action through which college personnel at RCC aimed to align resources to serve public assistance recipients.

The conceptualization of the New Visions program by RCC appears to have echoed the framework of previous programs emphasizing the relevance of the human capital approach (i.e., long-term education and training programs) to help welfare clients transition from economic dependency to self-sufficiency (Katsinas, Banachowski, Bliss, & Short, 1999). "New Visions' goals were to prepare welfare recipients for community college occupational training programs, foster lifelong learning, and promote job advancement" (Fein & Beecroft, 2006, p. viii). However, in its actual implementation, the program aligned with the work-first ideology of welfare reform by requiring welfare students to participate actively in occupational training and job advancement through their active participation in occupational mini-programs (Fein & Beecroft, 2006). The view of education/training as instrumental rather than as a personal good or benefit diluted the human capital elements in the conceptualization of the program. Participants were required to work a minimum of 20 hours a week and attend class for 12 hours a week for a six-month period for a total of at least 32 hours/week (35 hours for two-parent cases) in work and training activities. New Visions was a three-phased program designed to provide welfare recipients with education and training to facilitate their ability to acquire and hold a job while increasing general mathematical and English language skills among others.

New Visions was designed and intended to help welfare clients with high school diplomas or equivalency understand and navigate academic culture and develop occupational abilities to gain self-sufficiency. The program's first phase consisted of a one-week orientation. The second phase of the program was a 24-week core of special preparatory classes in key academic subjects, computer skills, and career/life planning. The design of this phase incorporated six principles considered to be optimal for non-traditional students: (a) short courses (i.e., three six-week segments) enabling students to realize progress and learning; (b) academic instruction offered on the basis of applied learning and hands-on assignments; (c) instillation of basic competencies such as critical thinking, problem solving, communication, and study skills; (d) use of flexible schedules to accommodate work and study simultaneously; (e) promotion of individualized instruction delivered in group settings; and, (f) maintenance of small class sizes (i.e., no more than 10 students). The last phase of the program was a period of occupational training based on a series of occupational mini-programs. In contrast to the previous two phases, the New Visions report notes that the third phase was not fully designed and much was left to the county welfare offices (Fein & Beecroft, 2006).

Although well-intentioned and based on some established principles, New Visions fell short conceptually in other areas. The program's philosophy, determined by welfare-to-work policy (and likely necessarily so for CalWORKs funding), that immediate and long-term benefits would accrue to welfare recipients if they bridged both work and college simultaneously did not prove to be feasible given student characteristics, including their weak academic skills, and their need to work for financial support. Bowl (2003), in a Great Britain study of a similar population, found that the pressures of family and personal responsibilities and lack of financial resources can overwhelm low-income adults to the extent that they cannot participate effectively in education and training. At RCC and elsewhere, institutional, organizational, and policy effects were present in both welfare recipients' experiences and program formulation, setting a course that was difficult for the welfare client-as-student to overcome.

In New Visions, conceptual problems were compounded by practical ones. New Visions courses did not count toward RCC degrees or certifications because the courses were tailored to welfare recipients' conditions of education under welfare policy. The program participants were isolated from other RCC students both because of the rigidity of welfare students' welfare-to-work individual plans and the place allocated for the New Visions program in the RCC campus. Furthermore, the criteria for inclusion in the program—a high school credential—was a poor predictor of academic ability, and the program's academic expectations were unrealistic. Multiple determinants of the program's outcomes underscore the notable influence of inputs on the program. Because the students selected possessed low academic skills (even though they had graduated from high school), student attainment and advancement were limited. Furthermore, the work requirements of the program and the policy framework were not consistent with circumstances contributing to academic performance (Levin, Montero-Hernandez, & Cerven, 2009).

Participants' economic needs and pressures from employers, as well as welfare time limits, led participants to work "far more than the 20 hours a week required by county welfare policy, and this made it substantially harder for them to complete the program" (Fein & Beecroft, 2006, p. xvi). Working while studying prevented the low-income students from engaging in continual interactions with college personnel that could enable them to define educational goals, develop study skills, and understand the academic culture.

Long-term potential aside, the majority of the documented short-term outcomes for the New Visions program were deemed weak and unsatisfactory: substantial drop-out rate; no signs of participants taking steps onto career ladders at a higher rate than nonparticipants; and no significant increase in participants' earnings (Fein & Beecroft, 2006). Explanations about the shortfalls of the New Visions program involved participants' personal and family-related issues, changes in program preferences, loss of eligibility resulting in variable work hours, leaving the TANF program, moving from the area, and working while studying (Fein & Beecroft, 2006). Although most of the program outcomes were not promising, program participants did report positive experiences with New Visions. Additionally, an increase of their academic skills in math and language skills by one grade level was documented as was increased likelihood to continue taking courses at RCC.

As is evident from the case of RCC, community colleges' design and implementation of institutional policies and programs to coordinate with welfare reform are challenging activities. Notably, education/training programs such as New Visions tend to take place in the midst of competing approaches advocated by policymakers at the state and local levels, as well as federally (Katsinas et al., 1999). At the institutional level, community colleges that become education and training providers for welfare recipients must comply with two evaluation systems and two institutional logics. They have to satisfy local welfare-to-work program requirements to qualify for federal training grants. Furthermore, they have to comply with the requirements stated by education regulatory agencies—that is, state higher education agencies and regional accreditation councils (Meléndez et al., 2004).

Ultimately, in addition to the overarching guidelines and requirements of state policy, community colleges' development of institutional guidelines and strategies may depend upon the nature of programmatic integration with welfare departments. This stems from the necessity of both welfare agencies and community colleges developing strong partnerships that foster mutual understanding of the purposes, goals, and strategies of action of the welfare-to-work program and of the two remaining in regular communication (Fein & Beecroft, 2006). However, Katsinas and colleagues (1999) note that in the 1990s, mutual understanding between welfare agencies and community colleges was lacking; neither knew sufficiently about the nature, goals, and resources of the other. More current literature (Shaw et al., 2006) suggests that these obstacles remain. Even when working in coordination, as with the New Visions program, it is difficult for the entities to retain momentum in relationships and programs. Furthermore, just as community colleges' mission-based practices are not aligned with federal and state policy, they are not likely aligned with the goals of individual welfare departments. In spite of this misalignment and the inadequacies of programs such as New Visions, community colleges have a particular responsibility to provide the education and training that welfare recipients desperately need. But, how can they fulfill this call in an environment where economic marketplace values are the priority?

SUPPORTING WELFARE RECIPIENTS AS COMMUNITY COLLEGE STUDENTS

We have argued that the construction of organizational contexts and programs aimed to support low-income people is problematic within a policy framework that is not concerned with development of human capital (i.e., knowledge and skills), and certainly not sensitive to broader student development. Yet, other actions at the state level can have salient effects. Policy changes in local income maintenance offices in the state of California during the 1990s expanded the state JOBS program and modified policies to increase employment incentives and support. In CalWORKs, the development of support programs encouraging personal attention and sustained communication with welfare recipients has been found to be more effective in engendering understanding of the regulatory system and preventing punitive damages. Providing personalized attention improved welfare participants' knowledge of the rules that governed permissions and sanctions; when communication with welfare recipients was established primarily through formal notifications, and not through individual staff–welfare recipient communication, the percentage of individuals who understood how the normative framework worked was smaller (Hasenfeld et al., 2004).

Accommodation of public welfare students demands continual efforts to create organizational structures and foster behaviors, both in welfare agencies and community colleges. Three actions seem critical to respond to the needs of public assistance recipients: 1. construction of collaborative networks among organizations at the local and state level to gather information and services that enable low-income people to overcome their constraints and problematic situations; 2. fostering of adequate levels of professionalization and staff training in welfare agencies and community colleges to comprehend and respond to the specific demands of disadvantaged social groups; and, 3. adjustment of organizational design and structuring to find additional sources of financial support, define staff role functions, and create intentional forms of interaction among participants.

According to two practitioners involved with New Visions (Camak & Aycock, 2009), in the effort to improve welfare-to-work student support, RCC took the project (referred to as a pilot) experiences and improved practices for CalWORKs students as a whole. For example, the college worked toward discipline "ownership" of developmental courses with CalWORKs student enrollees, including the disciplines of English and Mathematics. Consistent with CCC policy, these courses—basic skills—now carry standard credit and are both funded and counted as disciplinary courses/enrollments. Priority registration for low-income students was also instituted, and RCC's approximately 300 CalWORKs students presently have access to registration for courses two weeks before most other students.

Notwithstanding these marked improvements, considerable problems continue for welfare students at RCC. These include a marginalization of this student population through allocating them a peripheral physical location for the program offices and classrooms, out of the mainstream of the college, and limiting their access to course registration and planning systems because most CalWORKs students do not have home Internet access and must use campus or other shared facilities for access. This "digital divide" hinders the educational experiences of low-income students (Camak & Aycock, 2009). In spite of efforts at the campus level to serve low-income students, specifically welfare recipients, as was the case at RCC, mismatches between the goals of welfare policy and community colleges abound as do misalignments between expectations for low-income students and their actual performance.

The heavy responsibility falls upon community colleges to educate and train the workforce and provide poor people an opportunity for a reasonable standard of living or at least a living wage. Yet, there are federal, state, county, and institutional policies that limit or negatively affect the education and training of poor people. More generally, low-income students, especially welfare recipients, are disadvantaged in a host of ways and community colleges are poorly funded and structurally constrained to transform lives mired in poverty. We conclude that there is a necessity to develop a policy framework that supports the design and implementation of institutional programs aimed to understand and respond to the characteristics and needs of welfare recipients. That is, federal and state policy for low-income students—in this case welfare recipients—must take into account the customary practices of community colleges and the realities of their students. These practices and the conditions of students are well-amplified in the scholarly and research literature on community colleges.

The post-structural framework enables us to capture the socially constructed nature of the State's practices and approaches to addressing such problems as the education of poor people. The structural bases of poverty (Massey, 2007) suggest that "individual responsibility"—a concept tied to new capitalism and welfare to work ideology—is a construct that fails to match a fitting solution with the problem. Furthermore, social benefits—a well-educated workforce, economic well-being for individuals, and even national security—require attention to the whole of a society, to its health, education, and freedoms. Poor people need and deserve education and training in order to live productive lives and to benefit society. As the community college is the "poor people's college," its practices are critical in the social and economic development of the nation's economically disadvantaged, and this development will shape the future of the United States as a whole.

NOTE

1. Work-study, employment, on-the-job training, and community service can count toward the 32-hour work/education requirement for the welfare recipients. Class preparation (study-time) may or may not be an allowable welfare-to-work activity, depending on each county's policy.

REFERENCES

Bailey, T., Jenkins, D., & Leinbach, T. (2005). *What we know about community college low-income and minority student outcomes: Descriptive statistics from national surveys.* New York: Community College Research Center.

Bane, M. J., & Ellwood, D. R. (1994). *Welfare realities: From rhetoric to reform.* Cambridge, MA: Harvard University Press.

Best, S., & Kellner, D. (1991). *Postmodern theory: Critical interrogations.* New York: The Guilford Press.

Bloland, H. G. (1995). Postmodernism and higher education. *The Journal of Higher Education, 66*(5), 521–559.

Bloom, D., Anderson, J., Wavelet, M., Gardiner, K. N., & Fishman, M. E. (2002). *New strategies to promote stable employment and career progression: An introduction to the employment retention and advancement project* (ERIC Document Reproduction Service No. ED469576). New York: Manpower Demonstration Research Corporation.

Bombach, K. (2001). Moving welfare families into economic self-sufficiency: A model from El Paso Community College. *New Directions for Community Colleges, 116*, 73–81.

Bowl, M. (2003). *Non-traditional entrants to higher education.* Stoke on Trent, UK: Trentham Books.

Brock, T., & Harknett, K. (1998). A comparison of two welfare-to-work case management models. *Social Service Review, 72*(4), 493–520.

Camak, S., & Aycock, G. (2009). Personal communication. February 26, 2009.

Carnoy, M. (1984). *The state and political thought.* Princeton, NJ: Princeton University Press.

Cohen, A., & Brawer, F. (2008). *The American community college* (5th ed.). San Francisco: Jossey-Bass.

Cox, K. L. C., & Spriggs, W. E. (2002). *Negative effects of TANF on college enrollment.* Washington, DC: National Urban League Institute for Opportunity and Equality. Available online at http://www.eric.ed.gov/ERICDocs/data/ericdocs2sql/content_storage_01/0000019b/80/1a/b4/a3.pdf

Epstein, B. (1998). Interpreting the world (without necessarily changing it). *New Politics, 6*(4), (Winter), 107–113.

Fein, D. J., & Beecroft, E. (2006). *College as a job advancement strategy: Final report on the New Visions self-sufficiency and lifelong learning project.* Bethesda, MD: Abt Associates.

Fording, R. C., Soss, J., & Schram, S. F. (2007). Devolution, discretion, and the effect of local political values on TANF sanctioning. *Social Service Review, 81*(2), 285–316.

Goedegebuure, L., Kaiser, F., Maassen, P., & De Weert, E. (1993). Higher education policy in international perspective: An overview. In L. Goedegebuure, F. Kaiser, P. Maassen, L. Meek, F. Van Vught, & E. De Weert (Eds.), *Higher education policy* (pp. 1–12). New York: Pergamon Press.

Greenberg, D., Ashworth, K., Cebulla, A., & Walker, R. (2005). When welfare-to-work programs seem to work well: Explaining why Riverside and Portland shine so brightly. *Industrial and Labor Relations Review, 59*(1), 34–50.

Hartmark, L., & Hines, E. (1986). Politics and policy in higher education: Reflection on the status of the field. In S. Gove & T. Stauffer (Eds.), *Policy controversies in higher education* (pp. 3–26). New York: Greenwood Press.

Hasenfeld, Y. (2000). Organizational forms as moral practices: The case of welfare departments. *Social Service Review, 74*(3), 329–351.

Hasenfeld, Y., Ghose, T., & Larson, K. (2004). The logic of sanctioning welfare recipients: An empirical assessment. *Social Service Review, 78*(2), 304–319.

Horn, L., & Nevill, S. (2006). *Profile of undergraduates in U.S. postsecondary education institutions: 2003–04: With special analysis of community college students* (NCES 2006-184). Washington, DC: U.S. Department of Education, National Center for Education Statistics.

Jacobs, J. A., & Winslow, S. (2003). Welfare reform and enrollment in postsecondary education. *The Annals of the American Academy of Political and Social Science, 586*(1), 194–217.

Jewell, C. J., & Glaser, B. E. (2006). Toward a general analytic framework: Organizational settings, policy goals, and street-level behavior. *Administration and Society, 38*(3), 335–364.

Johnson, M. A., Ketch, V., Chow, J., & Austin, M. J. (2006). Implementing welfare-to-work services: A study of staff decision-making. *Families in Society, 87*(3), 317–328.

Katsinas, S. G., Banachowski, G., Bliss, T. J., & Short, J. M. (1999). Community college involvement in welfare-to-work programs. *Community College Journal of Research and Practice, 23*(4), 401–421.

Lens, V. (2008). Welfare and work sanctions: Examining discretion on the front lines. *Social Service Review, 82*(2), 197–222.

Levin, J. S. (2007). *Non-traditional students and community colleges: The conflict of justice and neo-liberalism.* New York: Palgrave Macmillan.

Levin, J. S., & Montero Hernandez, V. (2009). *Community colleges and their students: Co-construction and organizational identity.* New York: Palgrave Macmillan.

Levin, J. S., Montero-Hernandez, V., & Cerven, C. (2009). Overcoming adversity: Community college students and work. In L. Perna (Ed.), *Toward a more complete understanding of "work" for today's undergraduates.* Sterling, VA: Stylus.

Lurie, I. (2001). State implementation of TANF: Where do we stand in 2001. *Evaluation and Program Planning, 24,* 379–388.

Massey, D. S. (2007). *Categorically unequal: The American stratification system.* New York: Russell Sage Foundation.

Mathur, A. (2002). *Credentials count: How California's community colleges help parents move from welfare to self-sufficiency.* Washington, DC: Prepared by the California Community Colleges Chancellor's Office for the Center for Law and Social Policy.

Mazzeo, C., Rab, S., & Eachus, S. (2003). Work-first or work-study. Welfare reform, state policy and access to postsecondary education. *Annals of the American Academy of Political and Social Science, 586,* 144–171.

McCormick, L. (2003). Coping with workfare: The experience of New York City's community colleges. *Community College Journal of Research and Practice, 27*(6), 531–547.

Meléndez, E., Falcón, L., & Bivens, J. (2003). Community college participation in welfare programs: Do state policies matter? *Community College Journal of Research and Practice, 27*(3), 203–223.

Meléndez, E., Falcón, L. M., & Montrichard, A. D. (2004). Lessons from community college programs targeting welfare recipients. *New Directions for Community Colleges, 127,* 61–77.

Meyers, M. K., Glaser, B., & Donald, K. M. (1998). On the front lines of welfare delivery: Are workers implementing policy reforms? *Journal of Policy Analysis and Management, 17*(1), 1–22.

Morgen, S. (2001). The agency of welfare workers: Negotiating devolution, privatization, and the meaning of self-sufficiency. *American Anthropologist, New Series, 103*(3), 747–761.

Ortner, S. (2006). *Anthropology and social theory. Culture, power, and the acting subject.* London: Duke Univeristy Press.

Pusser, B. (2008). The state, the market, and the institutional estate: Revisiting contemporary authority relations in higher education. In J. C. Smart (Ed.), *Higher education: Handbook of theory and research* (Vol. XXIII). New York: Springer.

Rose, N. E. (2000). Scapegoating poor women: An analysis of welfare reform. *Journal of Economic Issues, 34*(1), 143–157.

Schlager, E., & Blomquist, W. (1995). A comparison of three emerging theories of the policy process. *Political Research Quarterly, 49*(3), 651–672.

Schram, S. (1993). Postmodern policy analysis: Discourse and identity in welfare policy. *Policy Sciences, 26*(3), 249–270.

Scott, W. R. (1998). *Organizations: Rational, nature and open systems* (4th ed.). Upper Saddle River, NJ: Prentice Hall.

Seccombe, K., James, D., & Battle Walters, K. (1998). "They think you ain't much of nothing": The social construction of the welfare mother. *Journal of Marriage and the Family, 60*(4), 849–865.

Sennett, R. (2006). *The culture of the new capitalism.* New Haven, CT: Yale University Press.

Shaw, K., Goldrick-Rab, S., Mazzeo, C., & Jacobs, J. A. (2006). *Putting poor people to work: How the work-first idea eroded college access for the poor.* New York: Russell Sage Foundation.

Shaw, K. M., & Rab, S. (2003). Market rhetoric versus reality in policy and practice: The Workforce Investment Act and access to community college education and training. *Annals of the American Academy of Political and Social Science, 586*, 172–193.

Skocpol, T. (1985). Bring the state back in: Strategies in current research. In P. Evans, D. Reuschemeyer, & T. Skocpol (Eds.), *Bring the state back in* (pp. 3–37). New York: Cambridge University Press.

Slaughter, S. (1990). *The higher learning.* Buffalo: State University of New York Press.

U.S. Department of Health and Human Services: Office of Family Assistance. (2009). *Caseload data 2008.* Retrieved July 10, 2009, from www.acf.hhs.gov

Weick, K. (1976). Educational organizations as loosely coupled systems. *Administrative Science Quarterly, 21*, 1–19.

IV

Persistence, Success, and Graduation

8

DEMOGRAPHY IS NOT DESTINY

*What Colleges and Universities Can Do to Improve
Persistence Among Low-Income Students*

JENNIFER ENGLE AND MARY G. LYNCH

A college education is widely considered the key to achieving economic success and social mobility in American society. Higher levels of educational attainment are related to higher incomes and lower rates of unemployment, and the earnings gap between high school and college graduates only widens over time (College Board, 2004; Institute for Higher Education Policy, 2005). While access to higher education has expanded dramatically in recent years, students from low-income backgrounds remain at a distinct disadvantage. By age 24, only 12 percent of students from low-income families will earn a Bachelor's degree, compared with 73 percent of their higher-income peers. This gap in college degree attainment is explained partly by lower college-going rates among low-income students. However, even low-income students who do enroll in college are less likely to persist through degree completion than their higher-income peers (Mortenson, 2007).

Traditionally, higher attrition rates from college for low-income students have been explained as almost entirely due to factors related to the students themselves. Previous research has shown that low-income students do tend to have fewer academic, social, and financial resources available to them than their peers, which negatively affects the extent to which they can interact with and succeed in the college environment. Academically, low-income students have often not been prepared well for college by their K-12 schools. Socially, low-income students may not have the support systems in place that other students do, particularly if they are the first in their families and communities to go to college. Financially, many low-income students have to work to support themselves and their families in order to afford college. Furthermore, low-income students tend to have fewer choices about where to attend college due primarily to financial constraints. As a result, they are more likely to attend less selective public colleges, which themselves have fewer economic resources, serve students with greater academic and financial need, and have lower overall graduation rates (Berkner, He, & Cataldi, 2002).

More recent research has shown, however, that student and institutional "input" characteristics do not fully explain lower graduation rates for low-income students and the institutions that serve them. Mortenson (1997) found that considerable variation in graduation rates remained even after controlling for characteristics such as the academic profile of incoming freshmen and the typical enrollment patterns of students (e.g., how many students attended part-time). According to his analyses, some colleges and universities perform better than expected given the characteristics of their student body, while others perform worse. Mortenson attributes the differences between such "higher-" and "lower-performing" schools to institutional efforts (i.e., policies and practices) to provide supportive academic and social environments that foster student persistence and degree attainment.

Using this type of analysis, a new body of research—including the study discussed in this chapter—has sought to identify and study "higher-performing" colleges and universities in order to determine and describe the conditions that contribute to student success at these institutions (AASCU, 2005; Carey, 2004, 2005a, 2005b; Kuh, Kinzie, Schuh, Whitt, & Associates, 2005; The Pell Institute, 2004, 2007). Thus, while most of the existing literature focuses on the student "input" characteristics that cannot change, we propose a new research emphasis on factors that institutions can control because what colleges do matters—a lot—to whether their students succeed.

This chapter will discuss major findings from research conducted by the Pell Institute (2007) to study public four-year institutions that serve large numbers of low-income students and that graduate their students at better than expected rates after taking the diverse academic and economic backgrounds of their student bodies into account. By conducting case studies of these institutions, we were able to identify policies and practices that improve overall retention and graduation rates at colleges and universities that serve large populations of low-income students, which we will share in detail here.

We also will discuss our recommendations for how colleges and universities can improve on these practices, some of which are already widely used on many campuses, to better serve low-income students. Despite the large numbers of low-income students enrolled in the colleges we studied, many of them designed programs focused on improving *overall* retention and graduation rates, assuming that all students would benefit equally from institutional efforts. By talking with low-income students themselves, we learned that these programs cannot be fully effective unless they specifically account for the needs of low-income students. As Paul Thayer (2000) has said, retention "strategies that work for first-generation and low-income students are likely to be successful for the general student population as well. By contrast, strategies that are designed for general campus populations without taking into account the special circumstances and characteristics of first-generation and low-income students will not often be successful for the latter."

In light of Thayer's claim, this chapter reviews the practices and policies that proved effective in promoting overall student success at the institutions in this study and deconstructs whether they work for low-income students and how they could work better.

WHAT ARE THE CONDITIONS THAT SUPPORT STUDENT SUCCESS?

In 2005, the Pell Institute set out to identify promising retention practices by studying 14 higher educational institutions that serve large numbers of low-income students. A diverse group of institutions with different characteristics, missions, geographic locations, and demographic compositions was selected to reflect the breadth of American higher education. Extensive research, including site visits and interviews with administrators, faculty, staff, and students, was conducted at each institution to help develop an understanding of the policies and practices that support student success. These findings, with support from the existing literature on student retention, provide a strong understanding of existing retention policies and practices and how they can support student success. These promising practices can be categorized into several areas: 1. focus on the first year, 2. monitoring student progress, 3. improving instruction in gatekeeping courses, 4. special programs for under served populations, and 5. creating a culture of success.

Focus on the First Year

Building on Tinto's research, the high-performing institutions in the study have directed many of their retention efforts at improving the freshman year experience in order to help entering students become "integrated into the social and academic communities of the college and acquire the skills and knowledge needed to become successful learners in those communities" (Tinto, 2003). Previous evaluations of first-year programs have demonstrated largely positive effects on student performance and persistence (see Lotkowski, Robbins, & Noeth, 2004; Pascarella & Terenzini, 2005; Smith, MacGregor, Matthews, & Gabelnick, 2004; Upcraft, Gardner, & Barefoot, 2005). Accordingly, almost all of the high-performing institutions in this study had well-developed first-year programs—such as freshman orientation programs, freshman success courses, freshman interest groups, and first-year learning communities—in which student participation was mandatory or high.

For example, at one high-performing research institution, the Provost initiated a Freshman Focus program in response to scores on the National Study of Student Engagement (NSSE) that indicated low levels of student engagement in class and on campus. The purpose of this living and learning community for first-year students is to integrate students' academic and student life experiences by linking academic affairs and student affairs programmatically. As part of the program, freshmen are enrolled in at least two courses with other students who live on their floors in the residence halls. A major goal of the program is to help faculty change the way they teach by utilizing more active and collaborative learning methods to facilitate better connections between course material and students' experiences on campus.

The President at one of the higher-performing institutions has made improving students' curricular and co-curricular experiences during the freshman year the centerpiece of the university's master plan to improve retention and graduation rates. The President's newly implemented First Year Experience (FYE) program consists of three major initiatives. The first is a mandatory summer orientation program where all freshmen receive advising, take placement tests, and register for courses prior to the fall semester. The second initiative involves enrolling every freshman in one FYE course per semester during the first year. FYE courses are general education classes that limit enrollment to 20 students, which allows for more engaging and active teaching styles that increase interaction between students and faculty, as well as among students. FYE classes also integrate involvement in co-curricular activities into course content in order to connect student learning inside and outside of the classroom. Juniors and seniors serve as peer mentors to freshmen, and as teaching assistants to faculty in FYE courses. FYE peer mentors and faculty are "hand-selected" to participate in the program and receive extensive training and support. The third initiative involves residence hall living and learning communities, which provide support services such as counseling and tutoring in the dorms to help students make the academic, social, and personal transition to college.

Monitoring Student Progress

According to Thomas (1990), advising is the most important component of any institutional retention effort. However, a recent survey by ACT and the National Academic Advising Association (NACADA) found that many colleges and universities are underutilizing and poorly administering their advising programs as well as failing to promote advising as a way to increase retention (Habley, 2004 as cited in Lotkowski et al., 2004). Furthermore, several national studies indicate that the part of their educational experience with which students are least satisfied is advising (cited in Kuh et al., 2005). Recent large-scale studies have found that institutions with high graduation rates have proactive advising programs (i.e., "intrusive" advising and early warning systems) in place that actively monitor student performance, intervene early when students experience academic difficulty, and follow-up on student progress (AASCU, 2005; Kuh et al., 2005; The Pell Institute, 2004). Evaluation research of such programs, while limited, does suggest positive outcomes, particularly for low-income and other under-resourced students (Abrams, Krotseng, & Hossler, 1990; Karp & Logue, 2002–2003; Mann, Hunt, & Alford, 2003–2004; Volp, Hill, & Frazier, 1998; Willett, 2002).

Most of the institutions in the study that proved successful at graduating students had systems in place to monitor student progress and to intervene when student performance was low. These monitoring programs took a variety of forms. In some institutions, strict academic progress and probation policies alerted students to problems at the end of the semester, although intervention was often voluntary and sometimes too late. Other institutions took a more proactive and less punitive approach with early warning systems in place that alerted students and advisers to problems in time to develop a plan of action to improve performance. Students on academic probation at these schools often were required to sign performance contracts that committed them to receiving advising, counseling, and tutoring and/or enrolling in study skills workshops/courses.

One example of a successful monitoring program is an intensive advising system developed at a high performing institution for students committed to graduating in four years. As part of this program, the university ensures freshmen that they will graduate in four years if they meet the program requirements, or the rest of their tuition is free. Students involved in the program must sign a contract that commits them to meeting with their adviser at least once a semester prior to registration and to consulting their adviser before making any changes to their schedule. Participants must declare a major upon entry to the program, maintain a full-time schedule each semester with courses that apply toward degree requirements, and meet the grade point requirements defined by their academic programs. Students also accept responsibility for registering on time for classes and financial aid.

In return, the university guarantees that the courses students need to complete degree requirements will be offered when they need to take them. If graduation is delayed due to course unavailability, the university will either allow students to substitute a comparable course or waive tuition to allow students to take the course for free the next semester. Advisers—and students—can keep track of progress to degree using online technology that supports the program. One adviser says she continuously evaluates each student's degree plan and notifies the student if he or she is not on track. This process helps to identify and address problems earlier. Internal research shows that students who participate in the program are nearly twice as likely to graduate in four years.

Another high-performing institution in the study developed an effective advising program for students who are at risk for attrition because they have not declared majors. This institution offers a structured program that allows students who enter the university without a major to explore different fields of study. Typically, 20 to 30 percent of all freshmen enter through the program. Academic advisers work closely with students in the program to help them identify their interests, values, and abilities through extensive career and personal counseling. Students may remain in the program through the first-semester of their sophomore year, at which point they must declare a major in order to register for the next semester.

Improving Instruction in "Gatekeeping" Courses

Institutions provide a wide range of academic and social support programs, many of which are geared toward under-resourced populations like low-income students. Developmental education programs, when properly administered and well-designed and taught, have been shown to improve persistence and graduation rates for underprepared students. Recent research also demonstrates the effectiveness of Supplemental Instruction (SI) programs, which provide peer-assisted academic support to students in introductory "gatekeeping" courses with traditionally high failure rates (see Lotkowski et al., 2004; Pascarella & Terenzini, 2005; Upcraft et al., 2005).

A number of the successful institutions in the study have focused attention on these "gatekeeping" introductory courses with low attendance and high failure rates. Many of them also have undertaken efforts to improve student success rates in general education and developmental courses by increasing opportunities for individualized instruction and interaction between faculty and students as well as among students. Despite the large size of the institutions in the study, the majority of higher-performing institutions offer relatively small classes taught by full-time faculty members, even at the introductory level. Most of the institutions also keep class sizes "small" in introductory courses by offering supplemental instruction.

For example, one Hispanic-Serving Institution in the study developed an initiative to improve instruction in general education and remedial courses through the Building Engagement and Attainment in Minority Students (BEAMS) program. At this school, a BEAMS team—comprised of seven academic faculty and student affairs staff—devised and implemented a plan to use a block roster model to combine the first-year experience course with developmental and introductory math courses for freshmen. Under the direction of the BEAMS team, the Title V funds were used to recruit and train faculty to teach the linked courses. Faculty were provided with stipends from grant funds to attend three one-day workshops in which they collaborated with each other to develop common syllabi and assignments for the linked courses. The BEAMS team "hand-picked" faculty members who were "motivated to make change" to participate in the project. Internal research shows that students who enroll in the linked courses have higher grade point averages and retention rates than those who do not enroll. The institutions would like to expand the program to include more students (less than half of incoming students currently participate), but lack the resources to do so at this time.

Another higher-performing institution has undertaken a major effort to improve the introductory algebra curriculum with a focus on addressing the low attendance and high failure rates in algebra as well as students' tendency to "put off" the required algebra course until their senior year. The lead faculty assembled a team of math instructors and graduate assistants to revise and standardize the algebra curriculum; the team continues to meet on a monthly basis to review implementation of the new curriculum and other aspects of the program.

The program includes more accurate placement testing and continuous assessment of student progress throughout the semester, with the chance to re-take exams, as well as additional faculty-student contact hours through required tutorials. Faculty are further encouraged to conduct one-on-one tutoring sessions, participate as math lab tutors, request homework online, and conduct homework problem sessions. Internal research demonstrates the program has increased students' grades and pass rates in the algebra course.

Special Programs for Underserved Populations

A number of colleges and universities offer comprehensive support programs to at-risk students. For example, Student Support Services (SSS), one of the federally-funded TRIO programs, provides services such as tutoring; academic, career, and personal counseling; and mentoring to low-income, first-generation, and disabled college students. A national evaluation found that SSS programs, which operate on more than 900 campuses across the country, have a positive impact on participants' performance and persistence in college (Chaney, Muraskin, Cahalan, & Rak, 1997).

Based on the proven success of such targeted programs, almost all of the institutions in the study provided programs for underserved and under-resourced student populations that incorporated many of the "best practices" in the retention literature. Such programs provide structured and intensive support to participants through bridge and orientation programs, intrusive advising with early warning systems, mentoring and tutoring programs, and, in some cases, grant aid. As a condition of their participation in such programs, students also often are required to attend full-time, live on campus, enroll in freshman seminar courses, and/or join campus organizations. Internal program evaluations show that students who participate in these programs have much higher retention and graduation rates than the overall student population.

For example, one research institution in the study participates in a long-running state-funded program that was created in the 1960s to increase access to and success in higher education for economically and educationally disadvantaged students. In an effort to recruit low-income students, the institution works with guidance counselors in high schools in economically depressed areas and provides transportation for low-income students to visit the campus. Once admitted, program participants are required to attend a residential summer bridge program and orientation to ease the transition to college life. The program continues during the academic year, when the students receive grant aid and support services such as personal, academic, and career counseling, tutoring and study skills workshops, and peer mentoring. Additionally, the program sponsors a student organization that allows participants to organize and advocate for themselves, both on campus and with the state legislature. Student satisfaction with the program is high, and so too are student outcomes. Participants graduate at higher rates than low-income peers who do not participate in the program and within 10 percentage points of the overall student population.

Creating a Culture of Success

In the institutions we studied, we found that the programs described above are necessary but not sufficient to improve student retention. As Tinto (2003) has said, "the ability of an institution to retain students lies less in the formal programs they devise than in the underlying commitment toward students which directs their activities" (p. 7). The high-performing institutions in this study do not merely "plug-in best practices" from the retention literature to improve their graduation rates; rather, these institutions are characterized by an organizational culture that promotes student success (AASCU, 2005; Carey, 2005a; Kuh et al., 2005). Creating this type of culture requires strong leadership from top college administrators. Campus leaders must prioritize improving retention as an institutional goal and consistently demonstrate their commitment to it through their words and actions. In the words of one Chancellor, "We recruit graduates, not just students. We make a commitment to students and we provide the resources they need—we genuinely want them to succeed."

Informed by the research literature as well as by internal data, the best of the administrators on the study campuses have assessed the problem, set benchmarks, created an action plan, and allocated the necessary resources to achieve their retention goals. These leaders demonstrated the level of their commitment to retention by not only allocating the necessary resources (even when scarce) to retention programs, but also by incentivizing and rewarding all members of the campus community, particularly faculty, to participate in as well as take ownership of retention efforts.

In addition, campus leaders in high-performing institutions also worked to ensure that quality collaboration and coordination occurred throughout their campuses. To be successful, top administrators must strive to organize their retention efforts into an intentional, structured, and proactive campus-wide program that requires coordination and collaboration among all units focused on the shared goal of improving student success (AASCU, 2005; Kuh et al., 2005; Pell Institute, 2007). This often manifests itself through campus-wide committees, task forces, or offices, which were present on nearly all of the high-performing institutions in this study.

Together with committed leadership, these coordination efforts can help contribute to an overall culture of success on a campus. Many high-performing institutions, in our study and others, do not necessarily perceive their success as a product of a "student retention effort" per se, but rather a focus on improving the student learning environment (AASCU, 2005). The colleges and universities in these studies were decidedly committed to an institutional mission that put students and learning at the center. There was a pervasive belief on these campuses that all students have the potential to succeed and should be held to high expectations; the campuses reinforced this belief by recruiting and hiring faculty and staff who were also committed to student learning and success. There was also the sense that the colleges and universities in these studies were "comfortable with the mission of serving their current students" (AASCU, 2005). While all of these institutions expressed a desire to improve themselves, they felt that they—and their students—were special (AASCU, 2005; Kuh et al., 2005).

DECONSTRUCTING AND RECONSTRUCTING LOW-INCOME PRACTICES AND PROGRAMS

The higher-performing institutions in our study were all graduating their students at higher than expected rates—even after accounting for the diverse academic and economic backgrounds of their student bodies. All of the institutions had, as discussed, implemented successful policies and practices to increase their retention and graduation rates. In most cases, there was also strong commitment from top leadership to make improving retention a top priority on their campuses.

Yet, when we spoke to low-income students themselves, we found that the institutions had work left to do to ensure that their efforts more effectively targeted and assisted low-income students. Here, we recommend that institutions deconstruct the policies and practices they have designed to boost overall retention and graduation rates in order to ensure that they meet the needs of their low-income students as well.

Reach-Out to Students About the Services That Exist

As the first in their families to go to college, many low-income students told us that they either weren't aware of the programs and services that existed on campus, or they didn't understand the function these programs served or how they could benefit from them. As one student said, "I know what offices there are, but I don't know what they do." As a result, low-income students often do not know where or who to turn to when they need help.

For instance, we were told that when low-income students on one campus receive a notice that they are not making satisfactory academic progress or when they incur unexpected financial hardship, they often believe they have to drop out because they are not familiar with the resources available that could help them improve their performance and/ or secure emergency aid.

Colleges need to reach out to low-income students—early and often—with information about the services available on campus. Orientation is not enough, as we discuss below. Faculty—as well as advisers—need to be well-informed too in order to make appropriate referrals to their students since for many low-income students the only time they spend on campus is in the classroom. As the director of the Student Support

Services program at one of the institutions said, "You have to take it to the students."

Address Cost as a Barrier to Using the Services

A number of programs and services, such as orientation and tutoring, available on the campuses in our study charge a fee for participation. With regards to summer orientation in particular, students often reported that they could not afford the cost of participating in the program and/or they and their parents could not afford to take time off work in order to participate. While a number of institutions offered fee waivers to participate in orientation, students said they were unaware of the waivers or did not believe they would qualify. In addition, there were other costs associated with attending the orientation program (i.e., related to travel) that were not waived that low-income students could not afford.

When low-income students do not attend orientation, they miss an important opportunity to learn about the programs and services the institution has to offer. When low-income students do attend orientation, we were told they often attend the last summer session or the session offered right before the term begins, which causes them to "miss out" in terms of the course scheduling and housing options that are still available. They also miss the chance to take placement exams early enough to enroll in remedial courses over the summer, which can put them behind in their studies before they even start.

At one of the institutions in the study, students who apply late and/or attend the last orientation session often "get stuck" in the least desirable dorm on campus. According to student affairs staff, these late enrollees also often face greater challenges to persisting in college, including academic under-preparation or inadequate financial resources. The effect is that there is an entire dorm on campus with a large population of under-resourced students. In response, the institution plans to provide extra resources, such as tutoring and computer and writing labs, to the entire dorm. The institution also plans to use "an intrusive advising model" to track the progress of dorm residents. The staff involved in the project hope that offering additional services and support to the entire dorm will reduce the stigma that students may experience when asking for and receiving extra help.

Offer Services at Convenient Times for Working Students

Low-income students who live and work off-campus often told us they cannot take advantage of services or programs available at their institutions because these are not offered at times that are convenient for them.

Students described the offices on one campus as "shutting down at 4pm," even though many courses are offered in the evening to accommodate students' work schedules. Students at another institution said they relied on the services offered by the ethnic programs because these were open until midnight, while other offices on campus closed at 5pm. Low-income students also said they are often unable to attend events or join organizations on campus due to time constraints. At least one institution was making an attempt to increase the availability of services to its commuter student population by extending the hours of operation at the learning center to include evenings and weekends. This institution also offers events during a scheduled "free hour" between morning and afternoon classes twice a week to help its students connect with campus life. Institutions might also try to incorporate or coordinate more services or events with classroom activities in order to make use of the only time that some low-income students spend on campus.

Remove the Stigma Associated with Using Such Services

Staff members who work with underserved populations often told us that low-income students face difficulties with seeking and asking for help. As the Director of a provisional admissions program said, "Students need help dealing with their anger about being in a special program." Staff members also said that low-income students do not ask for help because they fear exposing or stigmatizing themselves as failures. Staff in several Student Support Services programs told us that they "provide students with scripts" or "conduct role plays" in order to help students get over the intimidation factor of asking faculty and others for assistance.

Furthermore, students and staff said that the services targeted toward under-resourced populations may be stigmatized themselves because the programs that offer them operate "on the margins" of campus. Separate programs for under-resourced populations can also segregate low-income and minority students, which can make it more difficult for them to integrate into campus life at the conclusion of the programs, many of which only support students through the end of the freshman year.

Offer All Services to All Students

At a number of the universities in our study, not all students were offered the same options to participate in programs and services that may improve their chances of success. At some of the institutions, such programs and services may only be available in certain departments or colleges or these may only be offered to students participating in special programs.

At other universities, the services or programs may not be aligned with the advising systems, for instance, which limits the number of students who are referred to them. Some institutions also lack adequate resources to provide the services to all students who need them. As we observed, low-income and other students may "fall through the cracks" when services and programs lack centralization, coordination, or resources. We were also told that low-income students are less likely to participate in "voluntary" or "self-service" programs than their peers. At one institution in particular, staff estimate that almost 90 percent of freshmen attended the voluntary summer orientation program. However, when asked, they said that the 10 percent who did not were likely low-income students who could not afford to travel to or take time off work to attend it, which the students confirmed for us. Thus, programs and services intended to improve retention are most likely to reach low-income students when they are offered to and/or mandatory for all students. However, it is important to recognize and remove the barriers that limit the participation of low-income students before making it mandatory.

To reiterate Thayer, we recommend that colleges and universities design retention strategies that work for first-generation and low-income students since these are likely to be successful for the general student population as well. The reverse, however, is not necessarily true.

CONCLUSION

The large, public universities in this study were instituting some of the best practices that we know from the research are successful at increasing student retention and graduation rate— such as first-year programming, intrusive and early advising models, and course redesign for developmental and entry-level classes. These universities also had top leaders in place who were committed to creating an institution-wide culture of student success. Yet, despite their best intentions, these efforts were not always reaching as many of the low-income students on their campuses as possible. Using the post-structural framework provided by this book, institutions can and should deconstruct their retention practices in order to ensure that they are designed for and accessible to low-income and other under-served students.

In this era of college rankings, there is an increasing amount of pressure on public universities to compete for prestige—amongst themselves and with more heavily endowed private institutions. As a result, the leaders of many public institutions are focusing on improving their graduation rates—and their standings in the rankings—by admitting so-called "better" students rather than serving their current students better. Yet, as we found in our study, there are institutions that are serving large numbers of low-income students and serving them well. While there is room for improvement, it is important to acknowledge that it is indeed possible for public institutions to serve as both a point of access for low-income students and an exemplar of excellence. Unfortunately, few of the institutions in this study recognized, or were recognized by others for, their success with low-income students given "objective" graduation rate standards, which fail to account for student "inputs" as we did in our analysis. This needs to change.

As the President of one of the study universities said, "The national rankings should acknowledge differences in inputs and measure the quality of outputs in terms of the value added." Several efforts to revise ranking systems are currently underway. For example, an alternative ranking system developed by the *Washington Monthly* (2006) magazine ranks colleges and universities based on how well they promote social mobility among low-income students. According to the editors, "Rankings reflect priorities and they also set them. By enshrining one set of priorities, such as those set by *U.S. News*, colleges neglect the ones we think are most important." While such efforts are laudable, the real impetus for change must come from the state and university systems. Large, public universities are more likely to re-align their priorities toward access if systems and states provide better incentives and rewards for serving and graduating underrepresented populations. Given the rapidly changing demographics of the pool of future college students, with growing numbers of low-income and other under-served populations, such realignment is imperative.

REFERENCES

Abrams, B., Krotseng, M., & Hossler, D. (1990). Using retention research in enrollment management. In D. Hossler & J. P. Bean (Eds.), *The strategic management of college enrollments* (pp. 202–224). San Francisco: Jossey-Bass.

American Association of State Colleges and Universities (AASCU). (2005). *Student success in state colleges and universities: A matter of culture and leadership.* Washington, DC: Author.

Berkner, L., He, S., & Cataldi, E. F. (2002). *Descriptive summary of 1995–96 beginning postsecondary students: Six years later.* Washington, DC: National Center for Education Statistics.

Carey, K. (2004). *A matter of degrees: Improving graduation rates in four-year colleges and universities.* Washington, DC: Education Trust.

Carey, K. (2005a). *Choosing to improve: Voices from colleges and universities with better graduation rates.* Washington, DC: Education Trust.

Carey, K. (2005b). *One step from the finish line: Higher college-graduation rates are within our reach.* Washington, DC: Education Trust.

Chaney, B., Muraskin, L., Cahalan, M., & Rak, R. (1997). *National study of Student Support Services.* Washington, DC: U.S. Department of Education.

College Board. (2004). *Education pays 2004: The benefits of higher education for individuals in society.* New York: Author.

Habley, W. R. (Ed.). (2004). *The status of academic advising: Findings from the ACT sixth national survey* (Monograph No. 10). Manhattan, KS: National Academic Advising Association.

Institute for Higher Education Policy. (2005). *The investment payoff: A 50-state analysis of the public and private benefits of higher education*. Washington, DC: Author.

Karp, R., & Logue, R. (2002–2003). Retention initiative for unscheduled sophomores and unscheduled readmits. *Journal of College Student Retention: Research, Theory, & Practice, 4*(2), 147–172.

Kuh, G. D., Kinzie, J., Schuh, J. H., Whitt, E. J., & Associates. (2005). *Student success in college: Creating conditions that matter*. San Francisco: Jossey-Bass.

Lotkowski, V. A., Robbins, S. B., & Noeth, R. J. (2004). *The role of academic and non-academic factors in improving college retention*. New York: ACT.

Mann, J. R., Hunt, M. D., & Alford, J. G. (2003–2004). Monitored probation: A program that works. *Journal of College Student Retention: Research, Theory & Practice, 5*(3), 245–254.

Mortenson, T. (1997). *Actual versus predicted institutional graduation rates for 1100 colleges and universities*. Oskaloosa, IA: Postsecondary Education OPPORTUNITY.

Mortenson, T. (2007). *Bachelor's degree attainment by age 24 by family income quartiles, 1970 to 2005*. Oskaloosa, IA: Postsecondary Education OPPORTUNITY.

Pascarella, E. T., & Terenzini, P. T. (2005). *How college affects students: A third decade of research*. San Francisco: Jossey-Bass.

The Pell Institute for the Study of Opportunity in Higher Education. (2004). *Raising the graduation rates of low-income college students*. Washington, DC: Author.

The Pell Institute for the Study of Opportunity in Higher Education. (2007). *Demography is not destiny: Increasing the graduation rates of low-income college students at large, public universities*. Washington, DC: Author.

Smith, B. L., MacGregor, J., Matthews, R., & Gabelnick, F. (2004). *Learning communities: Reforming undergraduate education*. San Francisco: Jossey-Bass.

Thayer, P. (May 2000). Retention of students from first-generation and low-income backgrounds. *Opportunity Outlook*. Washington, DC: Council for Opportunity in Education.

Thomas, R. O. (1990). Programs and activities for improved retention. In D. Hossler & J. P. Bean (Eds.), *The strategic management of college enrollments* (pp. 186–211). San Francisco: Jossey-Bass.

Tinto, V. (2003). *Student success and the building of involving educational communities*. Higher Education Monograph Series, Syracuse University, No. 2. Syracuse, NY: Syracuse University.

Upcraft, M. L., Gardner, J. N., & Barefoot, B. O. (2005). *Challenging and supporting the first year student*. San Francisco: Jossey-Bass Higher Education Series.

Volp, P. M., Hill, T. L., & Frazier, C. L. (1998). Using telephone calls as examples of care to promote student success and retention. *Journal of the Freshman Year Experience & Students in Transition, 10*(1), 73–88.

Washington Monthly. (September 2006). *The Washington Monthly's annual college guide*. Retrieved on June 13, 2009 from www.washingtonmonthly.com/features/2006/0609.collegeguide.html

Willett, T. (2002). *Impact of follow up counseling on academic performance and persistence*. Gilroy, CA: Gavilan College Office of Research.

9

MINORITY SERVING INSTITUTIONS—WHAT CAN WE LEARN?

ALISA CUNNINGHAM AND LACEY LEEGWATER

As has been described in previous chapters, many institutional policies and practices negatively impact the higher education attainment of low-income students. Most research in this area is directed toward "mainstream" institutions that serve a relatively small fraction of racial/ethnic minority students, who are more likely than their peers to be from low-income backgrounds. However, a number of higher education institutions exist that directly focus on minority students and promise to support those students along their path toward academic success. These are Minority-Serving Institutions (MSIs), including Historically Black Colleges and Universities (HBCUs), Hispanic-Serving Institutions (HSIs), and Tribal Colleges and Universities (TCUs). The goal of this chapter is to highlight the role of MSIs in serving low-income students, with a special focus on the institutional policies and practices that may differentiate them from other colleges and universities.[1] The following sections will define MSIs and provide context for their role in higher education through an overview of their student and institutional characteristics. Then, using a post-structuralist analysis, the chapter will highlight positive MSI practices, potential barriers, and recommendations for supporting low-income student success.

WHAT ARE MSIs?

MSIs are colleges and universities that enroll a high proportion of students of color. These institutions are all unique, defined by their own cultural histories, leadership, student bodies, and educational purposes. However, they do share common elements, such as strong ties to communities and large numbers of students enrolling from the immediate surrounding areas. For example, HSIs are located in communities with high concentrations of Hispanics, and TCUs—most of which are located on reservations—serve large numbers of American Indians from various tribes living on federal trust lands (Clinedinst, Redmond, & O'Brien, 2000). At HBCUs, many draw students from all over the United States, but a number enroll students primarily from neighboring communities (O'Brien & Zudak, 1998). In addition to being more physically accessible, many MSIs have open admissions policies, providing access to students who otherwise might not enroll.

MSIs are often different from other college and universities through their history and legal framework. Their unique history positions MSIs as post-structural alternatives to the dominant higher education model in the United States. As noted by Wolanin (1998), the federal government has a special obligation to MSIs; for HBCUs and TCUs, this obligation stems from the federal government's for the welfare and education of African Americans due to discrimination and segregation dating back to the pre-Civil War era and the trusts between the federal government and sovereign American Indian tribes. The federal obligation to HSIs is rooted in the government's broader concern for equal opportunity to participate in education.

Until recently, MSIs were relatively unnoticed in the sphere of higher education. However, over the past decade these institutions have come to be recognized as important in serving the nation's students of color. Part of this recognition has been actively fostered by the Alliance for Equity in Higher Education, which represents the majority of MSIs—HBCUs, HSIs, and TCUs.[2] Combined, these MSIs educate more than one-third of all students of color in the United States, and will be the focus of this chapter.[3]

Student Characteristics

Together, MSIs enroll about 2.2 million students, including 1.3 million Hispanic, Black, and American Indian students. In fact, they enroll almost one-third of these students despite the fact that they comprise a small proportion of all higher education institutions (NCES, 2007). At the same time, MSIs graduate a substantial proportion of minority students. In 2007–08, MSIs awarded almost 187,000 college degrees and certificates to African American, American Indian, and Hispanic students; this included 49,000 associate's degrees and 85,000 Bachelor's degrees (NCES, 2007).

Many students who attend MSIs come from educationally disadvantaged and/or low-income backgrounds; often, they are the first generation in their family to attend college. For example, in 2007–08, 42 percent of students attending a Historically Black College or University or a Hispanic-Serving Institution were first-generation students, compared to 32 percent of students enrolled at other institutions. In addition, and most important for this chapter, 36 percent of students enrolled at these institutions were from families in the lowest income quartile, compared to 25 percent enrolled at other institutions; two-thirds of students were below the median (NCES, 2008).[4] These students were also more likely to be living with their parents and less likely to attend exclusively on a full-time basis, illustrating the non-traditional nature of many students enrolled at MSIs. See Table 9.1 for more details.

Institutional Characteristics

Currently, there are almost 350 MSIs in the United States, representing less than 5 percent of all higher education institutions. This includes over 110 HBCUs, almost 200 HSIs, and more than 30 TCUs. They tend to be located in three regions of the country—the Southwest, Southeast, and Far West. As a whole, MSIs share many similarities with other institutions, but there are some key characteristics that differ from the universe of higher education institutions. The majority of MSIs are public institutions, whether four-year or two-year, although this differs for each community.

In order to better serve their targeted populations, more than half of MSIs have open admissions to encourage students from all backgrounds and abilities to attend. In addition, MSIs are more likely to offer a wider arena of services to their students in comparison with all higher education institutions, including distance learning opportunities, remedial services, adult basic education, weekend/evening courses, and on-campus daycare. See Table 9.2 for exact percentages. These services reflect the

Table 9.1 Characteristics of Undergraduates Attending MSIs Compared to All Undergraduates, 2007–08

	Students attending MSIs	All undergraduates
% lowest income quartile	36%	25%
% first-generation	42%	32%
% living with parents	33%	24%
% attending full time	36%	48%
% receiving Pell grants	34%	27%
% 24 and over	46%	40%
% taking remedial math	45%	36%

Source: NCES, 2008.

Table 9.2   Percentage of Institutions That Offer Selected Services

	MSIs	All institutions
Offers remedial services	88%	55%
Offers adult basic/GED	43%	19%
Offers distance learning	73%	42%
Offers weekend/evening courses	47%	31%
Offers on-campus daycare	51%	17%

Source: NCES, 2007

characteristics of students attending MSIs, in that they help meet the needs of part-time, first-generation, older, and low-income students on campus. These non-traditional students are more likely to need various support structures on campus to help them stay in school. Other supports will be discussed below.

Also, faculty at MSIs tend to reflect the students served more than is true at mainstream institutions. For example, more than half of instructional staff at HBCUs are Black, 24 percent of staff at HSIs are Hispanic, and 41 percent of staff at TCUs are American Indian. In comparison, for all institutions, 5 percent are Black, 4 percent Hispanic, and less than 1 percent American Indian (NCES, 2007). Students often react positively to teachers who look like them, and engage in behavior they might not otherwise have done. By better aligning the student and staff racial and ethnic profiles, the institutions provide their students with increased opportunities for role modeling, mentoring, and other activities important for student success. Research studies have suggested that such opportunities can contribute to students' sense of interaction on campus (Allen, 1992; Nelson Laird, Bridges, Morelon-Quainoo, Williams, & Holmes, 2007).

Lastly, in general, MSIs try to keep their prices low as they tend to serve students from lower-income backgrounds that find it difficult to pay for tuition and other expenses. On average, tuition and fees are lower at MSIs in comparison with other institutions—in 2007, in-state tuition and fees averaged $5,343 at MSIs and $10,740 at all institutions (NCES, 2007). This is also true with total revenues and endowments, which tend to be lower than at other institutions. The latter impacts many aspects of how MSIs operate and the ways in which they can serve their students.

LEARNING FROM MSIs: PRACTICES THAT PROMOTE LOW-INCOME STUDENT SUCCESS

The remainder of this chapter provides a post-structural analysis of institutional practices and policies that impact low-income students at

MSIs, deconstructing current practices and offering recommendations for reconstructing policies and practices to better support low-income students at these campuses. MSIs serve as key models for improving student success for underserved student populations, offering a post-structuralist alternative to mainstream institutions. We provide a range of positive practices that can guide institutional change at other institutions seeking to address barriers to low-income student success. However, MSIs also struggle with their own impediments to low-income student success.

To a large extent, MSIs were created to address failures in mainstream postsecondary education and account for emergent demographic realities. In large part, MSIs are a post-structural reaction to the structural impediments of demographic-specific policies and practices in mainstream institutions. In practice, this often means putting in place specific policies that address the needs of these populations, including low-income students. As expressed in Clinedinst et al. (2000):

> Whether the focus is on African Americans, Hispanics, or American Indians, the missions of all MSIs embrace the needs of the communities they serve. The commitment to supporting cultural values and traditions and to preserving and recognizing the past even as they strive to make an impact on the future sets MSIs apart from mainstream institutions. (p. 16)

This commitment results in a number of practices that positively impact low-income students by addressing underlying assumptions in the mainstream community about what the students should know and do.

Here, we concentrate on several themes: decreasing financial barriers while increasing financial literacy; using culturally relevant curricula and learning resources; cultivating student engagement; reaching out to local communities; and student-centered support services. Although each MSI is different, taken as a whole one can see a pattern of support for students they serve. Often these practices are targeted to the whole population but are particularly important to low-income students.

Reduced Financial Barriers and Increased Focus on Financial Literacy

MSIs have a history of keeping tuition costs low to account for the low-income status of most of their students. These policies provide a structural alternative to higher priced, mainstream institutions. They foster college going among low-income students and reduce the differentiation between low-income and higher-income students that tuition discounting often fosters at mainstream institutions.

Given the backgrounds of their students and the difficulty many face in meeting the costs of attending, financial issues have prompted additional attention. For example, many MSIs provide prospective and current students with information on higher education financing options and broader issues of credit and financial stewardship, which helps to reduce power and language barriers low-income students face. MSIs recognize that students often enter their institutions with little or no knowledge about how to properly manage their finances and that potential students may avoid attending their college based on incorrect conceptions of college costs. By recognizing these barriers and addressing them early— often through high school based programs or freshman orientations in advance of the freshman semester—MSIs give low-income students the resources they need to address potential financial barriers to their postsecondary success.

Many such programs also recognize the important role families play in the financial success of their students and therefore include family financial literacy in many of their initiatives. In addition, such programs often include extra measures for supporting low-income students such as emergency funds, scholarships for books and materials, and fee waivers for students in extreme financial distress.

For example, Southwestern Indian Polytechnic Institute (SIPI), a TCU in Albuquerque, New Mexico, offers a series of community-based workshops that link "native knowledge, values, and lifestyles" with college-going financial literacy programs (IHEP, 2008). At Dillard University, a private HBCU in New Orleans, Louisiana, the financial literacy program draws on students to facilitate peer sessions related to scholarships and financial aid.

Culturally Relevant Curricula and Learning Resources

Within post-structuralism, issues of identity and systemic barriers are intertwined with situational history. MSIs, particularly those with culturally based missions, weave the cultural heritage of their communities into the learning experiences for their students. A key goal for TCUs is the transmission of tribal customs and knowledge to new generations of Native Americans; therefore, most imbed cultural components throughout their curricula. For example, the Institute of American Indian Arts (IAIA), located in Santa Fe, New Mexico, is linking its general education program to "native cultural approaches to the learning process," beginning with a Native Foundation for College success course for first-year students (Overton-Adkins, 2008, p. 2).

HBCUs celebrate and integrate African American history into a range of campus practices such as the hosting of African American heritage celebrations at their institutions, the development and maintenance of civil rights archives, and the honoring of prominent African American figures through institutional and building names, scholarship programs, endowed chairs, etc. HBCUs also leverage current practices within the African American community—particularly volunteerism and community service—to support and enhance the student learning experience (Hazeur, 2008). Tennessee State University, a public institution located in Nashville, Tennessee, and Morris College, a private college in Sumter, South Carolina, are two examples of HBCUs that honor this cultural heritage through classroom-based service learning initiatives.

For HSIs, where language barriers often underscore cultural boundaries, many institutions embrace these cultural differences by offering "classes in English as a Second Language (ESL) instruction for non-native English speakers in the Hispanic adult and migrant community, as well as courses for attaining a General Equivalency Degree (GED) for high school completion" (Clinedinst et al., 2000, p. 17).

For all three institutional types, a focus on the history and culture of respective communities invariably includes a focus on the socioeconomic realities and historical triggers that have led to the low-income status for many within these communities. Such a focus provides opportunities for offering community-based solutions for addressing the economic and social factors perpetuating poverty, helping the students—and the faculty and staff at the institution—better understand the systemic, situational, and identity issues impacting their lives.

Student Engagement

Student engagement, or the degree to which students are engaged in educationally purposeful activities, has become an important framework for considering institutional policies and practices that support student success (Kuh, 2001). Student engagement includes such issues as crafting a supportive environment, fostering meaningful undergraduate learning opportunities, and building relationships between students and faculty to promote academic success. Results on TRIO programs and student engagement seem to suggest that TRIO-eligible students benefit more from active and collaborative learning activities and faculty–student interaction than do their non-TRIO eligible counterparts, although both populations benefit to some degree (Filkins & Doyle, 2002). Student engagement—and institutional practices that support student engagement—are important for low-income student learning and success.

Given the positive relationship, then, between student engagement activities and low-income student success, it is useful to analyze MSIs through this lens. Given that MSIs' missions are based on honoring student context and history, one might expect student engagement practices at MSIs to look differently than those at mainstream institutions. A 2007 study of student engagement at HBCUs and HSIs provides new insight into the student engagement differences between MSIs and predominantly White institutions (PWIs) (Nelson Laird et al., 2007). This study shows that both HBCUs and HSIs are doing a better job than their PWI counterparts of serving students with characteristics that could impede student engagement.

Examples of these institutional practices have been documented through the national initiatives noted previously and other key studies. California State University-Northridge, a public HSI, integrates active and collaborative learning activities into their first-year learning communities (Evenbeck, 2008). A number of institutions, such as the University of the District of Columbia (UDC), a public HBCU, and California State University Dominquez Hills, a public HSI, are emphasizing active and collaborative learning practice and the importance of faculty–student interaction in their comprehensive faculty development programs (Malnarich, 2008). A key strategy for MSIs working to improve student success in science, technology, engineering, and math (STEM) disciplines has been the integration of undergraduate research opportunities into major requirements (Kee, 2007), a practice that prompts both faculty–student interaction and active learning strategies.

In addition, MSIs provide unique learning opportunities and engagement through community-development initiatives (U.S. Department of Housing and Urban Development, 2003). Such activities provide students with hands-on experience in translating classroom theory into real-world practice. By basing these experiences within the context of their own communities, students are able to use their personal experiences to address community problems and have increased motivation to succeed. Thus, MSIs provide key student engagement activities that align with those found to be important to low-income student success.

Community Activities and Outreach

MSIs play an important role in their local communities, helping students maintain their connections with family and other networks. As noted above, many MSIs draw students locally or regionally, and their students may live at home while taking classes in college. For example, many TCUs offer courses that focus on strengthening the economy and promoting workforce development specific to the local reservation. They also offer programs such as literacy training, GED preparation, childcare, and substance abuse counseling. Leech Lake Tribal College promotes Project Grow, a program that encourages tribal members to cultivate traditional crops, in order to combat the high rates of diabetes on the reservation (Cunningham & Parker, 1998).

In addition, many HBCUs are involved in outreach activities to encourage African American high school students to enroll in college, informing them about the benefits of earning a degree (Clinedinst et al., 2000). As noted above, HSIs may provide materials in Spanish in order to reach out to local populations, or host community meetings. Such activities help MSIs build local solutions to local problems.

A number of model programs were highlighted in a 2003 (U.S. Department of Housing and Urban Development) HUD report. Through HUD HBCU funds, Texas Southern University, a private institution in Houston, linked job training for the city's unemployed workers with providing housing options for the significant number of homeless participants they were serving. Turtle Mountain Community College, a TCU in North Dakota, used HUD funds to develop a wellness center on the Turtle Mountain reservation to foster culturally sensitive health and wellness education programs for the tribal members.

The model programs noted here honor their communities—and the low-income populations in these communities—through sustained and systemic efforts to sustain and grow innate community resources. In addition, the programs often provide service learning, internship, research, and other experiential learning opportunities for their student body that directly connect community support goals to student learning outcomes and cultivate ongoing commitment to community outreach within the student body. Through these efforts, MSIs honor the history and circumstances of their low-income students and work with them to seek solutions to low-income community issues.

Student-Centered Support Services

As noted above, MSIs often provide services that directly recognize and meet the needs of the students they serve. But for many low-income students who must work full-time, live at home, or attend at night or on the weekends to support their higher education goals, accessing these services can be a major barrier. For example, these services are often physically located on the campus, may be scattered in buildings throughout campus, and are typically only available during regular office hours. This can be especially true of student support services—programs such as academic advising, tutoring, faculty mentoring, and writing and math labs—that are in place to support students' academic success. Many MSIs have worked to reduce these barriers by providing alternate or extended access to critical academic support services.

Acknowledging the hardships traditional student support services and faculty office hours were putting on their significant number of commuter and working students, Florida International University, a public HSI, created a Virtual Student Center that serves as

> a one-stop-shop repository for students to gain 24-hour access to major-specific and department information; a forum for communicating with faculty; a portal for online academic tutoring; and a central hub for students to communicate about academics, transportation, careers, and a number of different topical areas. (Chough, 2008, p. 2)

This approach has been adopted by a number of institutions, including New Jersey City University.

Kentucky State University, a public HBCU, physically clusters student support services offices on campus so that their students can more efficiently access the services, in addition to providing a centralized information center for "basic information on financial aid, registration, housing, counseling, and tutoring" (Bridges, 2008). The University of New Mexico, another public HSI, provides a third approach, by developing paper and online tools to help students better navigate the available services.

These and other initiatives underway at MSIs directly support low-income student success by recognizing the time constraints these students often face with working part- or full-time; commuting to campus; and attending classes online, at night, or on the weekends. Instead of forcing students to adapt to institutional policies and practices, these institutions have altered their policies and practices around the students needs in order to better ensure access to services vital to student success.

DECONSTRUCTING MSIs: PARADOX OF COMMITMENT

Despite their goals of providing a welcoming environment for students of color and other disadvantaged students, MSIs still include policies and practices that negatively impact the low-income students they serve. These may be internally driven, or influenced by external pressures.

Internal

MSIs have many of the barriers to low-income student success outlined in other chapters of this book. Barriers may include the lack of access to programs such as study abroad and internships; the absence of or few on-campus dormitories (Kezar, Chapter 1); difficulties in communicating financial aid information effectively (Perna et al., Chapter 4); and mis-alignment of colleges and state practices on accreditation and other poli-cies (Levin et al., Chapter 7). Such programs and practices may privilege middle- and upper-income students. Further, many of these barriers are exacerbated at MSIs because of the general lack of resources found at most MSIs in comparison to other institutions. In addition, MSIs often use language about disenfranchisement and disadvantage due to important historical factors and continuing discrimination. In this volume, Colyar (Chapter 6) suggests that focusing on lacks may have the side effect of re-privileging the norm. Often, however, MSIs' use of this language is necessary to gain increased funding and sometimes to validate their existence as institutions. Our research found less attention to the low income, first generation of students compared to race and ethnicity. All MSIs need to direct more attention to low-income and first-generation status and not privilege race so dramatically.

External

Many policies and practices at MSIs are impacted by federal or state governments, historical factors, or even market forces. These factors often limit or work against MSIs in their efforts to serve their students, especially low-income students. As mentioned above, MSIs as a whole lack the resources of many of their peers; this may be the most important challenge faced by MSIs. Underfunding is chronic among many MSIs, which impacts the students who need institutional services and supports the most. In order to keep tuitions low, many MSIs look to other, nontu-ition sources for revenue, and try to cultivate institutional endowments. Private MSIs have had greater experience—and greater success—with endowments but even among this group increases in endowments still leave them trailing mainstream institutions. Most MSIs lack alumni that come from wealthy backgrounds, which limits an institution's capacity to use this source; this is especially true of some recently founded MSIs that have a relatively young alumni body. At the same time, many states have reduced their commitment to higher education institutions, includ-ing public MSIs. Given these financial difficulties, MSIs often look to the federal government to help fill in the gaps. Several categories of federal programs, including institutional development, pre-college preparation, and financial aid, help MSIs. However, the resources are generally not enough to raise MSIs to the levels of their peers. This, in turn, impacts the ways in which MSIs can fulfill their mission and help the students who need it most.

MSIs' limited financial resources lead to their inability to address other external pressures, such as the increasing call for accountability for all higher education institutions. These accountability pressures may originate at the federal or state level, or through the accreditation process. Often accountability measures are not appropriate for the student bodies served by MSIs; for example, using the six-year graduation rate measure for MSIs as a measure of their success is misleading because many of their students take longer to complete their degrees. This is especially true for low-income students, who tend to have more risk factors for persistence such as attending part-time or working full-time while enrolled. Efforts aimed at improving student and institutional performance often have unintended negative consequences that put low-income students at MSIs at risk.

A related issue is that even if measures of success existed that more accurately reflected MSIs' mission, data collection is often an issue. According to a recent report:

> Without experience in data-based campus change, MSIs may encounter problems with regional accreditation agencies. They also have difficulty instituting practices grounded in evidence of need and impact that aid the support and retention of their students. (Del Rios & Leegwater, 2008, p. 12)

Without the ability to evaluate and target specific groups of students, it becomes difficult for the institutions to deliver the appropriate services to low-income students in particular, and they may be forced to use a broader, less efficient tool.

The highlighting of these policies and practices, though, should not limit the degree to which MSIs can provide importance guidance for low-income student success. In fact, they show that despite facing significant barriers often not faced by other institutions, MSIs continue to work on behalf of underserved student populations, particularly low-income students, to provide avenues for their academic success.

RECONSTRUCTING MSI POLICIES: RECOMMENDATIONS FOR SUPPORTING LOW-INCOME STUDENT SUCCESS

This review of MSI policies and practices through a post structural lens demonstrates that, to a large extent, MSIs were formed to mitigate the problematic structures in mainstream higher education and foster social change. Toward this goal, they have turned to alternative practices that more effectively support the success of their students. Where mainstream institutions have often ignored or not been able to meet the needs of low-income students of color, MSIs have tried to raise their students up to the implicit standards of White, middle- and upper-income students.

They have done this by targeting the specific needs of their students, understanding that their students may not have the tools they need to successfully negotiate college.

Nonetheless, their commitment leaves many students financially strapped. Students often do not have access to the facilities and support programs that other colleges have. Although tuition may be lower than at other institutions, low-income students may still face financial burdens that MSIs cannot cover. At the same time, MSIs often cannot target the resources they have on low-income students due to lack of capacity in collection and analysis of data.

These findings suggest that a number of new policies and practices could be put into place to expand the support of low-income students at MSIs. These recommendations can provide important guideposts for how MSIs can both continue to support the academic success of large numbers of underserved students—including low-income students. These recommendations also address how MSIs themselves can confront some of the issues raised through a post-structuralist review of their practices. Key recommendations include:

- *Increased federal and state support for MSIs:* MSIs serve significant numbers of low-income students while keeping tuition and fees low. To maintain and build capacity for serving low-income and other underserved populations, MSIs need additional federal and state funding. Funding for infrastructure development and capacity as well as social and academic support programs is particularly important.
- *Improved data capacity for understanding and meeting the needs of specific student populations:* MSIs have been increasing their capacity for data-informed decision-making; however, it continues to be limited. To address disaggregated needs of specific student populations, especially low-income students, MSIs need enhanced capacity for collecting and using institutional data. Recognizing this need, the BEAMS project report calls for the expansion of Title III and Title V funding programs to include support for institutional assessment and research offices, expanding the programs' current focus on institutional capacity building efforts in the areas of "academic quality, institutional management, and fiscal stability" (Del Rios & Leegwater, 2008) . With funds from Title III and Title V directed to institutional research and assessment, MSIs would have the resources needed to enhance data gathering and analysis technology, participate in national surveys to gather comparison data, and develop staff capacity to use data to improve services for specific student populations. In addition, federal stimulus dollars

have included efforts to improve longitudinal data systems, and it is important that MSIs play a part in this process.

- *Accountability measures that take into account short-term data capacity needs:* In the short-term, until MSIs have the resources they need to effectively collect and report institutional accountability data, national calls for increased institutional accountability must take into account the varying degrees of data collection capacity at MSIs and other under-funded institutions with significant underserved student populations. At the same time, MSIs must reiterate their commitment to measures that address student outcomes.

- *Continued attention to and support for student financial literacy programs:* As student loan guarantors, such as USA Funds, have provided significant resources to MSIs and other institutions to support financial literacy efforts, any proposed changes to student loan programs that change the degree to which current organizations provide these services must provide viable alternatives for sustaining financial literacy programs at MSIs. MSIs, and the low-income students they serve, benefit greatly from these resources and the sustaining of these activities remains a key driver for attracting, retaining, and graduating low-income students at MSIs.

CONCLUSION

MSIs serve a valuable role in higher education in educating a significant number of low-income, minority students and offer valuable models for effective ways of supporting low-income student success. At the same time, in order to support their mission, they need to ensure long-term viability. Thus, the efforts described in this chapter should be continued and strengthened through additional resources. Government and other programs that fund MSIs already see the importance of these institutions in recognizing a large-scale social problem and attempting to utilize creative ways to address specific barriers. However, their support is frequently not enough. MSIs themselves are becoming increasingly proactive in finding resources to support their activities. For MSIs to continue to make a difference for social change, they will need to adapt to new realities and communicate their unique contributions to higher education opportunity.

NOTES

1. Portions of this chapter are based on research and programmatic initiatives previously conducted by the Institute for Higher Education Policy (IHEP).
2. The Alliance, a program managed by IHEP, was established in 1999 by the American Indian Higher Education Consortium (AIHEC), the Hispanic Association of Colleges

and Universities (HACU), and the National Association For Equal Opportunity in Higher Education (NAFEO) to represent the shared interests of TCUs, HSIs, and HBCUs. Alliance initiatives incorporate the common goals and priorities of AIHEC, HACU, and NAFEO in order to speak with one voice about the issues critical to MSIs and the communities they serve.

3. We have chosen to focus on members of the Alliance given our long-running relationship and the fact that most of the research on MSIs has focused on these three groups of institutions. Other institutions are essential in serving students of color and are likely to share many of the same characteristics and institutional practices as those described in this chapter.

4. It is difficult to obtain information on MSIs as a whole using the sample surveys of the National Center for Education Statistics, given their relatively small proportion of the institutional population. Because the population is particularly small, the NPSAS data includes only HSIs and HBCUs.

REFERENCES

Allen, W. (1992). The color of success: African-American college student outcomes at predominantly White and historically Black public colleges and universities. *Harvard Education Review, 62*(1), 26–44.

Bridges, B. (2008). *Student Support Services: A practice brief based on BEAMS project outcomes.* Washington, DC: Institute for Higher Education Policy.

Chough, A. (2008). *Leveraging technology in campus change initiatives: A practice brief based on BEAMS project outcomes.* Washington, DC: Institute for Higher Education Policy.

Clinedinst, M., Redmond, C., & O'Brien, C. T. (2000). *Educating the emerging majority: The role of minority-serving colleges and universities in confronting America's teacher crisis.* Washington, DC: Institute for Higher Education Policy.

Cunningham, A., & Parker, C. (1998). Tribal colleges as community institutions and resources. In J. Merisotis & C. O'Brien (Eds.), *Minority-serving institutions: Distinct purposes, common goals.* New Directions for Higher Education, No. 102. San Francisco: Jossey-Bass.

Del Rios, M., & Leegwater, L. (2008). *Increasing student success at minority-serving institutions: Findings from the BEAMS project.* Washington, DC: Institute for Higher Education Policy.

Evenbeck, S. (2008). *First-year programs: A practice brief based on BEAMS project outcomes.* Washington, DC: Institute for Higher Education Policy.

Filkins, J., & Doyle, S. K. (2002). *First generation and low income students: Using the NSSE data to study effective educational practices and students' self-reported gains.* Paper presented at the 2002 Association for Institutional Research Annual Conference. Toronto, Ontario, Canada.

Hazeur, C. (2008). *Purposeful co-curricular activities designed to increase engagement: A practice brief based on BEAMS project outcomes.* Washington, DC: Institute for Higher Education Policy.

Institute for Higher Education Policy (IHEP). (2008). *Synopsis of the symposium for financial literacy and college success at minority-serving institutions.* Washington, DC: Institute for Higher Education Policy.

Kee, A. (2007). *Model institutions for excellence: A model of success—The model institutions for excellence program's successful leadership in STEM education (1995–2007): 2007 national report.* Washington, DC: Institute for Higher Education Policy.

Kuh, G. D. (2001). Assessing what really matters to student learning: Inside the National Survey of Student Engagement. *Change, 33*(3), 10–17, 66.

Malnarich, G. (2008). *Increasing student engagement through faculty development: A practice brief based on BEAMS project outcomes.* Washington, DC: Institute for Higher Education Policy.

National Center for Education Statistics (NCES). (2007). *Integrated Postsecondary Education Data System (IPEDS)*. Data Analysis System (DAS). U.S. Department of Education.

National Center for Education Statistics (NCES). (2008). *National Postsecondary Student Aid Survey (NPSAS) 2007–08 Undergraduates*. Data Analysis System (DAS). U.S. Department of Education.

Nelson Laird, T. F., Bridges, B. K., Morelon-Quainoo, C. L., Williams, J. M., & Holmes, M. S. (2007). African American and Hispanic student engagement at minority serving and predominantly White institutions. *Journal of College Student Development, 48*(1), 39–56.

O'Brien, E., & Zudak, C. (1998). Minority-serving institutions: An overview. In J. Merisotis & C. O'Brien (Eds.), *Minority-serving institutions: Distinct purposes, common goals*. New Directions for Higher Education, No. 102. San Francisco: Jossey-Bass.

Overton-Adkins, B. (2008). *Aligning multiple campus initiatives: A practice brief based on BEAMS project outcomes*. Washington, DC: Institute for Higher Education Policy.

U.S. Department of Housing and Urban Development (HUD). (2003). *Minority-serving institutions in higher education: Developing partnerships to revitalize communities*. Office of Policy Development and Research, Office of University Partnerships. Washington, DC: Authors.

Wolanin, T. (1998). The Federal investment in minority-serving institutions. In J. Merisotis & C. O'Brien (Eds.), *Minority-serving institutions: Distinct purposes, common goals*. New Directions for Higher Education, No. 102. San Francisco: Jossey-Bass.

Wolanin, T. (2003). *Reauthorizing the Higher Education Act: Issues and options*. Washington, DC: Institute for Higher Education Policy.

10

THE HIDDEN CURRICULUM

The Difficulty of Infusing Financial Education

ADRIANNA KEZAR AND HANNAH YANG

> I had constant underlying stress about money (as a low income student and faculty member). Overspending to fit in, yet feeling the need to be frugal all the time. Not understanding knowledge debt and basic financial issues. (hooks, 2003, p. 37)

> Not only do the vast majority of the rich keep their knowledge of basic economic skills from the poor, they invest in all forms of cultural reproduction and encourage endless consumption on the part of those who do not have class privilege. (hooks, 2003, p. 77)

Low-income students generally have little knowledge about finances and lack financial literacy. Studies have demonstrated that most students in college lack adequate skills about finances and that the low-income individuals' scores and knowledge are significantly behind those of middle- and high-income (Chen & Volpe, 1998; Jump$tart, 2008; Lyons, 2004, 2007). hooks' quotes express the stress and concern that lack of financial knowledge creates in the lives of students. In high school, low-income students do not have an understanding of the financial obligations to attend college—often choosing not to go to college because they are unable to navigate the financial aid system. Those that choose to go to college often drop out because they misunderstand that they have to pay back loans, take out more loans or credit card debt than they can handle, or mismanage their finances. Finances are key to access and success of low-income students as finances play an important role in whether or not they remain in college (Lyons, 2004; Paulsen & St. John, 2002, Tinto, 1993). The cost to attend postsecondary institutions continues to rise, merit-based aid programs have replaced needs-based aid in many states, and loans are on the rise (Reed, 2008). A study by Paulsen and St. John (2002) also found that due to tuition increases financial aid (loans and grants) was insufficient in helping low-income students persist. The authors also found that as unmet need increases, student persistence decreases.

In addition to the increasing amount of loan debt, college students also fall victim to credit card debt. One study found that college students graduate with more than 2,000 dollars in credit card debt (Nellie Mae, 2005). Along with the stress of financial difficulty due to loans and credit card debt 75 percent of college freshmen confess to making mistakes with their finances (KeyBank and Harris Interactive, 2006). And about one-third of the freshmen said that they are financially unprepared to manage their money at college. We believe that financial education could help low-income students to better manage their money and subsequently help them to remain in college.

hooks' (2003) second quote speaks to another important point which is that society and the higher education system are set up in a way that financial knowledge is limited or out of the reach of low-income students. Systematically, the higher education enterprise offers little, if any, meaningful financial education. As will be discussed in this chapter, few policies and practices are in place beyond federally mandated financial aid loan training or one-time, optional, short workshops on financial education. In fact, the system is set up to prey on this lack of knowledge and to put poor students into greater debt and financial despair. The growth of credit card companies on campus and their unprecedented access to students is part of this trend to make students consumers and dependent on banks.

If we know that lack of financial education creates incredible stress for low-income students, impacting their access and success, why are few campuses offering meaningful financial education? This chapter will examine why financial education is generally not a part of the higher education system and ways that financial education can be integrated thoughtfully into the system to help increase low-income student success. We draw on a study we conducted on a federal policy aimed to assist low-income students gain access and be retained in college. This chapter will be divided into four parts: 1. describe the study from which the themes and chapter ideas about financial education are drawn; 2. review existing policies and practices related to financial education; 3. identify hidden assumptions and biases that emerged in our research that helped us to understand why financial education may not be a part of the higher education system; and 4. note ways campuses can create exemplary financial education programs including resources and model programs.

RESEARCH STUDY

The study explored the potential of integrating Individual Development Accounts (IDAs) for low-income youth into the higher education system. IDAs are a financial tool that includes a matched savings account, financial education, and case management. Most IDA programs include about 8–10 hours of financial education for their enrollees. While the federal policy has been in place for over a decade, few campuses offer or partner with nonprofits to offer IDAs. The goal of the project was to better understand what barriers existed to capitalize on this federal tool for improving the lives of low-income students. In addition, we were interested in understanding aspects or structures that would support and enhance the integration of this federal policy. We wanted to better understand why IDAs were not being adopted or used within the postsecondary sector.

IDAs can be used for three primary purposes—postsecondary education, homeownership, and microenterprise. At present, IDAs have been used primarily by individuals interested in buying a home. The idea of IDAs is to provide incentives to save (matched savings fund) to low-income individuals and then give them access to asset building tools that are normally only available to middle-income individuals, potentially breaking the cycle of poverty. IDAs are available to only the poorest of the poor with families being 200 percent of the federal poverty level. IDAs are more than a matched savings account funding, but also provide new skills and life patterns learned through saving and financial education sessions. Demonstration project research on IDAs showed that low-income people can save, purchase assets, and often moved to self-sufficiency (Schreiner, Clancy, & Sherraden, 2002).

One major reason why IDAs have not been adopted by postsecondary institutions is that the Department of Health and Human Services (which distributes grants for IDAs through the Assets for Independence Act) marketed IDAs primarily to nonprofits working with housing and housing authorities. We soon realized that there was an opportunity to market IDAs through the research project and to find out what postsecondary leaders, administrators, and policymakers thought about IDAs and relatedly financial education. We asked about whether they would consider adopting this tool once they had a greater understanding of the tool through the research. We conducted focus groups where we presented this information and worked to understand postsecondary leaders' opinions and beliefs about IDAs and all its component parts including financial education. In total, we held 12 regional focus groups with approximately 144 postsecondary leaders and policymakers from national associations, think tanks, and policy organizations. We conducted a national survey of TRIO staff about offering financial education, case studies at eight campuses, and interviewed close to 100 campus administrators and staff about their views of IDAs. We spoke with and went out to case study sites ranging from research universities, comprehensive doctoral institutions, Master's institutions, community colleges, for-profit institutions, land-grant institutions, technical and vocational colleges, and liberal arts colleges.

There was a major difference in our data between institutions that served large numbers of low-income students such as rural community colleges and vocational institutions (which we will call low-income serving institutions) and campuses with fewer low-income students such as land-grant institutions and universities (which we will call middle-income serving institutions).[1] We summarize the findings between these two groups: 1. low-income serving and middle-income serving institutions have the same practices and policies of offering little financial education; 2. low-income serving institutions have greater openness to change their practices and policies than middle-income serving institutions; and, 3. middle-income institutions have significant biases and assumptions in place that prevent them from seeing the need to offer financial education while low-income serving institutions and staff that work with low-income students within middle-income serving institutions tend not to have these biases or they are less entrenched. These findings are elaborated on to help understand the perspectives and practices of campuses related to financial education and helping low-income students.

It is also important to define financial literacy and education as we found that higher education constituencies are not familiar with these terms. The President's Advisory Council on Financial Literacy in 2008 defines financial education as:

> the process by which people improve their understanding of financial products, services and concepts, so they are empowered to make informed choices, avoid pitfalls, know where to go for help and take other actions to improve their present and long-term financial well-being. (p. 35)

Financial education is those efforts aimed at addressing financial illiteracy and moving people to be financially literate. The Council defines financial literacy as "the ability to use knowledge and skills to manage financial resources effectively" (p. 35). To help provide some direction for postsecondary institutions as they consider what they should offer to their students we will highlight some of the research conducted on best practices when delivering financial education.

DESCRIBING AND DECONSTRUCTING FINANCIAL EDUCATION POLICIES OR PRACTICES

While very few policies or practices exist around financial education, we describe the few practices that postsecondary leaders described; some of which they even agreed were weak in conceptualization and implementation.[2] We recognize that there are some model institutions nationally that focus on financial education; however, what we present below is the "norm" for most campuses in how they approach (or do not address) financial education.

We asked institutions about any efforts they had in place for addressing financial education and we found a few vehicles that individuals identified. Most campuses have financial courses being taught within certain disciplines—for example business schools or public policy—but they are restricted in enrollment and do not have a practical orientation. The course(s) generally have a theoretical orientation and are aimed at students who plan to major in finance.

The most common broad approach to financial education is that financial aid offices are now mandated by federal law to offer entrance and exit counseling to students who are taking out federal loans; therefore, this excludes students who take out private loans. Low-income students are often in a position to take out private loans because of their poor credit histories and miss out on this training opportunity. Both entrance and exit counseling can be offered in-person or online and provide students information about the repayment obligation and plans, interest, debt management strategies (offered in the exit counseling), and the terms and conditions of their loan packages. Financial aid officers on many campuses noted that this information was usually offered through an online course that students click through in 30 minutes to an hour. Some campuses offer counseling through group workshops that last about an hour. When probing staff about the ability of such one-hour online or in-person courses to help students (particularly low-income students) develop financial literacy, postsecondary leaders recognize that clearly this one vehicle is insufficient. They acknowledged in-person sessions are better to engage and communicate material but that cost concerns were driving decisions to offer online training. Campus leaders also recognize this is an act of compliance on their end, not a meaningful financial education opportunity. In our conversations, some leaders began to realize that the very narrow scope of the financial aid sessions (which do not touch on financial literacy at all) needed to be rethought.

Some campuses also offer some financial basics in their first-year seminar. The majority of such sessions are offered a single time and not reinforced with any material later. Student and academic affairs leaders that offered these workshops in first-year seminars recognize that the short duration and narrow coverage of material are insufficient to create financial literacy in students. Planners of seminars noted that the courses are packed with so many different topics and skills that it is hard to go into any particular topic in-depth. However, first-year seminars represent an important vehicle to build from since many campuses offer this course, it is taken by a large number of students on a campus, and is likely to reach low-income students that are often hard to identify.

Also, some campuses have support student groups that offer financial education and training. Student groups invite community agencies with expertise in financial training to offer workshops. If students organize events, it comes at no cost to the institution, which seems critical in tight budget times. The staff spoke about the ways students can reach other students more effectively and actually get larger audiences for such events. While student programming is extremely important, this approach may not help to institutionalize financial education and make it a value for the campus.

Some TRIO and GEAR UP programs offer financial education within their outreach programs to low-income and first-generation youth. Since TRIO and GEAR UP work with low-income students on campus it was particularly important for us to understand if financial education was offered as a part of these programs. Not all low-income students are able to participate in such programs, in fact, only a quarter of the institutions in the country have TRIO programs for example; however this is one place where we know institutions can reach a variety of low-income students.

Our survey identified that about 50 percent of TRIO programs offer some form of financial education either on campus or as part of their outreach program, e.g., Student Support Services.[3] However, most of the financial training in both college preparation and college success programs is not mandatory. A majority of the college preparation TRIO programs (e.g., Upward Bound and Talent Search who work with high school students) focus mainly on financial aid issues and lightly touch upon financial literacy issues such as budgeting, saving, planning, credit, debt, and other financial information critical to be successful in society. For more details about the results of our survey, please see our institutional policy brief available on our website: http://www.usc.edu/dept/chepa/IDApays/publications/Policy_Brief.pdf.

Some (but not many) middle-income serving campuses described interest in addressing what they began to see as a gap in the way they had constructed learning and education on campus, which excluded financial education. The need to address financial literacy stemmed from a concern about the increasing debt burden of students and their ability to pay tuition (maintaining enrollments) and the rising default rate at their institution. Their reasons for wanting to add financial literacy rarely acknowledged their responsibility for making financial education a learning outcome of college that breaks the cycle of poverty.

Even on low-income serving campuses, we did not find that they had created policies and practices to support financial education. We did find a general openness to the concept of financial education, and an understanding about the importance of financial education, but most of these campuses have been unable to find the time and energy to address the issue and suggested that they needed models and ideas in order to move toward better supporting low-income students. In the last section of the chapter, we hope to offer ideas, some of which we brainstormed and created in conjunction with leaders on campuses serving large numbers of low-income students.

While we can deconstruct the existing practices as narrow, insufficient, and piecemeal, what is even more significant is the general absence of campus policy or practices related to financial education. What the lack of policies and practices to support and integrate financial education into postsecondary institutions suggests is that financial education is not a priority or value. To better understand why it is not a priority or value, we examined people's underlying assumptions.

REVELATION: MIDDLE- AND HIGH-INCOME BIASES OR PRIVILEGES EMBEDDED IN HIGHER EDUCATION

We have just described the dearth of policies and practices related to financial education and wanted to present data that may help to understand or interpret this void. Also, in order to successfully reconstruct the higher education system so that financial literacy becomes an important component of campus operations, it is important to explore what assumptions or biases are in place that have prevented it from being integrated. We highlight some of the assumptions that emerged that prevent leaders from adopting practices that can make low-income students successful including: 1. financial education is not appropriate for higher education, and, 2. charity rather than empowerment. While we describe these generalized assumptions, we also note variations we saw by institutions that work most with low-income students and staff who work directly with low-income students such as TRIO and GEAR UP. These groups had some unique assumptions that are important to highlight and which do not support the prevailing middle-income biases entrenched across most of the academy.

Financial Education is not Appropriate for Higher Education

One of the first assumptions that was apparent in our conversations was that administrators and staff felt the financial education was inappropriate knowledge to include within higher education, even to low-income populations. Administrators and staff felt that financial education should either be taught at the home or in high school. When asked about whether they had surveyed their students to find out whether they were financially literate, almost all institutions did not have any idea about the financial literacy of their students. They assumed that financial education must be taught in the home and in earlier grade levels; if it was not, it was not postsecondary's responsibility. When presented with data that: only seven states require a personal finance course to graduate high school (with recent legislation and curriculum still pending), students are often not taught financial information in the home (particularly low-income students), and most college students are financially illiterate, postsecondary staff did begin to question some of their assumptions. However, they adamantly held to the view that higher education cannot be tainted by practical knowledge. Solutions were to be developed by reforming K-12 or parents and communities.

On the campuses that had first-year seminars or did integrate some form of financial education into first-year seminars, we brainstormed with staff about ways they could integrate financial literacy in deeper ways than a single workshop. For example, perhaps they could include it as a key issue within first-year seminars. They could bring in various disciplines such as economics or sociology to talk about finances in both a theoretical and practical fashion. Most campus leaders suggested that the general education curriculum is political and that it would be difficult to get scholars across disciplines to agree on financial literacy as a key topic. Finances was not considered one of those big issues or key questions like morality/ethics, sustainability, life and death, politics, decision-making, or love that are considered topics of focus within first-year seminars. Tell Marx that finances are not a key topic in a capitalist society!

We also explored less political territory—the co-curriculum. We asked about ways that finances could be integrated into student activities, advising, and other opportunities that students participate in outside the formal curriculum. While we recognize that the co-curriculum cannot reach all low-income students, there might be opportunities for targeting programs for low-income students and ensuring that many of them receive the knowledge. The co-curriculum was seen as a more appropriate place for financial education; but logistical problems seem to abound for considering ways that financial information could be included. For example, advisers are already at a premium and cannot even handle course scheduling and crisis questions that students have on campus. Campuses that tend to serve low-income students (community colleges, for example) have very few advisers. The most common response about a place in the co-curriculum where financial education might be appropriate was for the financial aid officers to consider offering workshops or one-on-one counseling. While they were not sure if the financial aid officers had the skills to teach financial literacy, they were open to having the staff members partner with some of the organizations in the community that we told them we could introduce them to who could train financial aid officers in financial literacy. However, quickly leaders would become concerned that financial aid officers are overburdened because of the scandal in the financial aid arena (in 2007) and the bad economy, which was making financial aid offices unduly busy. In the end, most campuses could not find a fit in their curriculum, co-curriculum, and services for financial education.

This general disregard for finances as a core source of knowledge and the relentless way that people could not see it as part of the curriculum, co-curriculum, or services suggests a hidden curriculum affecting low-income students. Silence about finances privileges those who can learn about it in their home and through their social network, keeping that knowledge for a select few. Not making financial knowledge accessible to a broader network limits the ability of low-income people to compete with their middle- and high-income colleagues, the illusion of a level playing field being burst again.

We did not find this pattern of assumptions across all of the campuses that we spoke with or visited. Campuses that serve large numbers of low-income students—for-profit institutions, vocational colleges, and some community colleges—were much more open to the concept of financial education. These leaders could not be sheltered in their middle- and high-income biases; there are simply too many students on campus who they can see direly need financial education and tools. These leaders also recognize that financial education—even if already offered in high school—would need to be reinforced in postsecondary education. Higher education provides many financial firsts from financial aid, scholarships, credit cards, balancing work and school, budgeting, and working with your own finances for the first time.

While the institutions often did not have the tools or expertise on campus, they were open to the idea of working with a tool that can offer them a way to reach and make low-income students more successful.

They were interested in following up with us about materials on financial education—now available on our website for the IDA-PAYS research project: http://www.usc.edu/dept/chepa/IDApays/. One TRIO director expressed this sentiment clearly:

> I myself was a low-income student and I still struggle with financial issues. As a student in high school and college, these issues were never addressed. I never learned about finances at home and I struggle to maintain my life existence even today. Being a student was incredibly difficult and if I can bring this knowledge to other low-income students, I'll do everything in my power to make that information available. Only now do I realize how my entire life has been affected by this lack of knowledge and I wish that someone had shared this information with me and the skills to be financially competent earlier in my life.

As this quote illustrates, campuses that are familiar with low-income students, or staff and personnel that work directly with low-income students or who were themselves low-income students, have a much better appreciation of the importance of this financial knowledge.

Charity rather than Empowerment

When we examined postsecondary leaders' views on IDAs as a matched savings account with a financial education component, most expressed concern that low-income students should *not* save money for their education. Middle- and high-income individuals believe that low-income people are incapable of saving. And while they are correct that it is difficult for low-income populations to save money, the IDA demonstration project illustrated that low-income families and students can save and this is an important lesson toward their journey to break out of poverty.[4] The middle-and high-income biases of administrators and staff members on campus reinforces a charity or dependency perspective where the poor are always waiting for the wealthy to provide for them. It is this perspective that many critics suggest has created a dependency and cycle of poverty and led to the lack of empowerment of many populations (Schreiner et al., 2005). While middle- and high-income individuals do not mean harm in their belief that low-income people cannot save, this belief can reinforce and keep people in poverty.

These biases about low-income students not being able to save and also not wanting them to help finance their education have translated into not providing these students with tools and knowledge to succeed in the financial world. For example, financial aid does not cover all of the costs at many institutions. Books and equipment are often not considered when postsecondary staff think about the cost of attending college. The middle- and high-income class bias is that the cost of an institution tends to be the tuition and that parents cover "other costs" or these other costs are invisible, which severely disadvantages low-income students. While middle-income people do not recognize this issue, there is typically no way for low-income populations to meet the costs of attending college without working and saving. For example, after federal grants are considered, Pell grant recipients still face an average unmet need of $8,873 for all institution types; after all aid received, including student loans, Pell grant recipients faced an average unmet need of $3,516 for all institution types (Cook & King, 2007). Low-income students are also hesitant to take out loans (Burdman, 2005). Without the proper education on financial topics like loans, work/school balance, and how to save and budget, low-income students will continue to drop-out of school due to financial reasons. Financial education can empower students to make more informed decisions about their personal finances and IDAs can take the some of the financial burden of low-income students.

On the middle-income serving campuses, individuals who work closely with low-income populations such as TRIO and GEAR UP programs were notable exceptions in their opinions about IDAs. TRIO and GEAR UP staff wholeheartedly believed in the value of youth and adult students saving toward their education and receiving financial education, and recognize that this could break the cycle of poverty. A GEAR UP staff member described the importance of low-income populations saving:

> Financial education is just not enough. The habits and patterns of good financial behavior need to be integrated into any approach to make low-income students more successful. This is why I like the idea of the IDA. Students don't have to save a lot of money, but they have to save some money. They have to learn to make those hard choices of delaying gratification, budgeting, planning, using financial institutions, and holding on to a long-term goal. All of these skills are part of savings and are a part of breaking out of poverty.

Also, campuses that have large numbers of low-income students were also likely to understand the value of students saving—and not just giving scholarships. Middle- and high-income serving institutions focused all attention on scholarship acquisition.

Clearly, the biases about what is appropriate for the curriculum, co-curriculum, and services at many institutions is developed on the class-based assumption that finances are not a particularly important knowledge base. The middle-class charity view prevents leaders from seeing the value of tools such as IDAs or other matched savings options. If these assumptions are not addressed, it will be difficult to convince postsecondary leaders to adopt new policies and make financial education more of a priority.

RECONSTRUCTION: NEW OR REVISED FINANCIAL EDUCATION POLICIES AND PRACTICES TO BETTER SERVE LOW-INCOME STUDENTS AND MODEL PROGRAMS

Thus far in this chapter, we have identified that few policies and practices around financial education exist. We have also examined some of the underlying assumptions that appear to prevent postsecondary leaders and policymakers from integrating financial education and financial tools such as IDAs into campus operations. For the rest of the chapter, we want to focus on ways that postsecondary institutions can rethink their policies and practices related to financial education to better serve low-income students. Our overall advice is: to create a meaningful financial education program will entail creating a campus-wide team drawing on existing resources and offices that understand financial education (that may entail bringing in outside agencies if inside resources are more limited); integrating financial education into the curriculum, co-curriculum, services, and programs particularly focused on low-income students; developing an ethic about the importance of financial education by providing professional development for campus faculty and staff, and learning about the wealth of resources and existing financial education models. Although there is little financial education happening on college campuses, during our research project we found a few promising models of financial education programs that we highlight in this section to provide ideas for reconstructing your programs. There is no single model of financial education and various models are presented for readers.

Forming a Campus-Wide Team with Campus Financial Expertise

As noted under the hidden assumptions or biases, campuses need to do a better job utilizing the existing expertise about financial education that they have on campus. An example is that the administration can establish an ongoing committee on financial education and resources and appoint the various members of the community with expertise in this area. This team could include staff from the following offices: financial aid office, faculty with expertise about finances and financial literacy, on-campus credit union/bank, business and education department, student support office, and academic advising offices. This group can be tasked with thinking about ways that the curriculum, co-curriculum, and services might better integrate information about financial education and campus resources. They can review the policies and practices we have recommended and determine which might work best on the particular campus given the financial issues that students face. For example, adult returning students have different financial concerns than youth. This network can also be used to advise campus leaders when making decisions related to financial education and/or issues that might impact low-income students. This is an initial important step to help effectively craft and design the ideas below.[5]

Curriculum

While postsecondary leaders suggested that the curriculum would be the most difficult place to gain support for financial education, we firmly believe that financial education needs to be part of the formal curriculum. In 2008 the President's Advisory Council on Financial Literacy also recommended that the U.S. Department of Treasury and the U.S. Department of Education work together to require a college course in financial literacy. As long as financial education is marginalized to a workshop, it will never get the time and attention of students in order to more fundamentally change their knowledge base and understanding. Given data suggesting that most students lack financial literacy, a case can be made that personal finance is important knowledge that should be integrated into the formal curriculum. It appears the one place that financial information is given to students is in first-year experience courses. This presents an opportunity for building in more rigorous and substantial financial literacy. Rather than having campuses just offer a single two-hour workshop on financial issues, financial education can be introduced in several different parts of the course and related to different material that is covered. Also, these course offerings can be enhanced by having lenders, the Internal Revenue Service, and other government and community groups come in that have expertise in financial literacy.

Another approach or complementary approach is to integrate financial education into a general education requirement or core course taken by many students that seems aligned with financial education. Math courses, business courses, and economics courses could all be made more practical and real if financial education was added in. This is also one way to ensure that the low-income students gain the financial resources they need in order to be successful and retained.

We highlight three different curricular models. The University of Wisconsin-Madison and Great Lakes Higher Education Guaranty Corporation developed a three-credit pilot financial education class and tested it during the 2006 spring semester.[6] Students in the study exhibited a marked and sustained improvement in two cash management behaviors: creating a budget and keeping a spending diary. The curriculum consists of 14 modules developed to meet particular learning objectives to improve financial knowledge and skills. Modules include lecture information along with supplementary materials and activities. The curriculum has been made available for use by other educational institutions in various formats.

Financial Literacy 101, a product of Decision Partners, is an online course for college students. The curriculum has a high degree of personalization, tailoring the learning experience of each student to his or her personal goals and learning needs. This program uses a prevention-based learning model by preventing predictable financial problems related to credit cards and budgeting as students transition to an unsupervised financial life at college. Postsecondary institutions can use this program in a variety of settings—in the resident halls or in a first-year experience course. Each institution only has to pay $1500 with unlimited use.[7]

The National Endowment for Financial Education (NEFE) also has a college financial education program for universities to offer to students called the CashCourse College Program.[8] It is a free, online program that covers important college topics like living at college, buying or leasing a car, replacing lost items, studying abroad, handling peer pressure, paying for fraternities and sororities, and paying for spring break. NEFE also allows postsecondary institutions to customize the website and marketing materials according to their school colors and logo.

Co-Curriculum

The co-curriculum offers a variety of opportunities for integrating financial education—residential halls, student groups, career center, leadership programs, orientation, and the like. We offer a few examples but there are literally hundreds of opportunities. Many campuses offer career courses through their career center. Campuses can include financial education as part of the career courses that are taken by many students across various majors and interests. Career counselors can draw on on-campus and external resources to offer such workshops. While career centers are one area to capitalize on, other campuses may use another center or office. When working with returning adult low-income students some community colleges now have Centers for Working Families. These centers are a strong match for offering financial education and supplementing curricular efforts. A Center for Working Families that participated in our study had created a unique financial literacy curriculum to fit the specific needs of the low-income students who were often in economic crisis and needed to get out of significant debt and chaos before they could move to other general principles of budgeting and saving.

Another opportunity is orientations and workshops for parents; many low-income serving institutions realize that the more that parents understand the importance of finances, the more they can help support on-campus efforts. Also, reaching out to parents can impact other students that might come to their campus and helps develop general knowledge in the community. This is an approach particularly important for community colleges and regional or local institutions. Extension services are another way to reach out to the community to develop awareness about financial literacy.

One of the ways to make the co-curricular experiences more relevant and beneficial is to create financial simulations and other video-based technological tools that are attractive to incoming students. For example, Brigham Young University has created an online education tool—financial path—that helps students to calculate how much they expect to make in the future and what debt burden seems safe to take out given this information. While this software is currently not available through open source, other campuses should consider creating similar software that might engage students.

Student groups represent an important opportunity for reaching low-income students. An example of a way to partner with students' groups is to host an awareness campaign. One campus has a campaign entitled "Someday." They use slogans to get students' attention such as: "Someday I'll have a Ferrari, but for now I'll hoof it. It pays to save." Working with students to design financial education is important because they can help make it relevant and connected to the student culture of the campuses and better aligned with the particular needs of the low-income students on campus.

The co-curriculum provides many opportunities to supplement knowledge learned in the curriculum, particularly by working with student groups, connecting to other goals that students find important such as employment (through career centers), creating awareness campaigns, infusing into orientation, and educating parents who can support students.

Services

While it may not be economically possible to hire certified financial counselors to work on campus, certified financial counselors can be hired as consultants to train staff (advisers, financial aid officers, career counselors, and others who run into low-income students as part of their work) to offer various financial education workshops. Many campuses also have credit unions that can be a critical partner and provide expertise for designing financial education and training staff.

Training advisers/academic counselors that offer financial education workshops and conduct crisis training and interventions for students in major financial trouble can help bolster financial education efforts. Academic counselors tend to get many questions related to student life—not just course scheduling—and broader training is necessary for them to be effective. Some campuses have designated counselors that work with first-generation college students and the National Academic Advising Association has a special interest group where these counselors meet and discuss common challenges. Financial education has been an emerging topic with this interest group. Having campus support for advisers to address issues of financial education is important in order that they can institutionalize changes based on the needs and interests of their students. Counselors/advisers are often told to narrowly focus on course scheduling and "academic" issues, which can severely affect low-income student success.

Financial aid offices should try to see their role as financial educators not just financial aid processors. They are the one office on campus that has a mandate around financial matters and the more they model an ethic of financial education, the more likely others on campuses are likely to also support this approach. On low-income serving campuses that we went to where the financial aid offices played this role, students actually sought out advice and support from these offices. Financial education can be encouraged through the financial aid office in many different ways. For example, they can help students watch out for alternative loan vendors, provide financial referrals, and they can help develop the online tools that help students calculate and understand debt burdens. Alternative vendors are currently aggressively marketing to students through every media—radio, MTV, and billboards—and campuses need to counter these messages.

The Financial Aid and Scholarship Department at California State University, Northridge[9] initially engaged in financial literacy efforts four years ago. Through an array of opportunities students engage in learning through individual counseling, presentations, websites, and campus events. One of their primary concerns is teaching students to make informed decisions to reduce cost, and finance their college education without sacrificing their academic focus or crippling their financial futures. The department's next step is to fully deploy Financial Literacy 101, the Decision Partners program highlighted under the curriculum section. A faculty member piloted it in a classroom last term, reporting that students enthusiastically embraced the tool. The tool will be available next year and fully implemented on the department's website for all students.

A recent trend in postsecondary institutions is opening a new office on their campus independent from the financial aid office and focused on student money management services. These offices being separate allows for the financial aid office to remain focused on advising students regarding financial aid issues and the student money management office to focus on financial literacy topics. This office provides students with workshops and one-on-one counseling on personal finance—understanding credit, managing credit card debt, budgeting, etc. The staff at these offices are trained in finance and some consist of graduate assistants who are studying finance. Using current faculty as directors, graduate assistants, and trained volunteers allows for schools to cut some of the major costs in opening a new office. One nationally recognized program is the Red to Black, an outreach of an academic program in personal financial planning at Texas Tech University.[10] The name represents the school's colors and the program goal to help students get "out of the red" in their personal finances. Red to Black provides free and confidential financial counseling and education for the Texas Tech community. Services include individual or couple sessions and presentations or workshops. Select trained volunteers who are upper division or graduate students in personal financial planning provide all services. Financial services have began to slowly spread among postsecondary institutions and have had positive responses from students.

One important component of these programs is the one-on-one counseling they offer. This is especially important for low-income students who may not feel comfortable discussing their financial situations to a large group of students. In addition, the advisers are trained in finance, so they may have information and resources for low-income students.

Institutional research offices can conduct research about financial education among students to help target campus efforts. What knowledge do students have and what are the greatest gaps in their financial knowledge? A few campuses conduct research to support their financial education efforts. For example, Brigham Young University conducted an internal study that suggested if parents set aside $400 for college, the students are less likely to take out a heavy loan burden. This is one of the reasons they were so excited about IDAs because their own research supports that small savings create expectation to go to college and makes students more wary of debt because they have parents who are more aware of financial choices.

One benefit of having financial education included in the services of postsecondary institutions is that services are offered through a student's education. Co-curricular programs are often compartmentalized to key parts of a student's educational process. For example, a student's first year is usually packed with activities including orientation and first-year experience courses; although it is important to cover financial education at this time, it is also key to reinforce learning each year. In addition, financial education being included as a service allows students to come to the office or department when they are going through a particular experience and receive help immediately.

Programs for Low-Income Students

Our survey results suggest that many programs that work with low-income youth can benefit from including financial education. As we described, 50 percent of TRIO programs offer no financial education and of the 50 percent that do offer it, much is optional and fairly narrow. Resources are beginning to emerge that can help. For example, the GEAR UP national office has recently developed a national financial education curriculum in both Spanish and English that can be adopted by programs. The GEAR UP Money Skills for Real Life financial education program on low-income students' needs is offered to middle and high school students. NEFE prepared this website for the National Council for Community and Education Partnerships (NCCEP). The website was made for GEAR UP students, but it is also available to the public.[11]

Because financial education is best learned over time, introducing it within outreach programs in middle and high schools is extremely important. Financial education can fundamentally improve access efforts. Various studies have demonstrated that if a family saves only a small amount of money—a few hundred dollars—the children are more likely to believe that they can attend college (Elliott, Sherraden, Johnson, Johnson, & Peterson, 2007). Therefore, reaching out to students and their parents in these early years can have significant payoff to access efforts. As Upward Bound staff noted: "Students often have fears that they will not be able to afford higher education and do not understand the financial implications of going to college. Financial education and IDAs can create a realistic plan for having students address the financial needs of college." Therefore TRIO pre-college programs may want to offer more personal finance topics in addition to financial aid education and TRIO in-college programs may want to consider being more systematic in the timing of their education. Spreading out the education over a student's four years in college could be very beneficial. Students in their first year of college are bombarded with a lot of new information about college and therefore may not remember the advice they received about credit card debt, for example. This also allows financial topics to be reinforced in the students over time and allows the staff to highlight particular topics according to the students' year in school.

The recent Higher Education Opportunity Act (HEOA) reauthorization included financial education as a required service of all TRIO programs (or, in the case of McNair, simply makes it permissible). We encourage the directors in these programs to capitalize on this mandate and make financial literacy mandatory for all their students, not just an optional workshop.

Faculty and Staff Development

Certainly with the current economic crisis, students are not the only ones who need financial planning and help. In order to generate a greater appreciation among faculty and staff about the importance of financial education, it is important to make training available to the overall university community. The campus-wide financial education team can help develop training appropriate for staff and faculty. Such training also helps to develop the ethic and support for financial education more broadly on campus. The more that conversation occurs about finance and members of the campus community increase their literacy, the greater the likelihood that this information will become communicated and part of the fabric of the campus.[12]

BEST PEDAGOGICAL PRACTICES IN FINANCIAL EDUCATION

One of the major findings from our study is that postsecondary institutions have little understanding about existing resources about financial education. In this section, we highlight best practices from the literature on delivering financial education and highlight IDAs as a tool to strengthen a financial education program.

When beginning to search for a financial education program or creating a curriculum there are two components that have been identified in studies of financial education programs as being important for producing positive learning outcomes: when to teach financial education (during key times—teachable moments) and a successful teaching method to use (active, experiential, and problem-based learning techniques).

Financial education experts have found that learning and change in financial behaviors is more likely when financial education is offered at the same time that individuals are making a specific financial decision—teachable moments (Lerman & Bell, 2005; Peng, Bartholomae, Fox, & Cravener, 2007). Based on this finding we recommend that postsecondary institutions consider offering financial education every year of college and choosing financial topics that are most relevant according to their year in school or age.

Recently financial education experts have begun to look at diversifying the teaching methods by using active, experiential, and problem-based learning techniques (Hilgerth, Hogarth, & Beverly, 2003; NEFE, 2004; Parrish & Servon, 2006). Financial education should also allow the student to actively participate in their learning through worksheets, discussing personal experiences, and case studies. These techniques go beyond the traditional lecture style and allow for students to be actively involved in their learning by sharing their experiences and reviewing case studies.

Individual Development Accounts or IDAs is a tool that maximizes teachable moments and active, experiential, and problem-based learning techniques. IDAs as covered earlier are matched savings accounts for low-income individuals to save toward a new home, a first business or postsecondary education. Students who save with an IDA are saving with a specific goal—to pay for their education-related expenses. This act of saving for their education is a teachable moment. For example, students are in the process of learning how to save and therefore the financial education they receive provides them with the information and skills they need to be successful by reaching their goal—savings for postsecondary education. The results have shown that attending financial education (up to 10 hours) while saving for an IDA has increased savings (Schreiner et al., 2002).

IDAs also maximize active, experiential, and problem-based learning techniques because students are actively participating in the information they learn in the financial education session by saving for their IDA. Instructors can also use this opportunity to talk to students about their experience saving and can work through any problems students are having by brainstorming the issue together. Each financial topic covered in a financial education program can be related back to the student's personal experience saving for an IDA.

Including this tool into a financial education program truly allows students to practice their learning while also increasing their chances for success by maximizing the best practices found in financial education research. Detailed information about how to offer an IDA, how to apply for an AFI (Assets for Independence) grant or partner with a nonprofit, the value of IDAs, and experience working with IDAs is offered on our IDA-PAYS project website at: http://www.usc.edu/dept/chepa/IDApays/.

CONCLUSION

In this chapter, we have tried to make visible the hidden assumptions about financial education that result in its absence from most postsecondary institutions, even from those that serve large numbers of low-income students and are open to offering financial education. Low-income serving institutions often take their cue from campuses such as research universities and comprehensive institutions that serve fewer low-income students and are deeply entrenched in middle- and high-income bias and assumptions. Also, we want to make apparent that even though many people have good intentions and some are open to offering financial education, people are unaware of resources, financial education models, and even on-campus resources for offering financial education. We hope that this chapter has offered a way to re-examine existing policies and practices and to develop some new and innovative ways of helping enhance the financial education skills of low-income students. We hope that fewer low-income students end up graduating without any knowledge of finances and that fewer feel the lifetime stress and strain that hooks expressed in her opening quote of the chapter.

From our research, we believe many postsecondary leaders' views may be out of touch with the general public and policymakers. The federal government has now mandated that financial aid offices offer some form of financial education for students who take out federal loans. Some policymakers and educational leaders have become concerned about the high level of debt among students because of credit cards and student loans, for example. The recent economic crisis has everyone concerned about the financial knowledge of United States citizens. While federal policy is unlikely to mandate the curriculum and co-curriculum, legislators and the general public are sending a clear message that financial education is indeed the work of postsecondary institutions. For example, in 2008 the President's Advisory Council on Financial Literacy recommended that the U.S. Department of Treasury implement an honor roll program for innovative financial literacy programs at postsecondary institutions in order to improve financial literacy among college students. In the future, postsecondary institutions need to be able to demonstrate that they are accountable and addressing policymakers' concerns that students are financially illiterate. In addition, many states are beginning to mandate curriculum in the K-12 area related to financial literacy, where they historically have more control over the curriculum. We believe that higher education is going to become increasingly accountable for issues of financial education and while our focus has been on meeting the needs of those who are the most disadvantaged by the current system, financial education is an issue that policymakers are concerned about for all students on college campuses.

NOTES

1. However, not all community colleges have large numbers of low-income students and not all land grants serve mostly middle-income students. Yet, there is a general trend

that they serve different numbers of low-income students.

2. While we base these generalizations on the survey of TRIO, case studies of campuses, and regional and national focus groups, it was difficult to get a national picture of financial education. It can be offered by so many different offices and varies by campus type. Therefore, we based our findings on several key sources of data, yet more systematic study of financial education is surely needed. We doubt that the general findings we present though would be disputed by a national and broader based study.

3. The survey went out to 2,000 respondents and 550 replied, giving us a 27 percent response rate.

4. Research on IDA demonstration projects found that: 1. low-income individuals can save money over a long-term basis (one to four is the typical IDA); 2. low-income individuals benefit through the purchase of key assets; and 3. some individuals become self-sufficient and move out of poverty (Schreiner et al., 2002). The demonstration projects were such a success that Congress authorized ongoing funds for IDAs the last 13 years through the federal legislation Assets for Independence Act.

5. One important resource for this team is "Get financially fit: A financial education toolkit for college campuses" that helps the team to think systematically. Available at: http://www.newyorkfed.org/regional/Fin%20Ed%20Toolkit%20for%20College%20Campuses.pdf. This tool provides easily accessible information on building a successful financial education program, marketing effectively, and evaluation considerations.

6. University of Wisconsin-Madison and Great Lakes Higher Education Guaranty Corporation website: https://www.mygreatlakes.org/about/content/about/press_release/rs_press_release/061120_gl_uw_financial_education report.html.

7. Decision Partners website: http://www.decisionpartners.org.

8. CashCourse College program website: http://www.cashcourse.org/.

9. Financial Aid and Scholarship Department at California State University, Northridge website: www.csun.edu/finaid/.

10. Red to Black program website: www.r2b.ttu.edu and personal financial planning academic program website: www.pfp.ttu.edu.

11. GEAR UP Money Skills for Real Life website: http://www.gearup-moneyskills.org/.

12. A summary of organizations that offer financial education and literacy programs is provided on our project website: http://www.usc.edu/dept/chepa/IDApays/resources.html. These online programs can be marketed through a campus brochure that explains the importance of financial education and how to sign up for the online program. Please note that some of these online programs may not be tailored to low-income populations, so it may be important to supplement these programs with other information (e.g., hand-outs) or a one-on-one counseling component in order to best meet the needs of these students. In order to keep cost down, some programs invite financial advisers from the local area to speak to their students, highlighting topics important to low-income students, such as credit card debt.

REFERENCES

Burdman, P. (2005). *The student debt dilemma: Debt aversion as a barrier to college access* (Paper CSHE 13 05). Berkeley, CA: Center for Studies in Higher Education, University of California, Berkeley.

Chen, H., & Volpe, R. P. (1998). An analysis of personal financial literacy among college students. *Financial Services Review, 7*(2), 107–128.

Cook, B., & King, J. (2007). *2007 Status report on the Pell grant program.* Washington, DC: American Council on Education.

Elliott, W., Sherraden, M., Johnson, L., Johnson, S., & Peterson, S. (2007). *College expectations among young children: The potential role of savings.* St. Louis, MO: Washington University,

Center for Social Development.

Hilgerth, M., Hogarth, J., & Beverly, S. (2003). Household financial management: The connection between knowledge and behavior. *Federal Reserve Bulletin*, 309–322.

hooks, b. (2003). *Where we stand: Class matters*. New York: Routledge.

Jump$tart Coalition for Personal Financial Literacy. (2008, April). Financial literacy still declining among high school seniors, Jump$tart Coalition's 2008 survey shows. Retrieved August 2009 from http://www.jumpstart.org/

Keybank and Harris Interactive. (2006, August). *One-third of college Upperclassmen admit being financially unprepared as freshman*. Retrieved August 2009 from http://www.harrisinteractive.com

Lerman, R. I., & Bell, E. (2005). *Financial literacy strategies: Where do we go from here?* (Policy Brief 2006-PB-10). Washington, DC: Opportunity and Ownership Project, The Urban Institute.

Lyons, A. (2004). A profile of financially at-risk college students. *The Journal of Consumer Affairs, 38*(1), 56–80.

Lyons, A. (2007). *Credit practices and financial education needs of Midwest college students.* (Working paper 2007-WP-23). Indianapolis: Networks Financial Institute, Indiana State University.

National Endowment for Financial Education (NEFE). (2004). *Motivating Americans to develop constructive financial behaviors*. Denver, CO: Author.

Nellie Mae. (2005). *Undergraduate students and credit cards in 2004: An analysis of usage rates and trends*. Retrieved June 12, 2009 from http://www.nelliemae.com/library/research_12.html

Parrish, L., & Servon, L. (2006). *Policy options to improve financial education: Equipping families for their financial futures*. Washington, DC: New America Foundation, Asset Building Program.

Paulsen, M., & St. John, E. (2002). Social class and college costs: Examining the financial nexus between college choice and persistence. *Journal of Higher Education, 73*(2), 189–236.

Peng, T. M., Bartholomae, S., Fox, J. J., & Cravener, G. (2007). The impact of personal finance education delivered in high school and college courses. *Journal of Family and Economic Issues, 28*(2), 265–284.

President's Advisory Council on Financial Literacy. (2008). *2008 Annual Report to the President*. Washington, DC: U.S. Department of the Treasury.

Reed, M. (2008). *Student debt and the class of 2007*. The Project on Student Debt, an initiative of The Institute for College Access & Success. Retrieved June 12, 2009 from http://projectonstudentdebt.org/files/pub/classof2007.pdf

Schreiner, M., Clancy, M., & Sherraden, M. (2002). *Saving performance in the American Dream Demonstration: A national demonstration of Individual Development Accounts*. St. Louis, MO: Washington University, Center for Social Development.

Schreiner, M., Sherraden, M., Clancy, M., Johnson, L., Curley, J., Zhan, M., Beverly, S. G., & Grinstein-Weiss, M. (2005). Assets and the poor: Evidence from Individual Development Accounts. In M. Sherraden (Ed.), *Inclusion in the American dream: Assets, poverty, and public policy* (pp. 185–215). New York: Oxford University Press.

Tinto, V. (1993). *Leaving college: Rethinking the causes and cures of student attrition* (2nd ed.). Chicago: University of Chicago Press.

V
Transfer and Moving on to Graduate School

11

IMPROVING TRANSFER ACCESS FOR LOW-INCOME COMMUNITY COLLEGE STUDENTS

ALICIA DOWD

This chapter reports on research of the Study of Economic, Informational, and Cultural Barriers to Community College Student Transfer Access at Selective Institutions, conducted in 2006 by the New England Resource Center for Higher Education (NERCHE) of the University of Massachusetts Boston and the Center for Urban Education at the University of Southern California. I wish to acknowledge the valued contributions of numerous colleagues to the study, particularly my co-principal investigator Glenn Gabbard, as well as Estela Mara Bensimon, John Cheslock, Jay Dee, Dwight Giles, Elsa Macias, Lindsey Malcom, Tatiana Melguizo, Jenny Pak, and Sharon Singleton. The study was funded by The Jack Kent Cooke Foundation, Lumina Foundation for Education, and Nellie Mae Education Foundation.

Patrick Sullivan, a community college English professor, asserts that poor and working-class community college students "understand that class is a powerful reality in America, and they feel its inequities sharply" (Sullivan, 2005, p. 145). He argues that these students "have been taught by harsh economic realities that classic American 'happy endings' do not apply to them" (p. 146). The findings from a national study of transfer conducted by me and others (Dowd, Bensimon, Gabbard, Singleton, et al., 2006) indicates that, indeed, happy endings are elusive when it comes to transfer from community colleges to selective four-year colleges and universities. In this chapter, I synthesize previously reported findings to suggest steps faculty members can take to improve transfer access for low-income students.

From interviews from our study with faculty, counselors, and students, I describe how faculty can act as "transfer agents," individuals who bring a critical consciousness to help students understand the specialized language of higher education and take advantage of the resources available to them. From our review of transfer programs, policies, and practices at eight pairs of community college and four-year college campuses selected as potential exemplars of equitable transfer practices, I describe how faculty can act as "transfer champions" to modify such transfer structures to facilitate transfer by low-income community college students. In large part this involves becoming aware of class-based inequities in transfer access and becoming willing to take responsibility for changing the programs, policies, and practices that disadvantage low-income students.

Among the solutions that are most often held up as strategies to improve higher education access for low-income students through the transfer function, those that attempt to make the structures of transfer more visible (namely articulation agreements) are the most prominent. However, such strategies will be insufficient if important institutional actors such as faculty are not involved in questioning the hidden assumptions and unquestioned norms that make those structures difficult for low-income students to navigate.

Before exploring the ramifications of overemphasizing structural solutions at the expense of attention to the faculty role in facilitating transfer access, I describe the scope of the problem of limited transfer access for low-income students based on statistical analyses from our study. For two reasons, I focus primarily on transfer to highly selective public institutions. First, public universities enroll the majority of community college transfer students (Dowd, Cheslock, & Melguizo, 2008) and many have a statutory obligation to enroll transfers. Second, the admissions practices of highly selective public flagship universities are of special importance when we consider whether the distribution of postsecondary opportunity is meritocratic (Bowen, Kurzweil, & Tobin, 2005; Gutmann, 1987) and whether community colleges are in fact a cornerstone of a democratic education system (Brint & Karabel, 1989). The socioeconomic and racial-ethnic composition of the elite student body is of special concern because elite institutions also function as gatekeepers to advanced, graduate, and professional education and to positions of civic and corporate leadership. The pursuit of "excellence" today may well be displacing a social commitment to equity in higher education, reducing access to highly selective institutions for students from less affluent families (Bowen et al., 2005).

LIMITED TRANSFER ACCESS FOR LOW-INCOME COMMUNITY COLLEGE STUDENTS

Although community colleges and the transfer function are often construed as the embodiment of democratic opportunities for access to higher education, transfer is primarily something affluent students do. Among high school graduates of the Class of 1992 who transferred to highly selective colleges and universities, 79 percent were from the two highest socioeconomic quintiles. Students categorized as having the lowest level of socioeconomic status (SES) contributed *a mere 2 percent* of the student body who transferred to this group of colleges assigned the highest prestige rankings based on information in the Barron's Profile of American Colleges. This suggests that fewer than one of every one thousand transfer students are low-income students. As we might expect, the share of low-income students increases when we look at transfers from community colleges to institutions of lesser selectivity. Even then, however, affluent students are greatly over-represented and low-income students are nearly absent. The two top SES quintiles still represent greater than half of the transfer enrollment (56 percent) and the lowest quintile *only 6 percent* (Dowd et al., 2008).

The two drivers creating an institutional openness to or demand for transfers are "market" and "mission." Not surprisingly, then, the preferences of four-year institutions for transfer students differs according to their governance and financing (public or private), selectivity, and type (liberal arts focus and federal research orientation) (Cheslock, 2005; Dowd & Cheslock, 2006). Trend analyses demonstrate that it became more difficult to transfer between 1984 and 2002, the most recent data available at the time of our study. Highly selective institutions and private institutions at all levels of selectivity decreased their transfer enrollments during this period. As shown in the transfer enrollment rate trend lines in the upper panel of Figure 11.1, the typical percentage of transfers in the entering class at private elite institutions declined almost by half, from 10.5 percent to 5.7 percent.[1] Private institutions of lesser selectivity admitted a much larger share of transfers, but there too transfers lost about a 5 percent share, as enrollments dropped from near 30 percent to 25 percent.

Transfer is part of the statutory role and mission of public universities. Not surprisingly then, and as shown in the lower panel of Figure 11.1, transfer enrollment rates at public institutions are much higher. From 1984 to 2002, transfer enrollment rates hovered around 20 percent at selective public universities, with a decline in the late 1990s that neared 15 percent before rebounding somewhat. At other public institutions, transfers contributed about a third of the entering class in 2002. Even in this less competitive public sector, by the mid-nineties transfer students were losing enrollment share. The only type of institution to increase transfer access from 1984 to 2002 was the least competitive public colleges and universities, which suggests that transfers may have been impacted by a "trickle down" effect (Astin & Oseguera, 2004). As entry to colleges

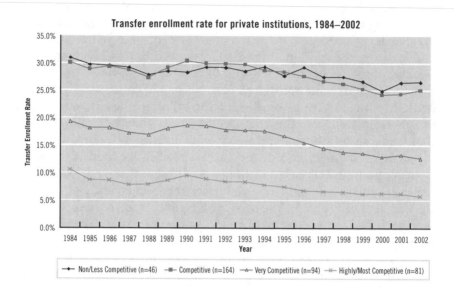

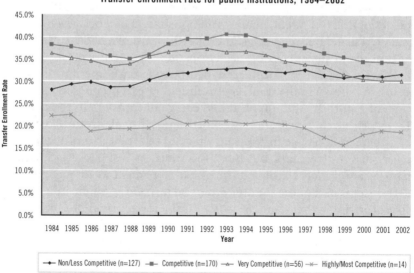

Figure 11.1   Transfer Enrollment Rates for Private and Public Institutions, 1984–2002

with any degree of selectivity became more difficult, transfers may have been redirected to open access four-year institutions. There is some evidence that the socioeconomic distribution of transfer enrollments became more skewed toward affluent students during this period (Dowd & Melguizo, 2008).

DECONSTRUCTING PROMINENT SOLUTIONS FOR TRANSFER ACCESS

The functioning of colleges and universities can be viewed through various lenses. In a bureaucratic mode, institutions rely on structures such as rules, regulations, hierarchies of decision making and information flow, formal divisions of labor and high levels of role specialization (Birnbaum, 1988). Today the most prominent efforts to improve transfer access involve legislating articulation agreements (articulating curriculum requirements and course numbering), creating public databases listing transfer requirements, and providing financial incentives for students to transfer. All of these solutions operate primarily in a bureaucratic mode, with political considerations adding to their perceived importance.

Notwithstanding the Jack Kent Cooke Foundation's Community College Transfer Initiative, for which my and my colleagues' research was conducted with the express purpose of drawing attention to socioeconomic inequities in transfer access (Wyner, 2006), the problem of the lack of transfer access for low-income students has largely been out of view. Although various forms of articulation have been treated as important policies to improve transfer (Anderson, Alfonso, & Sun, 2006; Long, 2005; "Transfer and Articulation," 2005; U.S. Department of Education, 2006; Wellman, 2002), articulation policies are mostly about improving the efficiency of the transfer of credits (Roksa & Keith, 2008), not about improving equity in the distribution of transfer resources. They are structural reforms touted by politicians and educational leaders to communicate the efficiency of transfer systems, largely to middle-class voters who, although feeling they are getting closed out of selective four-year universities, may be wary of enrolling their children in community colleges (Anderson, Alfonso, et al., 2006).

Articulation policies aim to improve transfer by canonizing transfer requirements (to regulate institutions) and publicizing them (to inform students of the classes they should take, when, and in what sequence in order to apply credits earned in community colleges to bachelor's degrees). California's ASSIST database, which is the state's official record of transfer requirements and agreements, illustrates the informational aspects of articulation policies. Students can use the data base to identify which courses to take in order to transfer to certain institutions and to earn degrees in particular programs or majors.

There are many challenges to effective articulation, including differences in course content across the two- and four-year sectors, curriculum sequencing, course numbering, the use of quarter versus semester systems in different institutions, and the inadequate supply of places in upper division classrooms for students in high demand programs. Articulation agreements can quickly become quite complex and managing them becomes as much a matter of "building and sustaining personal relationships" as of bureaucratic compliance. In the absence of strong personal relationships between faculty and administrators at two- and four-year campuses, the quality of articulation agreements is likely to erode (Gabbard et al., 2006, p. 35).

Perhaps not surprisingly then, it appears that articulation agreements have not been particularly effective at promoting transfer (Anderson, Sun, & Alfonso, 2006; Roksa & Keith, 2008). This is likely due to the fact that when articulation agreements and mandated transfer of credit requirements are instituted, they are treated as structural solutions and the interpersonal and relational aspects of making those requirements work are overlooked.

Transfer structures, like all social and bureaucratic systems (Kemmis & McTaggart, 2000), shape the occupational identities of those who work in them. From this view, when we create detailed transfer regulations, faculty no longer have expertise to advise students about transfer or the expectation that they should do so. They do not work in transfer centers—the domain of specialized counselors and administrators—nor do they have familiarity with transfer databases, which are designed for students to navigate independently. If low-income students lack transfer access, the faculty are removed from responsibility for this problem because the solution has been constructed almost entirely in terms of rules, regulations, and incentives for students.

Transfer requirements are complicated, so certainly informational transfer databases are needed and valuable. However, putting the information out there is a half-step at best. Many low-income students are first-generation students, unfamiliar with the specialized terms and resources of higher education. The experience of one student, related by Pak, Bensimon, Malcom, Marquez, and Park (2006; see also Bensimon, 2007) based on a life history and narrative analysis of ten low-income community college transfer students who successfully transferred to an elite institution, highlights this point. The life history narrative of Lisbeth Marian Giles (a pseudonym) illustrates that making information available about transfer opportunities is not the same as making students aware that those opportunities are available to *them*.

Even though Ms. Giles "surprised herself by earning a 4.0 grade point average in her first year at the community college," she still lacked confidence or an understanding that she was eligible for transfer because she had internalized the view of herself as not "smart enough" or "rich enough" to transfer to a four-year institution (pp. 28–29). She emphasized her own timidity in the college environment and the fact that she did not act on available information until an adviser finally took her under wing:

> Because when I was a 4.0 student that first year...I never got anything. I was never offered honors. I was never offered Phi Beta Kappa. I was never offered transfer information. There was transfer information on the walls in the transfer office for...local state colleges around here. But that all had to be initiated by the student. And if you're a timid little student who doesn't know anything, you wouldn't go anywhere.

An adviser, Mr. Rollins (a pseudonym), helped Lisbeth Marian Giles overcome her timidity. He "mentored and guided her in a very personal way, almost as a father figure" to help her "overcome psychological barriers" or her "own feelings of inadequacy" (p. 28).

An essential point to be taken from this story is that data are not "self-acting" (Cohen, Raudenbush, & Ball, 2003). Students are not able to consume information and make use of it until they realize its relevance to their own lives. Ms. Giles' educational experiences had already shaped her identity so strongly that it was hard for her to believe she was indeed elite "college material." The transfer center director at her community college, Mr. Rollins, acted as an "institutional agent," using institutionally based funds of knowledge (Stanton-Salazar, 1997) to enable her to make use of the transfer information and opportunities available (Bensimon, 2007).

Stanton-Salazar (1997) has argued that practitioners at colleges and universities have "institutionally based funds of knowledge" that include content about, among other things, academic subjects, career planning, and the organization of educational institutions. In addition, he emphasized that practitioners understand the specialized language, relationships, and networks of the people who work at colleges and universities in ways that students new to higher education cannot. When they use this specialized knowledge to help students, particularly racial minority students, to navigate academic and bureaucratic processes such as transfer, they are acting as institutional "agents" to enable students to make use of educational resources. Similarly, practitioners who play this role to facilitate the transfer of low-income students, African Americans, Latinas, Latinos, and other underserved ethnic groups act as "transfer agents" (Bensimon, 2007; Bensimon & Dowd, in press; Dowd, Bensimon, Gabbard, Singleton, et al., 2006; Pak et al., 2006).

RECONSTRUCTING SOLUTIONS FOR IMPROVED TRANSFER ACCESS

Today prominent strategies to improve transfer, including the various forms of articulation created through regulations, informational databases, and guaranteed transfer programs, neglect the key role faculty can play in facilitating transfer for low-income students. This omission is problematic because faculty can play an important role as "transfer agents" by mentoring students and providing role models (Bensimon, 2007; Bensimon & Dowd, in press; Dowd, Bensimon, Gabbard, Singleton, et al., 2006; Pak et al., 2006). As we found through our case study of eight pairs of community colleges and highly selective four-year institutions selected as potential exemplars of a transfer-amenable culture, faculty can also act as "transfer champions." In this role, apart from their direct interactions with students, faculty influence institutional policies in areas such as curriculum, counseling and advising, financial aid, and assessment of student learning and institutional effectiveness (Gabbard et al., 2006). They draw on their organizational funds of knowledge (Stanton-Salazar, 1997) to reshape institutional cultures and structures to make them more amenable to low-income transfer students.

The specific practices of transfer agents include advising students one-on-one to let them know which rules must be followed strictly and which ones are malleable; assisting students with preparing college application forms; identifying financial resources for transfer, for example by conducting an online search of financial aid databases with a student; alerting students to enhanced academic programming, such as Honors programs, teaching assistantships, research internships, or opportunities for independent study; introducing them to other faculty or staff who can serve as role models or mentors; and physically going with students to university campuses for guided tours.

Transfer champions act by representing the interests and interjecting the experiences of community college transfer students in their service on university committees and in their interactions with faculty colleagues. Gabbard et al. (2006) relate the experiences of community college and four-year college faculty who collaborated to offer extended academic programming, such as a summer research seminar, to community college students. Through the collaborations, faculty gained a better sense of the difficult transitions facing transfer students. They overcame perceptions of the "cultural divide" separating the two sectors that can create mistrust among faculty at institutions of unequal prestige and selectivity (Gabbard et al., 2006, p. 36). Their new knowledge translated into change in their practices. Some four-year college faculty became "sensitized to a greater variety of learning styles" and adopted new teaching techniques.

This played out at an institutional level because these individuals then shared what they had learned with their colleagues, which affected the "larger curricular landscapes" (p. 81). This type of change is particularly important in light of the finding that the four-year faculty respondents were likely to "reject programs and practices that they perceived as remedial" (p. 80). Through interactions with community college colleagues and students, elite college faculty reframed the problem of transfer access away from the prevailing deficit perspective focused on the lack of merit of community college students and the lesser quality of community colleges.

For their part, community college faculty involved in collaborative teaching and curriculum design with faculty at selective institutions learned that their students could succeed at competitive four-year institutions and broadened their sense of the community college transfer mission to afford students the chance to do so. They became more familiar with the admissions review processes at the four-year institutions, which enabled them to "become more skilled at writing letters of recommendation and helping students complete applications to four-year institutions" (p. 81). These insights translated into broader institutional changes in the form of orientation and academic development programs.

Given the powerful role faculty often play as formal and informal institutional leaders, changes in beliefs, attitudes, teaching practices, and personal interactions matter. As one faculty respondent put it, "anything that's going to work in a place like this has to be faculty-driven and faculty-owned" (p. 80). This means that curriculum committees, admissions committees, and faculty governance meetings at four-year institutions are essential venues for improving transfer access for low-income students. These committees determine what kind of curriculum counts when students transfer and how to determine the merit of a student's performance at the community college. In these venues, transfer champions are those who draw on their organizational funds of knowledge about the community college curriculum and community college students to negate unwarranted assumptions of a lack of quality. This is particularly important in the prestige-maximizing culture of many selective institutions. It is difficult to signal the academic accomplishments of potential community college transfers, many of whom are "late bloomers" (Pak et al., 2006), in environments where academic merit is so strongly defined by standardized test scores.

Based on the research my colleagues and I conducted for the Jack Kent Cooke Foundation's Community College Transfer Initiative, which ultimately awarded grants of approximately one million dollars each to eight highly selective universities to increase transfer access for low-income students, we recommended strategies for creating a "transfer-amenable culture" (Dowd, Bensimon, Gabbard, Singleton, et al., 2006). We arrayed these recommendations along four dimensions: structural, informational, relational, and cultural. We chose this configuration to emphasize that the role of faculty, in their relationships with transfer students and through their ability to shape institutional cultures, should be enhanced as a complement to the structural and informational supports for transfer provided through articulation policies.

In making these recommendations, we used the expression "extra mile advising" to characterize what faculty members do when they act outside of institutional norms and take responsibility for ensuring transfer access in very personalized ways. But, it is necessary to ask, what would motivate extra mile advising among faculty at selective universities, where many faculty are focused on their research, or at community colleges, where faculty have heavy teaching loads and little time for advising? Our case study findings highlighted two factors. Individuals who had been transfer students themselves were motivated by their own experiences and identification with the transfer experience. Others were motivated by a sense of empathy, gained through relationships with transfer students or through faculty collaborations that enabled them to understand the cultural shock transfer students experience moving from one sector to another (Gabbard et al., 2006).

But, what would lead faculty unfamiliar with transfer students to adopt such an empathic position, particularly given all the other pressures on faculty for research and teaching? Community college transfers are largely invisible to the majority of faculty at elite institutions and aspiring transfers are one of many different groups of students with differing ambitions at community colleges. First of all, elite college faculty would need to become aware that the problem of inequitable access for low-income transfer students exists and that they can play a role in rectifying it. At community colleges, faculty would need to accept that providing a transfer pathway to elite institutions for academically able students is part of their college's mission (along with transfer to comprehensive, non-selective universities, developmental education, and workforce development), and that they themselves are in the best position to identify and mentor students with the talent and ability to benefit at a prestigious public university.

One way to assist faculty in seeing the lack of transfer access for low-income students as a problem of institutional practice is to engage them in seeing for themselves how difficult it is to navigate the transfer process and how few human and material resources are allocated for assisting students in transfer. The findings I have reported above come from the Study of Economic, Informational, and Cultural Barriers to Community College Student Transfer Access to Selective Colleges (Dowd, Bensimon, Gabbard, Singleton, et al., 2006). In addition to generating statistical and interpretive results and examples of exemplary transfer practices, the study led to the creation of two institutional self-assessment protocols focused on transfer, one for community colleges (Dowd, Bensimon, & Gabbard, 2006a) and one for highly selective four-year institutions (Dowd, Bensimon, & Gabbard, 2006b).

These assessment instruments, which are a series of indicators grouped with appropriate assessment scales in categories of institutional practice, were designed to engage faculty (as well as of counselors and administrators) in "action inquiry"(Greenwood & Levin, 2005; Kemmis & McTaggart, 2000). Action inquiry involves the systematic use of data, collaboration, reflection, and deliberative practice to bring attention and resources to bear on rectifying problems of practice. The assessment instruments bring current practices into relief by providing indicators of exemplary practice for use in a diagnostic benchmarking process (Dowd & Tong, 2007). These indicators were developed through analysis and categorization of the case study results from our study (Gabbard et al., 2006). Through diagnostic benchmarking, teams of faculty, administrators, and counselors compare their own institutional practices against the indicators and exemplary practices to see what is and is not taking place on their campus to take institutional responsibility for transfer equity (Dowd, 2008).

For example, the section of the assessment instrument on institutional transfer policies and practices at community colleges includes indicators for transfer workshops, transfer credit evaluation counselors, board of trustee and alumni involvement. In regard to faculty involvement it lists professional development opportunities for learning how to assist transfer students. The same section on the four-year version includes indicators for policies enabling standardized test scores to be waived for transfer admissions, clear credit review policies, and training for assessing curriculum and credits earned at the community college. In regard to faculty, partnerships and collaboration with community colleges is highlighted, with indicators for joint faculty research and funding, pedagogy workshops, joint community service, and the presence of community college faculty on committees relevant to the transfer function.

NEXT STEPS

In new projects subsequent to the research reported in this chapter, Estela Bensimon and I have continued to develop and field test transfer self-assessment instruments (SAIs) for action research (on our part) and action inquiry (on the part of collaborating practitioner colleagues) (see Bensimon, Dowd, Alford, & Trapp, 2007; Bensimon, Rueda, Dowd, & Harris III, 2007; Dowd, 2008; Dowd, Bensimon, Bordoloi, & Watford, 2007). This work has involved our colleagues at USC's Center for Urban Education and faculty, administrators, and counselors at community colleges and four-year institutions in California and Wisconsin.

In field testing, we have been particularly attentive to issues of content validity, examining whether the transfer self-assessment indicators needed modification for the local contexts of action inquiry. This led to modifications of the community college version of the Transfer SAI for our study at Long Beach (CA) City College of transfer-eligible students who do not transfer (Bensimon, Dowd, et al., 2007). In our work in Wisconsin, we are improving the content validity of our transfer self-assessment tools by incorporating indicators of transfer access for racial-ethnic groups underserved by higher education (namely, in the Wisconsin context, African Americans, Latinas and Latinos, and Hmong students) (Dowd et al., 2007).

We also examined the theoretical construct validity of the use of self-assessment instruments to bring about organizational learning and change. In this respect, we adopt Greenwood and Levin's standards for the validity, reliability, and credibility of action research, which, they argue, are "measured by the willingness of local stakeholders to act on the results of the action research" (2005, p. 54). We find that the validity of our action research at Long Beach City College, for example, is demonstrated by the fact that some of the practitioners who collaborated with us in a variety of action research projects have adopted changes in their teaching and advising practices. In addition to these changes in individual beliefs and practices, a new program was instituted, called a Transfer Academy, to provide specialized transfer counseling and advising to potential transfers. This programmatic initiative was accompanied by news of transfer students and transfer requirements on the campus website, revealing new attention to transfer issues.

Practitioners who wish to conduct action inquiry to improve transfer access for low-income students on their own campuses can adopt the transfer self-assessment instruments that we have developed (available from the Center for Urban Education at USC, http://cue.usc.edu/) or examine their own institutional data and assessment practices as a starting point for inquiry. A number of articles by CUE researchers describe the rationale for creating a "culture of inquiry" (Dowd, 2005) and provide examples of the steps needed to do so (Bensimon, 2004; Bensimon, Polkinghorne, Bauman, & Vallejo, 2004; Bensimon, Rueda, et al., 2007; Dowd, 2008; Dowd & Tong, 2007; Pena, Bensimon, & Colyar, 2006). Today, the standards for accreditation self-study encourage inquiry as a strategy for organizational change and provide an important impetus to do so. Two questions should guide action inquiry in the area of transfer. First, are we framing the problems of the lack of transfer as a problem of practice, amenable to our own changes in practice, or are we assuming a lack of merit on the part of aspiring transfer students? And, second, are we acting as "transfer agents" and "transfer champions" to improve transfer equity?

The report from Long Beach City College's action inquiry project, called "Missing 87: A Study of the 'Transfer Gap' and 'Choice Gap'" (Bensimon, Dowd, et al., 2007), provides a detailed example of how to do this type of work and illustrates the potential outcomes (available at http://cue.usc. edu/). At Long Beach City College, approximately 20 faculty, administrators, and counselors divided up into two teams to gather data on the transfer culture and practices at their campus. One team interviewed students about their transfer aspirations and outcomes. Another reviewed documents and observed how transfer advising was conducted at transfer fairs and in the transfer center on campus. This qualitative data was discussed in meetings of the inquiry team, as was quantitative data showing the rates of student progress through the transfer curriculum. Based on what they learned, participants recommended steps for improvement in the project report. As noted above, a number of these changes were incorporated through individual changes in instruction and advising or through changes in institutional policies.

Faculty can spur this type of research on their own campuses by requesting an inquiry process as part of accreditation review or programmatic self-studies. More generally, simply asking for and relying on data about the outcomes of students who transfer or aspire to transfer—along with indicators of their socioeconomic status, such as Pell grant receipt or enrollment intensity (full time or part time)—can motivate attention to the experiences of transfer for low income students.

NOTE

1. The transfer enrollment rate is the proportion of transfer students among the total number of new freshmen and transfers in an enrolling class. The different levels of selectivity are based on the institutions' rankings in the Barron's Profiles of American Colleges. Elite institutions are defined as those with average combined SAT scores above 1,240.

REFERENCES

Anderson, G. M., Alfonso, M., & Sun, J. C. (2006). Rethinking cooling out at public community colleges: An examination of fiscal and demographic trends in higher education and the rise of statewide articulation agreements. *Teachers College Record, 108*(3), 422–451.

Anderson, G. M., Sun, J. C., & Alfonso, M. (2006). Effectiveness of statewide articulation agreements on the probability of transfer: A preliminary policy analysis. *Review of Higher Education, 29*(3), 261–291.

Astin, A. W., & Oseguera, L. (2004). The declining "equity" of American higher education. *Review of Higher Education, 27*(3), 321–341.

Bensimon, E. M. (2004, January/February). The diversity scorecard: A learning approach to institutional change. *Change,* 45–52.

Bensimon, E. M. (2007). The underestimated significance of practitioner knowledge in the scholarship of student success. *The Review of Higher Education, 30*(4), 441–469.

Bensimon, E. M., & Dowd, A. C. (in press). Dimensions of the "transfer choice" gap: Experiences of Latina and Latino students who navigated transfer pathways. *Harvard Educational Review.*

Bensimon, E. M., Dowd, A. C., Alford, H., & Trapp, F. (2007). *Missing 87: A study of the "transfer gap" and "choice gap."* Long Beach and Los Angeles, CA: Long Beach City College and the Center for Urban Education, University of Southern California.

Bensimon, E. M., Polkinghorne, D. E., Bauman, G. L., & Vallejo, E. (2004). Doing research that makes a difference. *Journal of Higher Education, 75*(1), 104–126.

Bensimon, E. M., Rueda, R., Dowd, A. C., & Harris III, F. (2007). Accountability, equity, and practitioner learning and change. *Metropolitan, 18*(3), 28–45.

Birnbaum, R. (1988). *How colleges work: The cybernetics of academic organization and leadership.* San Francisco: Jossey-Bass.

Bowen, W. G., Kurzweil, M. A., & Tobin, E. M. (2005). *Equity and excellence in American higher education.* Charlottesville: University of Virginia Press.

Brint, S., & Karabel, J. (1989). *The diverted dream: Community colleges and the promise of educational opportunity in America, 1900–1985.* New York: Oxford University Press.

Cheslock, J. J. (2005). Differences between public and private institutions of higher education in the enrollment of transfer students. *Economics of Education Review, 24*(3), 263–274.

Cohen, D. K., Raudenbush, S. W., & Ball, D. L. (2003). Resources, instruction, and research. *Educational Evaluation and Policy Analysis, 25*(2), 119–142.

Dowd, A. C. (2005). *Data don't drive: Building a practitioner-driven culture of inquiry to assess community college performance* (Research Report). Indianapolis, IN: Lumina Foundation for Education.

Dowd, A. C. (2008). The community college as gateway and gatekeeper: Moving beyond the access "saga" to outcome equity. *Harvard Educational Review, 77*(4), 407–419.

Dowd, A. C., Bensimon, E. M., Bordoloi, L., & Watford, T. (2007). *Does "2+2" still equal four? Examining the "new math" of transfer access from community colleges to the baccalaureate.* Presented at the Association for the Study of Higher Education, Jacksonville, FL.

Dowd, A. C., Bensimon, E. M., & Gabbard, G. (2006a). *Transfer access self-assessment inventory: For community colleges.* Retrieved May 5, 2008, from www.jackkentcookefoundation.org [links: Grants and RFPs/Community College Transfer Initiative/2006 National Forum]

Dowd, A. C., Bensimon, E. M., & Gabbard, G. (2006b). *Transfer access self-assessment inventory: For four-year colleges.* Retrieved May 5, 2008, from www.jackkentcookefoundation.org [links: Grants and RFPs/Community College Transfer Initiative/2006 National Forum]

Dowd, A. C., Bensimon, E. M., Gabbard, G., Singleton, S., Macias, E., Dee, J., et al. (2006). *Transfer access to elite colleges and universities in the United States: Threading the needle of the American dream.* Retrieved May 5, 2008, from www.jackkentcookefoundation.org [links: Grants and RFPs/Community College Transfer Initiative/CCTI Research Report/ Executive Summary]

Dowd, A. C., & Cheslock, J. J. (2006). *An estimate of the two-year transfer population at elite institutions and of the effects of institutional characteristics on transfer access.* Retrieved May 5, 2008, from www.jackkentcookefoundation.org [links: Grants and RFPs/Community College Transfer Initiative/CCTI Research Report/Section II]

Dowd, A. C., Cheslock, J., & Melguizo, T. (2008). Transfer access from community colleges and the distribution of elite higher education. *Journal of Higher Education, 79*(4), 1–31.

Dowd, A. C., & Melguizo, T. (2008). Socioeconomic stratification of community college transfer access in the 1980s and 1990s. *Review of Higher Education, 31*(4), 377–400.

Dowd, A. C., & Tong, V. P. (2007). Accountability, assessment, and the scholarship of "best practice." In J. C. Smart (Ed.), *Handbook of higher education* (Vol. 22, pp. 57–119). New York: Springer.

Gabbard, G., Singleton, S., Macias, E., Dee, J., Bensimon, E. M., Dowd, A. C., et al. (2006). *Practices supporting transfer of low-income community college transfer students to selective institutions: Case study findings.* Retrieved May 5, 2008, from www.jackkentcookefoundation.org [links: Grants and RFPs/Community College Transfer Initiative/CCTI Research Report/Section IV]

Greenwood, D. J., & Levin, M. (2005). Reform of the social sciences and of universities through action research. In N. K. Denzin & Y. S. Lincoln (Eds.), *Handbook of qualitative research* (3rd ed., pp. 43–64). Thousand Oaks, CA: Sage Publications.

Gutmann, A. (1987). *Democratic education.* Princeton, NJ: Princeton University Press.

Kemmis, S., & McTaggart, R. (2000). Participatory action research. In N. K. Denzin & Y. S. Lincoln (Eds.), *Handbook of qualitative research* (2nd ed., pp. 567–605). Thousand Oaks, CA: Sage Publications.

Long, B. T. (2005). *State financial aid policies to enhance articulation and transfer.* Boulder, CO: Western Interstate Commission for Higher Education

Pak, J., Bensimon, E. M., Malcom, L., Marquez, A., & Park, D. (2006). The life histories of ten individuals who crossed the border between community colleges and selective four-year colleges. Retrieved May 5, 2008, from www.jackkentcookefoundation.org [links: Grants and RFPs/Community College Transfer Initiative/CCTI Research Report/Section III]

Pena, E. V., Bensimon, E. M., & Colyar, J. (2006). Contextual problem defining: Learning to think and act. *Liberal Education, 92*(2), 48–55.

Roksa, J., & Keith, B. (2008). Credits, time, and attainment: Articulation policies and success after transfer. *Educational Evaluation and Policy Analysis, 30*(3), 236–254.

Stanton-Salazar, R. D. (1997). A social capital framework for understanding the socialization of racial minority children and youths. *Harvard Educational Review, 67*(1), 1–40.

Transfer and Articulation. (2005). SideNotes: *The Education Commission of the States (ECS).* Retrieved May 1, 2006, from www.ecs.org/clearinghouse/23/75/2375.htm

Sullivan, P. (2005). Cultural narratives about success and the material conditions of class at the community college. *Teaching English in the Two-Year College, 32*(2), 142–160.

U.S. Department of Education. (2006). *A test of leadership: Charting the future of U.S. higher education.* Washington, DC: Author.

Wellman, J. V. (2002). *State policy and community college-baccalaureate transfer.* San Jose, CA, and Washington, DC: National Center for Public Policy and Higher Education and the Institute for Higher Education Policy.

Wyner, J. (2006, February 10). Educational equity and the transfer student. *Chronicle of Higher Education,* p. B6.

12

POST-BACCALAUREATE PREPARATION AND ACCESS FOR LOW-INCOME STUDENTS AND THE MYTH OF A LEVEL PLAYING FIELD

ALEX JUN AND KRISTIN PAREDES-COLLINS

A great deal of research has demonstrated the importance and value of educating a diverse student body that includes those of varying socioeconomic and racial backgrounds (Chang, 1999; Hurtado, Milem, Clayton-Pederson, & Allen, 1998; Ibarra, 2001; Milem, Chang, & Antonio, 2005). Positioned within this book, this chapter presents the need for an extended focus on low-income students' persistence beyond the baccalaureate, and into graduate school. Each year, educators rightly celebrate the graduation of low-income students. Individual success stories are singled out, and students that have successfully navigated college to pursue a career in a worthwhile field are highlighted with great university pride. However, implicit in these celebrated stories is an assumption that the achievement of a Bachelor's degree is "good enough" for low-income students, as they overcame insurmountable odds to reach such an accomplishment.

Less than half a century ago, the United States was rife with the overt forms of injustice, such as state-mandated segregation, "separate but equal" laws, and other intentional forms of systemic racism. Although overt racism, blatant gender inequality, and intentional classism has been morphed into hidden forms of prejudice over the decades, we continue to live in a nation that is plagued with the stains of this social stratification. As Adrianna Kezar alludes in her introductory chapter, stratification has an impact on class, as the system of higher education privileges the wealthy and continues to oppress the poor. Correspondingly, Bowen, Kurzweil, and Tobin (2005) delivered a call to recognize the persisting effects of the sordid past of the United States and to engage in the morally just action of addressing the disparities that still remain. They submit that stratification has led to exclusionary barriers on, among other things, class. Sacks (2007) refers to a "great sorting" that continues to stratify students as they muddle through middle school, high school, college, and beyond.

In order to shed light on an area that is in great need of systemic change and reconceptualization, we explore the inequity of advanced learning at the post-baccalaureate level for low-income students through a lens of post-structuralism. We critique the current system of higher education that perpetuates the myth of meritocracy for the wealthy, while systemically oppressing the poor by preventing greater opportunities to explore graduate education. This systemic inequity continues to hold low-income students to a secondary standard—college attainment (a Bachelor's degree) is considered the pinnacle accomplishment for low-income students, while advanced degrees are considered as a viable and attainable option for high- and middle-income students. In an effort to make progress in this area, institutions need to identify low-income students as a significant priority and acknowledge their under-enrollment.

In this chapter we consider the importance of extending the pipeline achievement *beyond* the baccalaureate. To this end we first explore and deconstruct the Ronald E. McNair Post Baccalaureate Achievement Program, a federally funded program designed to serve low-income students. We then offer suggestions for the reconstruction of the current structure of higher education on both a programmatic and institutional level for low-income students, as it pertains to graduate preparation programs.

LOW-INCOME STUDENTS AND GRADUATE SCHOOL

In 1986 the Council of Graduate Schools (2004) declared a crisis, saying that the "end of the pipeline had been reached" because of the low participation of low-income students and students of color. This projected a decrease of qualified students of diverse backgrounds prepared to enter post-baccalaureate degree programs. According to the National Center for Education Statistics (1999), this situation has not changed markedly since 1985, when less than 12 percent of underrepresented students, including those from low-income families, chose to pursue education pathways that led to academic careers that required advanced degrees.

The emergent knowledge economy of today functions with educated individuals who are able to succeed in a diverse and culturally broad environment. In terms of expanding this body of educated individuals, diversity in social class is an important piece to the milieu of diversity. Most institutions of higher education largely support middle- and high-income student success. Graduate education has, in some respects, become the new Bachelor's degree of the previous generation—compulsory for the elite few, and a significant accomplishment for those of little means. Through the critical lens of post-structuralism, we see that the challenges for low-income students are embedded in the daily policies and practices of an institution.

During the 2005/2006 academic year, 45,596 research doctorates were awarded by U.S. universities. With a 5.1 percent increase over the previous year, this marks the year with the greatest number of doctorates awarded in the United States (Survey of Earned Doctorates, 2007). However, of the doctorates awarded, it is likely that a disproportionate number of students from low-income backgrounds persisted to earn a graduate degree. In a study of the Ph.D. pursuant behaviors of graduates from 31 highly selective colleges, Ehrenberg, Groen, and Nagowski (2005) found that an increase in university-distributed aid was associated with a "decreasing PhD propensity of graduates" of the institution. Likewise, an increase in a university's Pell grant eligible students was associated with a decrease in the number of graduates that pursued a doctoral degree (Ehrenberg et al., 2005, p. 7). High-achieving students in the bottom half of the national income distribution are 18 percent less likely to earn a graduate degree than those in the top income half (Wyner, Bridgeland, & Diiulio, 2007). Essentially, although it is difficult to assess the precise number of low-income students who persist to graduate with a doctoral degree, it appears that low-income students are much less likely to even attend graduate school.

According to the Survey of Earned Doctorates (2007), "First-generation college graduates appear to have faced greater challenges in terms of financing doctorate education, reporting higher rates of relying on their own financial resources and incurring higher levels of debt…than their counterparts from more highly educated parental backgrounds" (p. 41). Further, as first-generation students took an average of an additional semester to complete their schooling, they likely forwent more income as they earned their doctorate (Survey of Earned Doctorates, 2007). Additionally, amongst the 2002 cohort of doctoral graduates, first-generation students comprised a substantially smaller proportion of students, as compared to the number of first-generation undergraduate recipients (Wyner et al., 2007). While high-achieving college graduates in the bottom income half are two-thirds as likely to earn a Master's degree as their high-income counterparts, they are merely half as likely to graduate with a research doctorate (Wyner et al., 2007).

These disparities matter "because our society is deprived of highly-educated scholars and professionals from diverse backgrounds" (Wyner et al., p. 27). Further, they reveal a hidden assumption that the playing field is now level for low- and high-income students alike at the undergraduate level, simply because both now attend the similar institutions and have access to the same faculty, facilities, and libraries. The reality for low-income students is that they continue to remain disadvantaged when it comes to graduate school access. While high-income students benefit from family resources, increased opportunities for learning and enrichment, and encouragement toward post-baccalaureate education at an early age, children from low-income families are less likely to experience the same luxury. Further, high-income students have more resources to visit potential graduate schools, attend conferences, and pay for expensive test preparation programs. While some high-income children dream about professional careers that require post-baccalaureate education, low-income children dream of college attendance and graduation, and may have been unfairly socialized to believe that a Bachelor's degree is the highest form of education they can achieve.

As high-achieving, low-income, and first-generation students progress through the academic pipeline, they experience manifold challenges—likely perpetuating their socialized perceptions about graduate school being a distant reality. While many of these students excel in their academic coursework, they may struggle to find or are unaware of research opportunities and other scholarly activities that would better prepare them for careers in research and postsecondary teaching. They may also lack access to key services that would contribute to their success in the graduate application process (e.g., assistance with writing effective personal statements, obtaining letters of recommendation, and securing funding for graduate education). In addition to curricular and co-curricular challenges, these students may also struggle with feelings of isolation, given the intense nature of postsecondary education, and may find themselves alienated from family and friends who are unfamiliar with the demands of higher education (Allen, 1992, Maldonado & Willie, 1995). Next, we explore one particular federal program that has been specifically designed to improve low-income students' preparation for graduate education.

THE MCNAIR SCHOLARS PROGRAM

With the Economic Opportunity Act of 1964, Upward Bound, a program that serves to provide the opportunities and support necessary for low-income, first-generation high school students to complete high school and attend college, was created. As a part of the Higher Education Act, a second, federally funded outreach program called Talent Search was added the following year. Specifically geared toward disadvantaged high school students that have the potential to thrive in college, Talent Search provides academic and career support, as well as financial counseling. The program seeks to boost high school graduation and college attendance rates amongst these students. Student Support Services (SSS), a program established in 1968 with a goal to aid first-generation, low-income students and students with disabilities as they navigate the college admission process, was the third program established by the federal government. SSS also provides resources and assistance (both academic and financial) during college, in order to improve retention and graduation rates. These three programs were the initial "TRIO" programs, a moniker that was ascribed in the late 1960s. In the subsequent years, several other educational opportunity programs were added.

The McNair Scholars Program, the largest and most comprehensive federal program of its type, serves to prepare low-income or first-generation college students for doctoral studies, thereby increasing the number of PhD degrees received by underrepresented students. Student participants receive a variety of support services, including academic and financial aid counseling and tutoring. Mentorship and research opportunities, seminars, and summer internships are also important components of the program. Institutions of higher education that are interested in participating in the McNair Program are eligible to apply through the U.S. Department of Education. During the 2008 fiscal year, the 185 participating institutions received a total of $44,326,656. Participating institutions received an average grant of $239,604 and named a total of 5,067 students as McNair Scholars (U.S. Department of Education, 2008). Of the participating institutions, 13 are Historically Black Colleges and Universities (HBCUs), and 15 are Hispanic-Serving Institutions (HSIs) (U.S. Department of Education, 2005). While each school incorporates the aforementioned tenets of the program, they utilize school-specific models to facilitate the program.

In the most recent comprehensive assessment of the program, 70 percent of the student participants were low-income and first-generation, more than half of whom were also underrepresented minorities. The remaining 30 percent were other students also underrepresented at the graduate school level (e.g., underrepresented minorities that are neither first-generation nor low-income). Approximately 82 percent of the McNair participants were underrepresented minorities (in the 2001–2002 participant year), 47 percent of whom were African American and 24 percent of whom were Hispanic or Latino. According to graduation and enrollment data reported to the U.S. Department of Education by participant institutions, participation in the program was associated with increased entrance rates into graduate school. Further, McNair participants graduated from doctoral programs at nearly the same rate as nonparticipants (U.S. Department of Education, 2005).

Program Outcomes

In 2000/2001, 63 percent of active participants graduated one year after entering the program. This does not mean that only 63 percent of participants graduated, as students enter the program at different points during their academic career. Of those who completed their undergraduate education that year (n=1,069), 40 percent were admitted into graduate programs and 39 percent commenced their graduate studies the following academic year. Of those who entered graduate programs, 42 percent (n=258) of underrepresented graduates enrolled, versus 35 percent (n=811) of the low-income, first-generation graduates. Ninety-three percent of the McNair Scholars that enrolled in graduate school were still enrolled one year later (U.S. Department of Education, 2005). Further, with each year that passes, the number of McNair graduates that are enrolled in graduate school increases, indicating that many students do not enroll in doctoral programs immediately following graduation. Of the 2001/2002 participants, 56 percent earned a Bachelor's degree, 16 percent earned a Master's degree, 1.7 percent earned a doctoral degree, and 2.4 earned another terminal degree. Of the 18,714 students that participated in the McNair program through the 2001/2002 year, 478 students, or 2.6 percent, have earned a Ph.D. (U.S. Department of Education, 2005). As many McNair Scholars are both underrepresented and low-income, they have a multitude of obstacles to overcome, including "less financial and social support in graduate school, making an ambitious goal even more difficult for McNair participants," as compared to their less-disadvantaged counterparts (U.S. Department of Education, 2005, p. 26).

Pierre Bourdieu (1993) submits that members of nondominant groups, in order to avoid being silenced, have resisted characterizations that their competency and cultural codes are somehow deficient. Low-income students in this population enter the academic game because they have chosen a different trajectory than that predetermined for them by the dominant culture. The pursuit of graduate education, then, principally means an investment in their academic, cultural, and symbolic capital in ways that derive maximum benefit or profit from participation (Bourdieu, 1993). Entering the academic arena requires knowledge about the landscape that low-income students do not possess, and programs like McNair can facilitate their process of transformation by providing the information, knowledge, and training necessary to enter academic career paths.

As each of the more than 180 McNair institutions can choose how to implement the program, different schools experience varied levels of success in propelling students toward graduate school. Although the schools share the same programmatic elements (e.g., academic counseling, financial aid counseling, tutoring, mentorship and research opportunities, seminars, and summer internships), some institutions highlight specific benefits of the program. For example, the University of Minnesota emphasizes the importance of undergraduate research by requiring the McNair Scholars to participate in a nine-week summer research apprenticeship under the guidance of a mentor faculty member. As the university has identified a set of criteria for the McNair Scholar faculty members, the faculty mentors that oversee student projects are experts in their field, and many hold positions of leadership within their department. One criterion maintains that faculty members have a professed desire to serve students who are underrepresented, whether they are first-generation, low-income, and/or minority students.

The McNair Scholars at the University of Minnesota consistently note their relationship with mentor faculty members as particularly instrumental in encouraging them to attend graduate school. Faculty mentors also enjoy the mentorship experience, reporting a growth in personal satisfaction, intellectual stimulation, and an appreciation for the ability to work with a diverse group of students (Tellijohn, 2007). They set high standards for their mentees, and were rewarded with positive results. In the 15 years the university has participated in the program, more than 60 percent of the 300 student participants have continued on to graduate school. Further, several graduates of the University of Minnesota's McNair Program returned to teach at their alma mater following completion of graduate school. While summative reports such as the one in Minnesota are available, exploration of the effectiveness of the McNair faculty mentor relationship on students' continuation into graduate school has not been conducted.

DECONSTRUCTING GRADUATE PREPARATION PROGRAMS

While we acknowledge the important role that federal programs such as the McNair Scholars Program play in enhancing access, we also question the assumptions that such legislation often makes. In her recent study of low-income graduate students who participated in a McNair program as undergraduates, Spears (2007) found that as much as McNair participants were excited and anxious to get their graduate career started, the social transition was a difficult one for many of them. In relation to their social transition, low-income McNair alumni in graduate schools were out of place within both their family and academic cultures. Spears also found that the vast majority of students also struggled with finances, as well as meeting the burdens of appearance. Participants described feelings of isolation from their families, as they realized that the more education they received, the more they did not fit within the pre-existing family culture. In a form of double consciousness as being at once low income and well educated, they became border crossers, having to create new space between family and school culture in order to feel at home (Spears, 2007).

Low-income McNair Scholars in Spears' study talked about feeling connected to family and community out of a need for survival, a phenomenon that Spears refers to as behaviors necessary for graduate students in working-class families trying to occupy middle-class cultures. A lack of financial resources at both an individual and familial level left the students with a burden to meet the manifold financial obligations to provide for their families, and help out family members in other ways whenever possible, while feeling burdened to maintain certain kinds of appearances through dress and demeanor. The latter burden to maintain appearances was viewed as an important factor to students' successful social transition through graduate school, though many in the Spears study admitted to struggling with self-doubt and their ability to fit in as scholars in the new world of academia.

Overall the participants felt that exposure to research and other preparation activities helped them know what they needed to do to be successful academically, but they expressed surprise at not knowing about some aspect of the graduate school culture during their time as McNair Scholars as undergraduates. Programs such as McNair claim to successfully prepare students for academic preparation to and success in graduate school; the focus is on the tangible academic skills needed in graduate school (research skills, GRE [Graduate Record Examinations] test preparation, and writing); however, as evidenced in Spears' study regarding social transitions, low-income students struggled most with the hard to measure, invisible, social and cultural constructs of the graduate school experience. These issues for low-income students are aspects of graduate preparation rarely acknowledged or addressed in McNair programs nationally, and this may reveal the hidden assumptions of higher education administrators that all graduate students perform on an equal and level playing field once they matriculate beyond the baccalaureate.

The McNair Scholars Program has been in existence for over 30 years, but we have seen few low-income graduates pursue doctoral education. We question why TRIO programs such as McNair serve such small numbers of students, and only at a select number of institutions. The current model of federal assistance is not enough to combat the overwhelming challenges that low-income children face today. Furthermore, in response to the problem of low-income students' low participation in graduate school, programs like McNair seek to fix the student and celebrate individual accomplishments, in lieu of examining the larger system that privileges the wealthy class. This focus on individualism is grossly inadequate—we cannot resolve the issue of graduate school access by merely providing individuals with extra academic and financial support. Moreover, offering free test preparation services and graduate school admission advisement merely scratches the surface of what is necessary for low-income students to be competitive for top graduate programs around the country. In addition, the types of test preparation programs differ by company, but, by and large, middle- and high-income families can afford to spend significantly more for services that charge much more. Faculty and staff might expect that all students have the financial means to choose undergraduate research opportunities over part-time employment, although the two are mutually exclusive. Educators may assume that students can afford lab fees, textbooks, the latest software, and extracurricular activities typical of middle- and high-income students. While some will be able to afford such things, others simply cannot. More is needed by way of dialogues about the personal impact of graduate school on self, personal, and professional relationships.

RECONSTRUCTING GRADUATE PREPARATION PROGRAMS

While some institutions across the country have certainly expanded access to underserved (low-income, first-generation, and minority) students, it is important that these students must not be admitted and forgotten (Bowen et al., 2005). Typically, they enter college with a diverse set of needs that must be addressed so that they might be retained and persist to graduation, and even graduate school. Only then will the cycle of underrepresentation be broken, in graduate school and beyond. Programmatic moves to address the underrepresentation and hopeful success of low-income students like the McNair Scholars Program will likely contribute to an institution's progress in the area. However, simply becoming a McNair participant institution cannot qualify a school as one that considers low-income students to be a distinct priority. This may merely perpetuate the thinking that the problem can be fixed by addressing the needs of the individual, rather than focusing on the need to change a broader set of institutional assumptions and policies. While several change strategies and models of leadership are applicable to this issue, we primarily focus on change strategies that are optimal for moving institutions forward in the area of diversity—a shift that can experience a fair share of resistance from many campus stakeholders (Kezar, 2007). As a reminder, the expanded definition of "diversity" used in this chapter extends beyond race and ethnicity to include class. Further, as research has shown that students of color are disproportionally represented amongst low-income students and first-generation students, there is extensive overlap between the categories.

Formalize Orientation for Low-Income Students

Institutions, whether they have received a TRIO funded grant or not, should provide more formal orientation programs for new graduate students from low-income families. The primary goals of these orientation programs should be to assist students in making connections with faculty, staff, and other students. Through structured time spent together in an orientation, graduate students begin to build relationships with each other and form social networks of support. As part of the socialization process, institutions could provide all new graduate students with a peer mentor—an older graduate student to share his or her insights and help guide them through the transitional process of the first year of graduate school. This peer mentor serves as role model and assists the new graduate student in acquiring the cultural knowledge needed to successfully matriculate through their departments. Departments should help to facilitate the introduction and interaction among the student and peer mentor. Departments should also provide bridge experiences that engage students with working-class faculty and graduate students to talk about how to manage the transition. A bridge program's focus should be to engage low-income students in developing their awareness of the cultural capital valued and rewarded in graduate school.

Address Financial Knowledge for Graduate Students

For low-income students, college attendance alone does not equalize the playing field for access to graduate school. In some cases, low-income students graduate college with debts so significant that the prospect of taking out additional loans for graduate school may be a deterrent for consideration of further study. As middle- and high-income families might have the means to pay off or sustain a similar level of debt, they have the luxury to consider graduate education as a viable option. For low-income students, weighing the consequences of more debt and the opportunity costs of forgoing salary and wages until the completion of advanced degrees is much more consequential. As Laura Perna and her colleagues discuss in Chapter 4 of this book, the structural changes in "no loan" schools may significantly impact the financial burdens for low-income students, leaving fewer students saddled with debt. This is certainly a step in the right direction, and we applaud the efforts initiated by these institutions. In addition to taking more proactive measures to provide a range of funding options to all new low-income graduate students admitted in departments, individual departments should provide financial support to all students to ensure feasibility of being able to manage the financial implications of going back to school. Administrators should also take into consideration those students who must split their time looking for employment or financial support, and thus lose time spent for their studies and balancing graduate student life.

Focus on Cultural Socialization

Borrowing from Antony's (2002) theory of socialization, which views content as part of one's identity, whereas "professionalization" is the transmission of the content knowledge of a profession. Traditionally, graduate students are likely to seek entry into a profession if they take on the norms, values, and attitudes of the professional community. The internalization of the profession's norms replace those of the individual self-identity and self-image. In a revised framework, socialization allows awareness of a field without rejecting one's own values and norms; socialization has numerous methodological forms, while asserting individuality (Antony, 2002).

Graduate preparation programs such as the McNair Scholars Program need to do more to help low-income students to understand the cultural isolation that they might face in graduate school. Through additional classes, workshops, roundtables and informal conversations, administrators should understand students' need to critically engage in learning about ways their social class influences their transitional experiences in graduate school. Programs should also provide additional opportunities for students to talk about the ways class influences their perception of themselves and others. Low-income students should be offered more structured activities to reflect on their core selves, class differences between their home and intended graduate department and institution, and ways to minimize the feelings of isolation and anxiety.

Extend the P-16 Pipeline

A distinct focus on integration of diversity should be embedded into the curriculum, which includes implementing alternative pedagogical strategies that will reach students with different learning styles or levels of preparation. Advisement and guidance for graduate schools should start as early as the first year in college (and ideally earlier at the secondary level in terms of career exploration and professional schools), and college advisement offices should identify low-income students during orientation and offer programs embedded into the co-curriculum to ensure graduate school knowledge transmission to students, modeled like the successful college preparation programs at the secondary school level. Institutions who have reached the final phase of institutionalization have fully implemented monitoring practices and measurement mechanisms so that progress can be assessed and areas in need of improvement can be identified. Higher education scholars and policymakers have been able to bridge several gaps over the past decade (Perna, Fenske, & Swail, 2002; Swail & Perna, 2002; Tierney & Hagedorn, 2002; Tierney & Jun, 2001). The vernacular of the P-16 pipeline reveals acknowledgment of the chasm between secondary and postsecondary education, specifically as it concerns low-income student access. A P-20 pipeline model of education may be more reflective of the current challenges to extend opportunities for low-income students beyond the Bachelor's degree, so that institutions of higher learning can build a language that reflects greater expectations for low-income students into its policies, curriculum, and structures.

Reconsider Merit in Graduate Admissions

Graduate school admissions policies may need to reconsider notions of merit as it concerns applicants from low-income families and acknowledge the benefit of a diverse student body on the learning environment for all students. Just as undergraduate admission programs offer aid for low-income students, graduate schools should extend similar consideration. If graduate programs are willing to acknowledge the manifold benefits associated with a diverse learning community, they should initiate recruitment models that intentionally achieve that end. An increase in low-income student enrollment will not happen by accident—and special preparation programs like McNair cannot bear the responsibility alone. Institutions of higher education, both undergraduate and graduate, must be willing to initiate change on both the administrative and the programmatic level.

Expand Guaranteed Graduate Admissions Policies from High School

Programs such as Baccalaureate/M.D. (or other similar admissions schemes that guarantee graduate admissions to students out of high school) are highly publicized and lauded by academic leaders. These programs continue to perpetuate the myth of meritocracy. In light of possible institutional change that schools might establish to expand opportunity for low-income students, the policies of these programs need to be reconsidered. Admission into many of these programs is typically limited to incoming first-year students. This simple policy alone limits involvement from low-income students. As low-income seniors in high school are focused on the attainment of a Bachelor's degree, they are likely unaware of the possibility of such Baccalaureate/M.D. programs that guarantee medical school admission—forgoing their opportunity for participation. However, if institutions with five-year M.B.A. programs or Baccalaureate/M.D. or M.A. programs accepted applications throughout a student's undergraduate tenure, graduate programs would have more opportunities to raise the awareness and interest of low-income students. For example, if a low-income student majoring in education and social work learned of a five-year combined B.A./M.A. program during their sophomore year and applications were due during their junior year, they would have time to envision themselves in the program, and discuss the possibility with academic and financial aid advisers. As noted before, we predict that when low-income students can more aptly visualize themselves in graduate school, achievement will be much more realistic.

CONCLUSION

As noted above, low-income students' achievement of a Bachelor's degree is lauded and considered a great success. While this attainment is certainly worthy of commemoration, our academic expectations for low-income students should not end here. With fewer low-income students attending and graduating college, they are less likely to pursue a post-baccalaureate degree than their higher-income counterparts (Ehrenberg et al., 2005; Wyner et al., 2007). Many children of middle- and high-income families consider a bachelor's degree as merely the first step on their path to a profession such as medicine, law, or the social sciences, where an advanced degree is requisite. The crux of the matter is that the pipeline to terminal degrees for low-income students is profoundly sparse, rendering the potential systemic benefits of graduate school preparation programs as only a moderate interruption to the self-deprecating cycle of low graduate school enrollment for low-income students. While graduate preparation programs help, low-income college students continue to enter graduate programs at disproportionately lower levels.

Pursuit of individual and vocational calling may be a luxury reserved for those who have benefited from a structure that rewards those who may not think twice about the cost of graduate education. The illusion of meritocracy and the perception of students having a level playing field for graduate school may limit support for low-income students who obtained a Bachelor's degree but will find a paucity of support for graduate degree attainment. Simply stated, financial assistance for test preparation services, conference travel, and research stipends at the undergraduate level is not enough to level the playing field for low-income students. These myths may have contributed to the dearth in access and equity, making graduate school a new elitist symbol for the privileged, as it is designed for middle- and high-income children of families who can more realistically afford six or more years of postsecondary education. When support for low-income students does not extend beyond baccalaureate preparation programs and into graduate school preparation programs, it gives the perception that a Bachelor's degree is "good enough," in turn, lowering expectations of low-income youth. For low-income students, pursuit of graduate education involves much more than an individual choice or desire, as choices are often made in conjunction with encumbrances like high student loan and credit card debt.

Creating a broad and diverse learning community where students of varying backgrounds are represented is the best way to prepare people toward living, working, and engaging in a world where the social class of one's family will no longer lead to unequal treatment or a dearth of educational opportunity. While state-mandated segregation has disappeared and overt racism and classism has decreased, skin color and social class can still be cause for unethical treatment, both directly and indirectly. We maintain that higher education has the power to reframe race, ethnicity, gender, and class as something that contributes to an individual's worldview that is both valuable and worthy to be understood.

REFERENCES

Allen, W. (1992). The color of success: African-American college student outcomes at predominantly white and historically black public colleges and universities. *Harvard Educational Review*, 62(1), 26–44.

Antony, J. (2002). Reexamining doctoral student socialization and professional development: Moving beyond the congruence and assimilation orientation. In J. Smart (Ed.), *Higher education: Handbook of theory and research, Vol. XVII* (pp. 349–380). San Francisco: Jossey-Bass.

Bourdieu, P. (1993). *The field of cultural production: Essays on art and literature.* New York: Columbia University Press.

Bowen, W., Kurzweil, M., & Tobin, E. (2005). *Equity and excellence in American higher education.* London: University of Virginia Press.

Chang, M. (1999). Does racial diversity matter? The educational impact of a racially diverse undergraduate population. *Journal of College Student Development,* 40(4), 377–395.

Council of Graduate Schools. (2004). *Graduate enrollment and degrees: 1986 to 2004.* Washington, DC: Author.

Ehrenberg, R., Groen, J., & Nagowski, M. (2005). *Declining PhD attainment of graduates of selective private academic institutions* (Working Papers). ILR Collection: Cornell University ILR School.

Hurtado, S., Milem, J. F., Clayton-Pederson, A. R., & Allen, W. R. (1998). *Enacting diverse learning environments: Improving the climate for racial/ethnic diversity in higher education.* San Francisco: Jossey-Bass.

Ibarra, R. A. (2001). *Beyond affirmative action: Reframing the context of higher education.* Madison: University of Wisconsin Press.

Kezar, A. (2007). Tools for a time and a place: Phased leadership strategies to institutionalize a diversity agenda. *The Review of Higher Education, 30*(4), 413–439.

Maldonado, L., & Willie, C. (1995). Developing a "pipeline" recruitment program for minority faculty. In L. Rendon & R. Hope (Eds.), *Educating a new majority* (pp. 309–329). San Francisco: Jossey-Bass.

Milem, J., Chang, M., & Antonio, A. (2005). *Making diversity work on campus: A research based perspective.* Washington, DC: Association of American Colleges and Universities.

National Center for Education Statistics. (1999). *The condition of education.* Washington, DC: ED Pubs.

Perna, L. W., Fenske, R. H., & Swail, W. S. (2002). Sponsors of early intervention programs. *ERIC review: Early intervention: Expanding access to higher education, 8*(1), 15–18.

Sacks, P. (2007). *Tearing down the gates: Confronting the class divide in American education.* Los Angeles: University of California Press.

Spears, J. (2007) *Experiences of low-income students' transition to graduate school* (doctoral dissertation). Available from Dissertations & Theses: Full Text (Publication No. AAT 3291650).

Survey of Earned Doctorates. (2007). *National Opinion Research Center at the University of Chicago.* Retrieved September 2009 from: http://www.norc.org/projects/survey+of+earned+doctorates.htm

Swail, W. S., & Perna, L. W. (2002). *Pre-college outreach programs: A national perspective.* In W. G. Tierney & L. S. Hagedorn (Eds.), *Increasing access to college: Extending the possibilities for all students* (pp. 15–34). Albany, NY: State University of New York Press.

Tellijohn, A. (2007, Fall). Early opportunities: Research programs give undergrads a boost for the future. *Connect: University of Minnesota College of Education and Human Development.* Retrieved September 2009 from: http://cehd.umn.edu/Pubs/Connect/2007fall/opportunities.html

Tierney, W. G., & Hagedorn, L. S. (2002) *Increasing access to college: Extending possibilities to all students.* Albany: State University of New York Press.

Tierney, W. G. & Jun, A. (2001). A university helps prepare low income youth for college: Tracking school success. *Journal of Higher Education, 72*(2), 205–225.

U.S. Department of Education, Office of Postsecondary Education. (2005). *A Profile of the Ronald E. McNair Postbaccalaureate Achievement Program: 1997–1998 through 2001–2002.* Retrieved September 2009 from: http://www.eric.ed.gov:80/ERICDocs/data/ericdocs2sql/content_storage_01/0000019b/80/29/da/6a.pdf

U.S. Department of Education, Office of Postsecondary Education. (2008). *Ronald E. McNair Postbaccalaureate Achievement Program.* Washington, DC. Retrieved September 2009 from: http://www.ed.gov/programs/triomcnair/index.html

Wyner, J. S., Bridgeland, J. M., Diiulio, Jr., J. J. (2007). *Achievement trap: How America is failing millions of high-achieving students from lower-income families.* Lansdowne, VA: Jack Kent Cooke Foundation & Civic Enterprises.

13
RE-ORIENTING OUR UNDERSTANDING OF COLLEGES IN RELATION TO LOW-INCOME STUDENTS

ADRIANNA KEZAR

Having read this book, it is our belief that you will think differently about existing campus policies and practices in relation to low-income students. Our intent was to have the reader question traditional assumptions by disrupting typical approaches involving the conceptualization, research, and work with this population. It is our belief that you cannot change campus practices successfully unless you change your mindset about low-income students and issues such as access, success, and institutional responsibility. In this final chapter, I summarize ways that authors have asked the reader to rethink the orientation to studying and working with students, as well as concepts and theories applied to understand low-income students. I also highlight the themes and ideas that thread throughout all of the chapters of this book.

ORIENTATION TO THE STUDY OF LOW-INCOME STUDENTS

Almost every author in this volume describes the problem of a *deficit perspective*, where the low-income students are seen as lacking and need to change in order to fit into the middle-class assumptions and rules of the institution—as Walpole points out: they must live on campus, wear certain clothes, get certain grades to be in a major, attend certain social events, and obtain additional support to make up for their lack of knowledge. Several authors note the stigma created for low-income students due to campuses taking the deficit model or approach. Campuses create special programs to make low-income students fit into the norms of the campus and as a result they can feel different from other students. Each author encourages practitioners and researchers to see students as having assets that contribute to the campus, rather than focusing on a deficit perspective. Practitioners are cautioned to look at practices they might use that may end up stigmatizing students.

When moving away from the individual to the system, as chapter authors have done, there are different approaches to thinking about systemic analysis of the structure. First, several authors mention how *issues of money are overemphasized* with low-income students. Kezar's and Walpole's chapters, in particular, examine the plethora of ways that low-income students are disadvantaged unrelated to money. Second, often *the system focus can be narrow—mainly focusing on bridge programs.* Colyar and Walpole both express concern about the overemphasis on bridge programs as the one program that tends to be created and as a catch-all for all challenges. These narrow approaches also adopt a deficit model—changing the student rather than changing the institution—and will not and have not served students well. The careful analyses presented in the chapters by Engle and Lynch (Chapter 8), and Cunningham and Leegwater (Chapter 9), demonstrate the sort of systemic analysis and the complex series of programs and policies that can support low-income students cover areas such as community outreach, culturally relevant curriculum, support services, first-year programs, financial literacy, and the like. Another aspect of the systemic nature of the problem is the *inter-linking of federal, state, and institutional policies.* Levin et al. (Chapter 7), St. John (Chapter 2), and Chambers and Deller (Chapter 3) all look at how institutional policies are connected to and constrained by federal and state policies. Also, St. John examines how institutional policies can constrain and hamper a state policy—campuses not providing needed support to make programs work as effectively as they can. Chambers and Deller (Chapter 3) and Levin et al. (Chapter 7) demonstrate how federal ideologies can impose themselves on programs, and constrain the vision and approach of local practitioners, ultimately failing low-income students.

One last re-orientation is emphasized in the text—*people, not just structures,* need to be focused on in terms of their role helping students. While many of the chapters talk about a comprehensive approach, Dowd (Chapter 11) reminds us about the importance of people to bring the programs and policies to life. Without the right orientation and perspective among educational professionals, low-income students will likely still not be successful. Educational professionals can adopt the right perspective by getting to know and understand low-income students—Colyar (Chapter 6), Dowd (Chapter 11), and Chambers and Deller (Chapter 3) all make this same plea.

Lastly, many chapter authors remind us that we can *learn more by studying success stories rather than failures.* Much of the past research on low-income students has focused on institutional problems and failures; few, if any, have identified and studied institutions and programs that succeed and what we can learn from them—I applaud Engle and Lynch (Chapter 8) and Cunningham and Leegwater (Chapter 9).

CONCEPTS

Chapter authors presented new and different ways to think about commonly accepted and unproblematic concepts such as access, partnerships, transition to college, and agency to support low-income students.

Access

Access has been a major focus for researchers and practitioners focused on helping low-income students; without access there is no point thinking about retention, success, or graduation. Yet, as Chambers and Deller (Chapter 3) note, the concept of access is often presented as if there is an on-and-off switch. Policymakers can turn on the access switch and opportunities are automatically open for low-income students. They register concern that the process is much more dynamic and complex than simply creating or opening the doors to access. Even when the doors are open, when one person has a 1,000-pound rock on their back, getting through the door is just not the same. As they note, access is a complex and nuanced process, contingent on many factors related to social positionality. Those from a low-income status rarely have the opportunity to choose from all possible options, even though access policies tend to present the opportunities in this fashion. Low-income students typically have a more defined choice set than middle- and high-income students.

Partnerships

Various chapter authors describe how low-income student success is dependent on partnerships between various types of colleges, between K-12 and higher education, and between government and educational sectors. St. John (Chapter 2) questions the notion of partnerships between schools and colleges. For many years policymakers have spoken about alignment between schools and colleges, and thankfully this rhetoric has given way to actual partnerships which represent the relationship that is needed to foster student success between secondary and postsecondary institutions. However, St. John demonstrates how even the notion of partnership can be short shrifted in programs such as the Twenty-First Century Scholars where colleges do the least that is acceptable and stop short of what is really needed in terms of fulfilling their responsibilities. Colleges tinker with the environment rather than truly change their institutional structures to support low-income students. Elementary and secondary schools are expected to reform, but colleges remain relatively the same. The partnerships needed for low-income student success are true and authentic relationships, where partners are willing to learn from each other and change.

Transition

Colyar (Chapter 6) suggests that the notion of transition to college is often seen as a short-term and relatively easy process that can be facilitated with programmatic efforts. But the reality of transitioning to college when the concept is so foreign, and there are constant reminders that you are an outsider, means that you may never really transition to or become a member of campus. Transition processes are longer and involve much more in-depth socializing processes. Yet at the same time, Colyar suggests that we try to minimize the distance between the individual and the campus environment, but this minimizing is by changing institutional structures, not trying to change individuals.

Institutional Choice or Agency

Agency is a major concept within post-structuralism and one that is often casually assumed to be possessed by formal organizations. Levin et al. (Chapter 7) challenge the notion of institutions having an unconstrained choice to alter their structures to support low-income students. While institutions have autonomy over certain choices, in other areas they can be constrained by federal or state policies or even local norms. The staff at the community college they studied were constrained by federal work first welfare policies that prevented them from making low-income adult students successful in their efforts to return and persist in college.

Simple notions from access, partnerships, transition to college, and choice are all problematized in this book. It might seem that the deeper exploration into these concepts makes it harder to support low-income students; yet such exploration helps overcome easy solutions that have not helped students and have wasted resources. These are not the only concepts re-examined in the book and we invite readers to open themselves up to re-interpretation of many taken-for-granted concepts. I believe this review of a few would help the reader to see others that are addressed in the book. I hope readers are leaving the book with the notion that common and well-understood language and concepts may need further re-examination when it comes to low-income populations.

THEORIES

Another underlying theme is that authors in this book challenge simple theories that have been brought to understand low-income students. Many authors in this volume refer to human capital theory. Human capital theory has been used in two ways to conceptualize low-income populations as it relates to college going. First, human capital is the logic behind the importance of educating low-income students—because we need the full human capital of the United States to support our economy. Human capital theory is also used as a lens to understand low-income students' choice to attend college, because it will offer them opportunities to further themselves and move up in the social hierarchy. Human capital theorists believe that students weigh the costs of postsecondary education against the perceived economic benefits, and have agency to decide about their future. Clearly, most authors in this volume see human capital theory as problematic in its emphasis on student agency over the many institutional constraints that we have described. However, human capital theory does bring attention to the need for educating low-income youth, because the future economy depends on more people being college educated. Yet, as Levin et al. (Chapter 7) demonstrate, a human capital approach can be used to turn low-income students into servants or cogs in a capitalist machine—their role as workers foregrounded rather than as students and citizens. While middle-class students can pursue the liberal arts and better themselves, low-income students are consigned to the status of workers.

Social or cultural capital is another theory that chapter authors question when used in an overly simplistic way. The simplicity exists when scholars and practitioners do not reconcile two different theorists' conceptions of social capital—Coleman and Bourdieu. Coleman conceptualizes social capital as something that exists in social relationships and that can be drawn upon to further individuals' goals and objectives. Middle- and upper-income students draw on their parents, their parents' friends, and their peers to develop college-going knowledge, which helps them to be successful in accessing and persisting in college. This theory results in stressing the importance of networks and mentoring relationships, for example, which can help low-income populations gain important information that helps them further their educational goals. Researchers and practitioners influenced by theories of social capital attempt to create programs that will provide low-income students with the social capital that is often missing within their natural environment, because their parents did not attend college and their peers do not have information about college going.

Yet, Bourdieu believed that social capital is implicitly communicated and understood, and the notion that programs can be developed to teach this cultural knowledge might strike him as overly simplistic. Explicit efforts to teach something that is a nonconscious process and based more on feelings and lifestyle than rational choice may seem misguided. Also, his theory would suggest that as lower-income groups developed the cultural capital of the high-status groups, the high-status groups would simply change the habits that are necessary for being successful. According to Bourdieu, the purpose of the cultural capital is class distinction; therefore those with higher social status will continuously find ways to alter the system to benefit themselves. He did see the cultural capital and habitus of different social classes as being durable. However, this does not mean that he did not see agency for individuals to learn cultural capital and to move between social classes. Many authors in this volume draw on Bourdieu to question overly simplistic approaches to creating social capital among low-income youth.

Chambers and Deller (Chapter 3), for example, question the college-going knowledge offered in early intervention for college programs and whether this information can truly overcome the historical and social circumstances of students. They ask policymakers and educational professionals to think more deeply about the social circumstances of low-income students, and not be fooled that handing them a set of knowledge can overcome these life circumstances. They also ask educational professionals to better understand the social and cultural capital that low-income students have, and to build from this knowledge rather than ignore their worldview and offer up middle-class social capital alone as the only way to succeed. St. John (Chapter 2) points to the importance of developing college-going knowledge early and sustaining it over longer periods of time. Colyar (Chapter 6) also asks for leaders to think about and build programs based on the experiences of the low-income students, rather than simply the experiences and knowledge of middle-income students. Teaching these students to adopt middle-class practices and abandon their own social capital as a way to succeed is likely doomed for failure.

Perna et al. (Chapter 4) also suggest that as we develop programs and policies, we keep in mind the knowledge and understanding of low-income students. A no loan policy will be more effective if it is communicated in a way that low-income students can understand, and this communication should be based on understanding how students access and process knowledge. Practitioners should consider ways to develop practices and programs that acknowledge this more complex history and background of students, and make sure to include low-income students as they implement policies, so that these programs can best reflect their needs. Chapter authors are clear that past theories have limited our ability to help low-income students—our underlying assumptions, often captured in theories, are critical to challenge and re-examine.

FUTURE RESEARCH

While the authors in this volume covered many areas, there are many unresearched issues that impact low-income students' success and need further investigation including remedial education, early admissions policies, merit scholarships, impact of little social engagement, working colleges, textbooks costs and their impact, how working over 35 hours a week can affect experience and outcomes, and remittance to parents and family. Adult low-income students need to be the focus of more research. The overlapping experience of being a racial minority and low-income needs additional research.

We also know very little about institutional differences and lack of knowledge about low-income students in different contexts. Walpole (Chapter 5) explores selective liberal arts colleges, Levin et al. (Chapter 7)—community colleges, Perna et al. (Chapter 4) —large public and private research universities, Cunningham and Leegwater (Chapter 9)—minority serving institutions, Engle and Lynch (Chapter 8) and Colyar (Chapter 6) —large public comprehensives, and, lastly, Kezar and Yang (Chapter 10) and St. John (Chapter 2) —multiple institutional types. Therefore the book covers a range of contexts, yet the authors often did not focus on the impact of the institutional type or have comparative data. More research that examines difference by sector would help. Kezar and Yang's chapter suggests that there are important differences by institutional type and that certain institutions have better structures to support low-income students—for example less elite institutions, for-profit, vocational and technical colleges, and some community colleges. As Cunningham and Leegwater suggest, by studying minority serving institutions, we can learn from institutions that have historically had success with low-income students.

The authors in this volume have challenged conventional concepts and simplistic theories, opened up new lines of inquiry, and most importantly offered ideas for improving the lives and experiences of low-income students in higher education.

CONTRIBUTORS

EDITOR

Adrianna Kezar is Associate Professor for Higher Education, University of Southern California. Kezar holds a Ph.D. 1996 and M.A. 1992 in higher education administration from the University of Michigan and a B.A. 1989 from the University of California, Los Angeles. She joined the faculty at USC in 2003. Kezar was editor of the ASHE-ERIC Higher Education Report Series from 1996 to 2004.

Her research focuses on change, leadership, access, diversity, public purposes of higher education, and governance in higher education. She has published over 75 articles and books and is featured in the major journals for higher education including *The Journal of Higher Education, Research in Higher Education, The Review of Higher Education,* and *Journal of College Student Development.* Her most recent book is *Organizing Higher Education for Collaboration* (Jossey-Bass, 2009). Other recent books include: *Rethinking the "L" Word in Higher Education, Higher Education for the Public Good,* and *Creating Organizational Learning in Higher Education,* all with Jossey-Bass Press (2005), and a national report published by the American Council on Education: *Leadership Strategies for Advancing Campus Diversity.* She is currently working on a grant from the Lumina Foundation related to a federal financial program called Individual Development Accounts focused on low-income students.

She has participated actively in national service, including being on the editorial boards for *The Journal of Higher Education, The Journal of College Student Development, Change,* and *The ERIC Review* and serving as a reviewer for 11 journals in and outside higher education. She has received national awards for her editorial leadership of the ASHE-ERIC report series from ASHE, for developing a leadership development program for women in higher education from ACE, and for her commitment to service learning from the National Society for Experiential Learning.

co-authored with

Hannah Yang is a Research Associate for Dr. Adrianna Kezar. She received her Master's in Education specializing in postsecondary education and student affairs from the Rossier School of Education at the University of Southern California. Since the start of her time at USC she has had an active role in the Center for Higher Education Policy Analysis (CHEPA). She administered surveys in high schools for financial aid and access research, evaluated the SummerTIME program by conducting exit interviews with the staff, and assisted the Director of the Increasing Access via Mentoring program, in recruiting and supervising students for the program and mentored an underprivileged high school senior with his college and financial aid applications. As evident by her experience, Hannah has an interest in low-income students and using quantitative research to gain rich descriptive data to help this population gain access to and have success in postsecondary institutions.

CHAPTER 2

Dr. Edward P. St. John is the Algo D. Henderson Collegiate Professor of Education at the University of Michigan's Center for the Study of Higher and Postsecondary Education. He is interested in education, social justice, and public policy. As a Senior Associate of the National Center for Institutional Diversity, he directs Projects Promoting Equity in Urban and Higher Education, funded by the Ford Foundation. The Ford Foundation projects have supported research on academic preparation and college success in Michigan, DC, and other states, along with the development of state indicators of minority representation in higher education. He has authored or edited 27 books and published more than 200 articles, chapters, and book reviews. His recent books include *Education and the Public Interest: School Reform, Public Finance, and Access to College* (Springer Press, 2006) and *College Organization and Professional Development: Integrating Moral Reasoning and Reflective Practice* (Routledge, 2009). He serves as series editor for *Readings on Equal Education* (AMS Press) and has received awards for leadership from the Association for the Study of Higher Education and for scholarship from the National Association of Student Financial Aid Administrators. Dr. St. John holds an Ed.D. from Harvard University and M.Ed. and B.S. from the University of California-Davis.

CHAPTER 3

Dr. Tony Chambers is an Assistant Professor, Program Coordinator of the Higher Education Program, and Director of the Centre for the Study of Students in Postsecondary Education at the Ontario Institute for Studies in Education, University of Toronto. Previously at the University of Toronto, Tony served as the Associate Vice-Provost, Students. Tony was formerly the Associate Director of the National Forum on Higher Education for the Public Good and Adjunct Associate Professor of Education at the University of Michigan. His research and teaching focuses on factors influencing student success in higher education, and the social purposes of higher education. He has served as an administrator and faculty member at several higher education institutions over the past 28 years, including Illinois State University, the University of Florida, University of Missouri-St. Louis, Michigan State University, and the University of Michigan. He has his doctorate from the University of Florida and both Master's and Bachelor's degrees from Illinois State University.

co-authored with

Fiona Deller is a Ph.D. student at the University of Toronto in the Department of Theory and Policy of Higher Education. She is also Research Director at the Higher Education Quality Council of Ontario (HEQCO). She has worked in public policy related to postsecondary education for the last ten years, holding positions in both federal and provincial governments, as well as at the Council of Ministers of Education, Canada (CMEC).

CHAPTER 4

Dr. Laura Perna is Associate Professor in the Higher Education Management program in the Graduate School of Education at the University of Pennsylvania. Her scholarship uses an integrated theoretical approach and a variety of analytical techniques to understand the ways that individual characteristics, social structures, and public policies separately and together enable and restrict the ability of women, racial/ethnic minorities, and individuals of lower socioeconomic status to obtain the economic, social, and political opportunities that are associated with two aspects of higher education: access as a student and employment as a faculty member. Her research has been supported by grants from the American Education Research Association, the Association for Institutional Research, and the Lumina Foundation for Education and been recognized by the Association for the Study of Higher Education's 2003 Promising Scholar/Early Career Achievement Award.

co-authored with

Valerie Lundy-Wagner is a Ph.D. student in the Higher Education Management Program at the University of Pennsylvania. Her areas of interest relate to the role of institutions in promoting undergraduate degree completion, particularly for underrepresented students, using a variety of methodological approaches. She also has an interest in undergraduate achievement and outcomes for students in science, technology, engineering, and mathematics programs and at historically Black colleges and universities.

April Yee is a doctoral student in the Higher Education program at the University of Pennsylvania's Graduate School of Education. She received a Bachelor's degree in sociology from Smith College and Master's degree in Higher Education Management from the University of Pennsylvania. Her professional experiences as an academic adviser to students at elite colleges and universities, as well as an urban community college, directly inform her primary research interests, which relate to the impact of social class on undergraduate student experiences. Specifically, she seeks to explore the ways in which students from different social classes interact with institutional administration, faculty, and curricula and the role of colleges and universities in disrupting and/or perpetuating the reproduction of social inequality in American society.

Leykia Brill grew up in Bedford-Stuyvesant, Brooklyn, with her grandmother and older brother. A first-generation college student, Leykia was awarded a Posse Scholarship to attend Wheaton College (Norton, MA). Working for her alma mater as an Assistant Director of Admission allowed Leykia to cultivate her passion for working with college and college-bound students. In May 2009, Leykia graduated from the University of Pennsylvania's Graduate School of Education with a Master's degree in Higher Education Management. She now works as an Assistant Dean of Admission for Amherst College.

Teran Tadal received her Bachelor's degree from Union College (NY). After graduation, she took a job in the Admissions office of her alma mater. In May 2009 Teran received a Master's degree in Higher Education Management from the Graduate School of Education at the University of Pennsylvania. She now works as a Regional Director in the Undergraduate Admissions office at the University of Pennsylvania.

CHAPTER 5

Dr. MaryBeth Walpole is an Associate Professor in the Educational Leadership Department at Rowan University in Glassboro, NJ. She received her Master's degree in Administration and Policy Analysis from Stanford University, and her Ph.D. in Higher Education and Organizational Change from the University of California, Los Angeles. Her research interests include the effects of social class on college access and experiences, college access for underrepresented students, and organizational change.

CHAPTER 6

Dr. Julia Colyar is an Assistant Professor in the Department of Educational Leadership & Policy at the University at Buffalo, The State University of New York. Her research focuses on access and transitions to college for underrepresented students. Much of her work has examined college preparation programs, including program structures and characteristics, the theoretical frameworks that guide program practice, school/university ecology, and student experiences. She also writes about qualitative research methods; she is particularly interested in the methodologies of portraiture and cultural biography.

CHAPTER 7

John S. Levin is the Bank of America Professor of Education Leadership and the Director and Principal Investigator of the California Community College Collaborative (C4) at the University of California, Riverside. The California Community College Collaborative has recently completed an investigation of program practices in California community colleges. Levin's books in this decade, *Globalizing the Community College* (Palgrave, 2001), *Community College Faculty: At Work in the New Economy* (Palgrave MacMillan, 2006) with Susan Kater and Richard Wagoner, *Non-Traditional Students and Community Colleges: The Conflict of Justice and Neo-Liberalism* (Palgrave MacMillan, 2007), and *Community Colleges and Their Students: Co-Construction and Organizational Identity* (Palgrave Macmillan, 2009), with Virginia Montero-Hernandez, are empirically based examinations of community colleges. He is currently working on two research projects on university faculty, one in the U.S. and one in Mexico.

co-authored with

Virginia Montero-Hernandez is a Ph.D. candidate in the Program of Curriculum and Instruction in the Graduate School of Education at the University of California, Riverside. She obtained her B.A. in Education at the Autonomous University of the State of Morelos, Mexico. In 2005, she was awarded by the National Council of Science and Technology in Mexico to study abroad. She is part of the research team of the California Community College Collaborative (C4) at the University of California, Riverside and co-author of a book along with John S. Levin, Director of C4. Her research interests involve the use of qualitative methodology to study academic identity, student development, and organizational identity in the higher education system both in the U.S. and Mexican context.

Christine Cerven is a Ph.D. candidate in Sociology at the University of California, Riverside. Her dissertation examines how identity is linked to self-esteem via social integration, self-meanings, and identity verification. Her current research projects include the examination of women's identity development within the community college, and the development of a measure of ethnic identity using an Identity Theory framework.

Genevieve Shaker recently earned her Ph.D. from Indiana University. Named the 2009 Association for the Study of Higher Education Dissertation of the Year, her dissertation was a phenomenological examination of the lived experiences of full-time nontenure-track faculty in English. Her research interests center on faculty, particularly contract faculty, as well as other university employees who are ineligible for tenure. She is currently a member of a research team exploring how conditions of faculty appointments and faculty identity affect faculty, students, and institutions.

CHAPTER 8

Dr. Jennifer Engle is the Interim Director and Senior Research Analyst at the Pell Institute for the Study of Opportunity in Higher Education, the research arm of the Council for Opportunity in Education. The Pell Institute conducts and disseminates research and policy analysis in order to raise awareness, facilitate dialogue, and prompt action on important issues affecting postsecondary access and success for low-income, first-generation, and disabled college students. She was the lead investigator and author on *Demography is Not Destiny: Increasing the Graduation Rates of Low-Income College Students at Large, Public Universities* (Pell Institute, 2007), a large-scale study of the policies and practices that improve retention and graduation rates for low-income students, as well as *Straight From the Source: What Works for First-Generation College Students* (Pell Institute, 2006), a qualitative study of the transition from high school to college for this population. She is currently leading a study of community colleges that successfully transfer low-income populations in Texas. She is also the editor of the Pell Institute's new peer-reviewed research journal, *Opportunity Matters: A Journal of Research Informing Educational Opportunity Practice and Programs*.

co-authored with

Mary G. Lynch is a Higher Education Research and Policy Analyst at The Education Trust, which works for the high academic achievement of all students at all levels, pre-kindergarten through college, and closing the achievement gaps that separate low-income students and students of color from other youth. Her most recent project, the Access to Success Initiative, focuses on measuring and closing the college access and success gaps that separate low-income and minority students from their peers in 23 public, higher education systems. She holds a Master's in Public Policy, with a concentration in Education, Social, and Family Policy, from the Georgetown Public Policy Institute.

CHAPTER 9

Dr. Alisa Cunningham serves as Vice President for Research and Programs at the Institute for Higher Education Policy, which focuses on a number of issues related to higher education policy development. She oversees all of the Institute's content work and manages a staff of experienced policy researchers and analysts. Since joining the Institute in 1997, her work has addressed a broad array of topics, including higher education financing, student financial aid, minority-serving colleges and universities, student persistence and attainment, international higher education policy, and opportunities for student access and success. In her tenure at the Institute she has been involved in several cutting-edge national studies as well as more focused studies of access in several states.

co-authored with

Dr. Lacey Leegwater is Associate Director of Planning and Special Projects at the Institute for Higher Education Policy (IHEP). In this role, she is responsible for the structuring of new program and research initiatives, developing and monitoring budgets, and writing proposals. She also manages cross-departmental projects, such as its international rankings work and contributes to the organization's broader strategic planning. She also contributes to IHEP's programmatic work, including overseeing the National Articulation and Transfer Network (NATN) and the Building Engagement and Attainment for Minority Students (BEAMS) project. Prior to joining IHEP, she worked at the American Association for Higher Education (AAHE) where, in addition to beginning her work with BEAMS, she worked with such programs as AAHE's Communities of Practice Initiative and Urban Universities Portfolio Project. She holds a Master of Arts in Education from the University of Virginia's Curry School of Education, with a specialty in social foundations of education and Bachelor of Arts in Political Science and Economics from the University of North Carolina at Chapel Hill.

CHAPTER 11

Dr. Alicia Dowd is an Associate Professor at the Rossier School and Research Associate in the Rossier School's Center for Urban Education (CUE) at the University of Southern California. Previously she served as an assistant professor in the Graduate College of Education of the University of Massachusetts, Boston. Her research focuses on political-economic issues of public college finance equity, efficiency, and accountability and the factors affecting student attainment in higher education. She was the principal investigator of two national research and service projects, evaluating institutional assessment, effectiveness and student success at community colleges. Her most recent project, funded by the Jack Kent Cooke Foundation, Lumina Foundation for Education, and the Nellie Mae Education Foundation, focused on community college transfers to highly selective four-year colleges. She has authored articles focusing on the effects of financial aid on student persistence and degree attainment.

CHAPTER 12

Dr. Alex Jun is Professor of Higher Education at Azusa Pacific University. Prior to joining the doctoral faculty at APU, Alex was Associate Professor of Higher Education and Director of the Postsecondary Administration and Student Affairs (PASA) Program in the Rossier School of Education at the University of Southern California. He is the author of *From Here to University: Access, Mobility, and Resilience Among Urban Latino Youth* (Routledge Press, 2001), and has published several articles on access, retention, and college preparation. He conducts research on college access and equity for historically underrepresented groups in urban environments, and teaches courses in higher education and research methods.

co-authored with

Kristin Paredes-Collins is a doctoral student at Azusa Pacific University and the Director of Admission at Pepperdine University. She has previously published in the *Journal of Christian Higher Education* regarding her interest in the state of diversity at predominantly White Christian colleges and universities. Her research interests also include the benefits of diverse learning environments and access in higher education.

INDEX

1963 Robbins Report 59

A
Aboriginal and native youth 53, 57, 65, 67
academic coursework 257
academic merit 75, 97, 225
academic policies 112–113
academic preparation xi, 30, 54, 73, 89, 239
academic skills 130, 152–153, 239
academic support viii, xvi, 30, 32, 41, 43–45, 150, 166, 180, 184, 188
academic unpreparedness 54
access gap 54
accountability data 189
Achieving the Dream Project 7
active, experiential, and problem-based learning techniques 183
admissions x, xiv, xv, xvi, 19, 80, 41–42, 46, 65, 75–79, 82–83, 86, 91, 99–100, 103–104, 112–114, 127, 172, 177–178, 218, 225–227, 243, 253
adult basic education 178
advising 8, 16, 164–168, 171–173, 184, 199, 204, 207–208, 224, 226–229
African Americans 3, 36, 38–40, 177, 180, 223
AimHigher 60–64
Alliance for Equity in Higher Education 177
alumni support 75
American Disabilities Act 140
apprenticeships 61
articulation agreements 218, 221–222
assessment 34, 64, 69, 147, 167, 188, 224, 227–228, 236
ASSIST data base 221
athletic tradition 75

attrition xiii, xvi, 13, 66, 116, 124, 152, 161, 166, 170, 192, 202

B
benchmarks 169
best practices 168–169, 173, 196, 210–211
Boston University 74
Bourdieu, Pierre 5, 9–10, 52–54, 64, 126–128, 134, 237, 251–252
Brigham Young university 206
budgeting 18, 44, 197, 200, 202, 205–206, 208
Building Engagement and Attainment in Minority Students (BEAMS) program xviii, 167, 188

C
California xvii, 31, 41, 110, 135, 140–141, 143–145, 148–149, 151, 228
California State University Dominquez Hills 183
California State University-Northridge 207
CalWORKs 141–155
campus events 207
Canada 57–58, 60–61, 65
Canada Millennium Scholarship Foundation 60
career xi, xiii, 12, 31, 60–61, 101, 103, 111, 114, 123–124, 128, 147, 149, 151–152, 166, 185, 205–206, 223, 232, 235, 237, 243
career center 205–206
career tracks 101
cash aid 145
Centers for Working Families 14, 205
child care services 14, 19, 32, 146, 183
class cultures 126, 239
co-curricular xii, 18, 22, 164, 206, 208, 235
Coleman, James 52

collaborative networks 154
collaborative teaching 225
college access x, xi, 30, 45, 77
college aspirations 76
college choice xi, 31, 72–73, 77–79
college enrollment rates 31
college environment xviii, 102, 122, 161, 273
college preparatory curriculum 32–33
college preparatory diplomas 36
communication strategies 80–82, 86, 90, 92
community colleges xi, xvii, 7, 8, 15, 99, 139, 195, 200, 205, 206, 217, 219, 221, 224, 228, 253
community involvement 68
community outreach 184, 248
commuter student population 172, 185
computer and research skills 130
Consortium on the Financing of Higher Education (COFHE) institutions 72
Core 40 30, 32, 36–37
core course 20, 204
costs 14, 19, 31–33, 44, 53, 67, 87–90, 107, 115–116, 171, 180–181, 202, 208, 253
counselors and peer advisers 43, 90, 92, 146, 168, 207, 218, 222, 227–229
course scheduling 171–200, 207
credit card debt 192–193, 208–209, 245
cultural awareness 56
cultural barriers 217, 226
cultural capital 9, 10, 126–128, 241, 251–252
culturally-based missions 176–180
culture of success xviii, 163, 168–169
curriculum design 225
curriculum development 146

D
data-informed decision-making 188
Decision Partners, Financial Literacy course 205
default rate 198
deficit perspective 10, 63–64, 116, 126–128, 201–203, 247–249
degree attainment 31, 33, 41, 94, 161–162, 245
degree completion rates 45, 91
demographic composition xvi, 90, 163, 174, 180
department of Health and Human Services 140, 144
disabilities 53, 57, 67, 139, 236
distance learning opportunities 178–179
diverse learning community 243, 245
doctoral degree 234–237
drop courses 125
dropout *see* attrition

E
early information 33
Economic Opportunity Act of 1964 235
economic resources 50, 162
elite colleges and universities 72–81
emergency aid 170
employers 152
employment xvii, 63, 99, 116–117, 144–156, 206, 240, 242
endowments 72, 74, 76, 179, 186
England 49, 50, 56, 59–60, 61
English as a Second Language (ESL) 58, 123, 182
enrollment rates 31, 39, 126, 219, 220
entrance and exit counseling 124
ethnic and racial minority groups vii, xi, xiii, 3, 22, 38, 40, 53, 128, 135, 149, 176, 179, 218, 223, 232, 253
Expected Family Contribution 75
extension services 206

F
faculty role/mentors 18, 21, 218, 238
FAFSA 19
family resources 235
federal Free and Reduced Lunch program 31
federal policy viii, 23, 145, 193–194, 212
federal poverty level 43, 194
fee waivers 171, 181
finances 192, 199
financial aid xi, 72–80, 86, 114–116, 207
financial barriers 74, 180
financial education 192–212
financial literacy 180, 205, 212
first-generation youth 168, 234
first-year courses and programs 133, 163–164
Florida International University 185
four-year college and university 32–33, 38, 40, 43, 45, 73, 99, 101, 217
fraternities (sororities) 115, 205
freshman interest groups 164
freshman orientation 108, 164, 181
friends (peers) xii, xiii, 19, 55–56, 81, 92, 100–102, 108, 109–111, 116–117, 121, 124–125, 130–134, 161, 168, 176, 186, 235, 251
funding viii, xv, 29–33, 43, 55, 57–62, 105, 111, 152, 186, 188, 194, 227, 235, 242
Future to Discover 60, 63

G
gatekeeping courses xvii, 163, 166
Gates Millennium Scholars 42

GEAR UP 8, 14, 64, 197–198, 202, 209
gender vii, 3, 4, 8, 14–15, 17, 21, 37, 52, 232, 245
general education 20, 21, 133, 136, 164, 166, 167, 181, 199, 204
government 50, 53, 57, 58, 60, 61, 141, 177, 186, 204, 212, 236
Grade point average or GPA 100, 104–106, 112–113, 123, 135
grades x, 66, 105, 112, 113, 122, 125, 167, 247
graduate student x, xi, 45, 208, 238–242
graduation rates xiii, xviii, 99, 101, 124–125, 162–166, 168–173, 236
grant aid 44–45, 73–78, 83, 87, 89, 91, 168
guaranteed transfer programs 224

H

habitus xv, 51, 52–53, 63–65, 69, 126–128, 252
hidden curriculum 192–200
high-achieving 90, 234, 235
high school courses 112
high school graduation requirements 30
Higher Education Act 7, 235
Higher Education Opportunity Act (HEOA) reauthorization 210
Hispanic 3, 39, 40, 177, 180
Hispanic-Serving Institutions (HSIs) xviii, 167, 176, 178, 236
Historically Black Colleges and Universities (HBCUs) viii, xviii, 176, 178, 236
homeless 184
Honors diploma 30, 32, 36
Honors programs 224
Hossler and Gallagher's (1987) three-phase model 78
housing 18–21, 63, 102, 107, 114, 123, 130, 164, 183–185
Human Capital Theory 9, 77, 251

I

I have a dream program 29
immigrant youth 68
incentives 30, 42, 56, 60, 154, 174, 194, 221, 222
independent learning/study 101, 224
Indiana Career and Postsecondary Assistance Center (ICPAC) 31
Indiana Commission for Higher Education (ICHE) 33
Indiana University 42, 84
Indiana's Twenty-First Century Scholars program iii, xv, 29–46
Individual Development Accounts IDAs xviii, 194–195, 202–203, 209–211
information-seeking behavior 80

Institute of American Indian Arts (IAIA) 181
Institutional Financial Aid Policies 72–92
institutional policy 130, 197
institutional resources 52, 74, 82
institutional structures 5, 16, 100, 127, 143, 250
instruction xviii, 41, 43, 56, 146, 150–151, 163, 166–167, 179, 187, 229
Internet 80–82, 92, 155
internships 18, 22, 104, 185, 224, 236, 238
interventions 41, 56, 60, 61, 67, 68, 207

J

job development/placement 146

K

K-12 30, 41, 42, 161, 199, 212, 249
Kentucky State University 185

L

lab fees 240
land grant institutions and universities 7, 195
Latino see Hispanic
leadership (institutional) 148, 169, 170, 177, 205, 240
learning communities 41, 133, 164, 183
learning styles 225, 242
Leech Lake Tribal College 183
les collèges d'enseignement général et professionnel (CEGEP) 58
letters of recommendation 225, 235
libraries 129, 235
loan program 57, 79, 86, 189
local communities xvii, 7, 135, 180, 183
Long Beach City College 228–229
Lumina Foundation for Education 30, 33, 34, 38, 43, 217

M

major 19, 44, 75, 100–111, 117, 121, 129, 133, 166, 183
Manitoba 60
mass media 81
matched savings account see Individual Development Accounts
McNair Scholars Program 235–242
mentoring viii, 45, 61, 165, 179, 184, 224, 251
merit aid 31
meritocracy 63, 233, 243–244
Michigan 31, 41
minority 12, 35–38, 40–42, 53, 77, 78, 167, 172, 176, 177
Minority-Serving Institutions (MSIs) xviii, 176–190

Morrill Acts or land-grant legislation in 1862 and 1890 7, 8
Morris College 182
municipal colleges and universities 7, 8

N
National Academic Advising Association 165, 207
National Association for College Admission Counseling (NACAC) 81
National Postsecondary Student Aid Survey 75, 78
Native Americans 36, 181
new capitalism 142, 155
New England Resource Center for Higher Education (NERCHE) 217
New Jersey City University 185
New Visions Program xvii, 141, 151–153
New York University (NYU) 74
no loan policy 73, 82, 252
North Carolina Covenant 42

O
occupational mini-programs 151
on-campus credit union/bank 204, 207
Organization for Economic Co-operation and Development (OECD) 49, 56, 57
outreach 31, 41–46, 90–91, 183, 184, 197, 208–209, 235, 248

P
P-16 pipeline 242, 243
parental education 34
parents 18, 22, 32–34, 36, 44, 53–54, 63, 68, 79, 87, 88, 92, 102, 103, 106, 116, 124, 129, 171, 178, 199, 202, 206, 208, 251–253
part time 7, 76, 162, 179, 187, 240
participation rates 49, 55, 57
partnerships 41–44, 61, 65, 150, 153, 209, 227, 249–250
Pathways to Excellence 64
pedagogical style 21
peer see friends
peer mentoring 168
Pell grant vii, ix, xiii, 7, 8, 10, 46, 72, 83, 85, 178, 193, 232
Pell Institute xviii, 162, 163
People's Movement 6, 8
persistence xiii, xiv, 33–34, 45, 46, 60, 69, 77, 91, 162–166, 168, 183, 187, 232
personal development 141, 144
Personal Responsibility and Work Opportunity Reconciliation Act (PRWORA) 144

personal statements 235
postsecondary campus visits 33, 43, 61
post-structuralism ix, xiv, 4, 5, 9–16, 24, 113, 114, 141, 181, 233, 234, 250
pre-college experiences 122, 124
predominantly White institutions (PWIs) 183
prestige 23, 75, 173, 219, 224–225
pricing 32, 44, 100, 107, 114
Princeton University 73, 84
private colleges 33, 29, 40, 75, 76
private loans 196
probation policies 165
Project Grow 183
Purdue University 20, 42

Q
QuestBridge 91

R
race see ethnic and racial minority groups
racial bias 149
recruitment 43, 65, 243
remedial services 178–179
research stipends 245
residential experiences see housing
retention 22, 41, 45, 63, 66, 69, 117, 123, 162–173, 187, 236; see also persistence
Riverside Community College (RCC) 141, 150
role modeling 179
rural and remote locations/colleges 7, 8, 35, 37, 53, 65, 67, 135, 195

S
SAT score 30, 35, 37, 75–79, 102, 104, 113, 122, 152–153, 165, 168, 170, 225, 227; see also test scores
scholarships 5, 6, 7, 14, 56, 87, 91, 105–106, 181, 196, 200, 202, 253
school reform xv, 42, 44
science, technology, engineering, and math (STEM) disciplines 183
selective and highly selective campuses see elite colleges and universities
self-assessment instruments (SAIs) 228
self-motivation 80
short-training programs 147
skill-building 144
social capital xv, 51–52, 62, 64, 66, 126, 251–252
social context 57, 80
social engagement/interaction 11, 43, 107, 253
social organizations 100
sororities see fraternities

Spanish 184, 209
staff training 146, 154
standardized test scores *see* SAT score
state grants 31–33
state level/policy ix, 31, 146, 148, 153, 157, 244
stop-outs *see* attrition
structuralism 10–11
student affairs 164
student characteristics 68, 152, 177
student development 45, 148, 154
student engagement 164, 180, 182–183
student groups 197, 205, 206
student involvement 69, 101
student learning 164, 169, 182, 184, 224
student money management services 208
student progress xviii, 165, 167, 229
Student Support Services (SSS) xiv, 167, 172, 197, 236
student support 43, 44, 84, 185
students of color *see* ethnic and racial minority groups
study abroad xvi, 18, 104–106, 111–112, 185
summer bridge programs (also can be just bridge programs) 22, 103, 109, 111, 122–126, 130, 135, 248
summer school 61
Supplemental Instruction (SI) programs 41, 43, 166, 167

T
Talent Search 197, 235, 236
teachable moments 210–211
teacher recommendations 112
teaching assistantships 224
teaching techniques *see* instruction
Temporary Assistance for Needy Families (TANF) program 141, 144–145, 150, 153
Tennessee State University 182
test preparation services 240, 245
test scores x, 66, 112–113, 225, 227
Texas 41, 84
Texas Tech University 208
textbooks viii, ix, 20, 128, 240, 253
The 1998 Workforce Investment Act 144
the Dearing Report of 1997 59
the Education Act of 1870 59
the Education Act of 1944 59
the Higher Education Funding Council for England (HEFCE) 61
The National Endowment for Financial Education (NEFE), CashCourse College Program 205, 209, 211

The Servicemen's Readjustment Act (or G.I. Bill) 7, 8
The University of Wisconsin–Madison and Great Lakes Higher Education Guaranty Corporation 205
time management 123, 130, 131, 132, 136
Title III 188
Title V 188
transfer 23, 58, 217–229
Transfer Academy 228
transfer agents xix, 218, 223–224, 229
Tribal Colleges and Universities (TCUs) viii, 176, 183
TRIO programs viii, ix, xi, 7, 168, 182, 197, 209, 210, 236, 239
tuition vii, xi, xiii, xv, 5, 6, 29–33, 45, 57, 78, 85, 87, 90, 91, 103, 107, 112, 132, 136, 165, 166, 179, 180, 186, 188, 193, 198, 202
Turtle Mountain Community College 184
tutoring 133, 135, 164, 167, 171, 184, 185, 236, 238

U
underrepresented students 50, 57, 58, 122, 126, 233, 236
unemployed 184
University of Massachusetts Boston 217
University of Minnesota 238
University of the District of Columbia (UDC) 183
University of Virginia 79, 90
unmet need 74, 193, 202
Upward Bound 197, 209, 235

V
vocational programs/majors 58, 101

W
Washington Monthly 174
Washington State Achievers 42
websites xv, 73, 81–92, 207
welfare recipients/students 139–156
welfare reform 139, 141, 142, 144, 146, 149, 151, 153
welfare-to-work programs 139–156
Whiteness Movement19
Wisconsin 45, 205, 228
work habits 125
work opportunities 43
working class 20, 22, 23, 100, 126, 127, 217, 239, 241
work-study 6, 75–76, 110, 116, 146, 156